The Regulation of Accounting

Peter Taylor and Stuart Turley

Basil Blackwell

First published 1986

Basil Blackwell Ltd
108 Cowley Road, Oxford OX4 1JF, UK

Basil Blackwell Inc.
432 Park Avenue South, Suite 1503,
New York, NY 10016, USA

British Library Cataloguing in Publication Data

Taylor, Peter, *1929–*
    The regulation of accounting.
    1. Accounting — Standards — Great Britain
    I. Title   II. Turley, Stuart
    657'.0941   HF5616.G7
    ISBN 0–631–13878–1
    ISBN 0–631–13879–X Pbk

Library of Congress Cataloging in Publication Data
Taylor, Peter, 1947–
    The regulation of accounting.
    Includes index.
    1. Accounting—Law and legislation—
Great Britain.
    I. Turley, Stuart. II. Title
    KD2042.T39 1986   346.41'063   86–9627
    ISBN 0–631–13878–1   344.10663
    ISBN 0–631–13879–X (pbk.)

Typeset in 10/11½ pt Times by Oxford Publishing Services, Oxford
Printed in Great Britain by Butler and Tanner, Frome, Somerset

Contents

The Regulation of Accounting

Modern Developments in Accounting and Finance

This new series of accounting texts is edited by Professor David Cooper of UMIST. Aimed at intermediate students, the books distil recent theoretical and practical advances in aspects of contemporary accounting and are written by recognized experts in their field.

Forthcoming titles include:

Budgeting
Trevor Hopper

Social Accounting
Anthony Hopwood

Financial Modelling
Peter Pope

Planning and Control in Multi-Business Companies
Cyril Tomkins

Editor's Preface

Accounting and finance are rapidly changing. This series is designed to both reflect these changes and to help thoughtful practitioners and students of the craft to appreciate better the nature of the changes and the possibilities for the future. In conditions of change, it is more valuable to appreciate the economic, social, political and technical dynamic of that change than the detail of current practices. It would also seem inevitable that the practices are somewhat fragmented and that the practitioners at the forefront of developments are seen as specialized.

The study of accounting and finance reflects these changes. The subjects are increasingly recognized as a part of social science, in part based on economic knowledge but drawing also on sociology, politics and administrative theory. It is also recognized that it is only through theory and conceptual thought that modern developments can be understood. In other words, theory is not to be seen as arid analysis of no practical consequences but as a systematic way of making sense of the complexity and dynamic of practice. Good theory should appeal to the thoughtful and reflective practitioner as well as to the student.

The books in this series, specially written by recognized experts, are designed for specialized and theoretically oriented courses in important modern developments in accounting and finance. Assuming a knowledge of the technical, they are intended to be well-defined and self-contained conceptual texts in developing and interesting areas of accounting and finance. Designed to be lively and flexible, they will stimulate the reader to consider the purposes, nature and future of accounting and finance.

Peter Taylor and Stuart Turley have produced a book that exemplifies the virtues of the series. Policy making in accounting is an area of topical interest and importance. The manner by which accounting regulations are developed is of interest because of their effect on the efficiency and accountability of organizations in society. The book provides a theoretical analysis which enables the reader to appreciate the significance of the technical whilst understanding the causes and likely development of practice. It demonstrates, in a lively and concise style, the significance of accounting regulations and how both individually and taken together, they interrelate with economic, social, legal and political areas. The current debates in the specialist literature are reviewed and analysed in order to provide a thorough grounding in the subject. To students it should demonstrate that good ideas and theories facilitate an understanding of practice in a way that is impossible through the detailed study of technical specificities. To the reflective practitioner, it provides the basis not only for understanding current practice but also a lever for changing practices in a manner which offers a more confident link between intentions and outcomes.

The quality of learning that any book achieves depends on the engagement of both reader and author. Both the authors and I would therefore value comment and reaction from the reader in order that we can all learn and hopefully produce even better texts in the future.

David Cooper

Acknowledgements

We are grateful to everyone who has helped us in the preparation and production of this book. The ideas it contains have developed over a number of years while we have been engaged in teaching and researching the regulatory aspects of financial accounting in the UK. We would like to thank our colleagues in the Department of Accounting and Finance at the University of Manchester for their contribution to our thinking on the subject. Thanks are due also to those outside Manchester who have aided us with their comments and other help on the various research papers which are reflected in the book. We would also like to thank our editor, Sue Corbett, for her confidence in commissioning the book, and Michael Bromwich and David Cooper for their helpful comments on the manuscript. Special thanks are due to Hilary Garraway, Julie Gorton, Kay Saunders, Irene Kelly and Anne Gleeson, who together produced the typescript. Finally we would like to thank Janet and Sue, our wives, for their support.

Peter Taylor
Stuart Turley

1

The Nature and Objectives of Accounting Regulation

The accounting statements which are prepared by the management of business enterprises and publicly disclosed have been subject to regulation for many years. Regulation has taken a variety of forms and has come from different sources. It is only in the relatively recent past, however, that there has been a significant growth of interest in the process of accounting regulation, as distinct from the content of the rules produced by that process. This book is about regulation. It describes and analyses the means by which accounting is regulated and examines the effects of such regulation. The book concentrates primarily on the framework of regulation in the UK but also makes comparisons with systems of accounting regulation in other countries both in terms of the regulatory institutions and the means and extent of regulation.

Few economic or social activities escape regulation of some kind and the scope of regulatory activity defies easy definition. The term 'regulation' may encompass the activities of governments, regulatory agencies established by governments, trade or other associations in the private sector, or loose industrial groups which pursue collusive activities. Consequently, we shall take a broad interpretation of regulation as it affects accounting statements by defining it as the imposition of constraints upon the preparation, content and form of external financial reports by bodies other than the preparers of the reports, or the organizations and individuals for which the reports are prepared.

THE FINANCIAL REPORTING ENVIRONMENT

Financial reporting by enterprises is currently conducted in an environment which may be described by Figure 1.1. The basis of figure 1.1 is the supply of accounting statements from enterprises to the users of these reports. These statements are influenced by the accounting and auditing policies required by accounting regulations which are chosen by regulatory institutions. These institutions are, in their turn, influenced by the preferences expressed by users and producers for alternative regulations and regulatory arrangements, and by data on the costs and benefits experienced by users as a result of accounting reports and the regulations thereon. Costs and benefits arise as a result of decisions made by users of financial reports, either based upon such reports or other information. Thus, the environment of financial reporting comprises four interrelated elements: production, regulation, use and consequences.

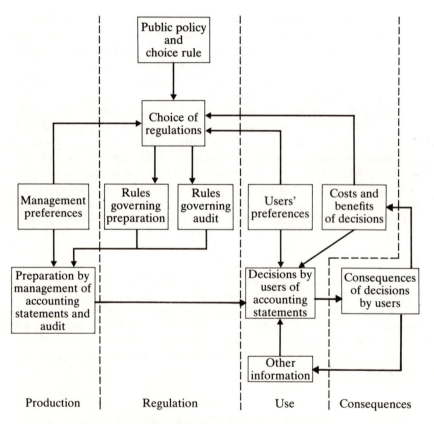

Figure 1.1 The financial reporting environment (adapted from May and Sundem, 1976)

Figure 1.1 is prepared on the assumption that some form of accounting regulation exists and influences the preparation of financial reports. The regulation of the market for information could be undertaken in different ways and to different degrees. For example, government might adopt a prescriptive approach by which detailed principles, rules and procedures are laid down and enforced by law. If the degree of prescription is high there might be no place for private sector bodies in accounting regulation. Less extremely, government could establish less detailed rules, and private sector bodies might emerge to become involved in additional regulation. As we shall see in chapter 2, there is a range of possible relationships between government and private regulators. Alternatively, legal regulations may provide only general requirements and private regulatory bodies to assist in their interpretation, and implementation may not be needed. In such circumstances much reliance is placed, either explicitly or by default, upon the independent judgement of those qualified by training and experience to confirm that, within the legal and social framework, financial reports follow the general requirements prescribed by law (Flint, 1982).

In this chapter we shall examine the nature and objectives of accounting regulation and introduce the various forms which such regulation may take. This examination involves two main issues. The first concerns the justification for regulating accounting. During a long history of accounting regulation, the means of regulation have changed and it is useful to examine the arguments that have been put forward in support of regulation. Although most authorities see a need for some form of regulation, there is no shortage of critics of both the content of regulations and the way they are decided, and in recent years arguments favouring an unregulated system of accounting have grown in force if not influence. These criticisms will be set out and evaluated.

The second major theme concerns the form which accounting regulation should take. Four broad approaches may be recognized. The first is regulation by the accounting profession through convention, precedent and training. This is potentially the most informal and least stringent means of regulation. A second approach is regulation by private sector regulatory institutions. Such institutions may be associated with the accountancy profession (e.g. the Accounting Standards Committee (ASC)), or may exert an influence over accounting as part of their other activities (e.g. the Stock Exchange). The third approach involves public sector regulation. This can be through governmental bodies (e.g. the Department of Trade in the UK or the Securities and Exchange Commission (SEC) in the USA) or through company law. Fourthly, a mixed system involving aspects of some or all of the other three approaches may be adopted.

Each approach can be further subdivided or elements variously combined, and this variety is reflected in the regulatory experience of different countries. The advantages and disadvantages are claimed for the alternative approaches to accounting regulation and in evaluating their relative merits it is useful to consider how accounting regulation fits in with more general considerations of public policy (May and Sundem, 1976). The regulatory institutions of accounting are considered in more detail in later chapters.

The case for or against regulating the supply or consumption of any commodity rests ultimately upon conclusions about the way that freely operating markets allocate resources. Such conclusions may involve considerations of either efficiency or equity or both. Consequently, we shall examine the case for regulating accounting statements by evaluating the characteristics of market allocation. In this context accounting information may be considered from two distinct but interrelated viewpoints: as a commodity in itself, traded in a market for information; and as an input into the decision processes of markets for other commodities.

MARKET ALLOCATION OF COMMODITIES

According to neoclassical economic theory, markets are capable of effecting an efficient allocation of resources through a series of decentralized decisions based upon the equation of marginal values relevant to the substitution of goods and services in production and consumption. This process ensures efficiency in each market, and through interrelationships between markets, a general equilibrium for the economy as a whole. The generally accepted criterion for judging efficiency is that of Pareto optimality, whereby an allocation is efficient if no person can be made better off without someone else being made worse off. There is no unique Pareto optimum solution for resource allocation. Instead, many alternative optima are possible since a particular Pareto optimal solution depends upon an initial assumption concerning the distribution of resources. Varying this assumption produces alternative solutions. In this manner, the Pareto criterion separates issues of efficiency from those of equity: economic theory can identify efficient allocations of resources, but non-economic criteria must be applied to choices between alternative efficient allocations because of the interpersonal comparisons implied by equity and distributional considerations.

In recent years considerable attention has been given to the application of economics based ideas to the provision of the commodity of accounting information (Watts and Zimmerman, 1985; Bromwich, 1985). We will examine the need for regulation of accounting from this perspective. Some have argued that unregulated markets for accounting information may allocate resources satisfactorily (Benston, 1969, 1973). In the following section we consider some of these arguments and go on to examine the counterview that there is a strong case for regulating the market for accounting information.

THE CASE AGAINST ACCOUNTING REGULATION

Accounting information relevant to enterprises is produced primarily by the management of the enterprises and by investment analysts and similar sophisticated users who might reanalyse the information disclosed by management into different forms. Opponents of regulations argue that both the suppliers and consumers of accounting information experience sufficiently strong incentives to trade in information to ensure that trading will take place in the absence of regulation or compulsion. On the demand side, users bid for information which is relevant to their decisions, while on the supply side, management has strong incentives provide adequate and reliable information in order to attract resources and to ensure beneficial effects on economic indicators such as share prices. Enterprises not providing information deemed useful by users, or not conforming to generally accepted standards of disclosure, would not attract or keep resources.

Two related motivations may be recognized for information trading. Users of information have incentives to obtain information to assist them in making decisions about trading in markets. Having obtained the information and taken up speculative positions, users have an interest in releasing the information to the market in order for it to be impounded in prices and gains realized. To ensure that the information has the expected effect on market prices, the private user has an interest in having the information verified by an auditor. Thus, private incentives may guarantee public disclosure. The ability of any individual to make such gains, and the processes by which such information is impounded into share prices, is the subject of capital market theory which is considered in greater detail in chapter 7.

A second motivation for trading in information is provided by the relationship between managers and shareholders in enterprises. A growing number of writers have applied agency theory to this relationship (Jensen and Meckling, 1976; Watts and Zimmerman, 1978; Leftwich, 1983). One of the conclusions which is suggested by agency theory is that mutual benefits are perceived by management and shareholders from the disclosure of audited financial information. According to an agency theory view, management (the agent) possesses superior information concerning the enterprise, and shareholders (the principal) cannot directly observe management behaviour. This assymetry of information supply creates the problem of 'moral hazard'. Moral hazard refers to the potential which the agent has for engaging in activities which are not in the best interests of the principal, such as fraud or suboptimal decisions. In order to solve the problem of moral hazard, the principal may seek to ensure that the agent's objectives are congruent with those of the principal by divising incentive schemes, such as profit sharing or share option schemes. Alternatively, the principal may seek information with which to monitor the agent's behaviour. The generation of information is a costly exercise and the agent has a comparative advantage in its production. Hence, agents will have an interest in providing such information in order to reduce the cost of monitoring the agent–principal relationship (Watts and Zimmerman, 1978). In addition, they will wish to provide such information in order to reduce the principal's reliance on incentive schemes which may involve the agent in undesirable risk taking. For similar reasons, the agent will favour an external independent audit (Watts, 1977). The audit of an agent's financial report to principals, both actual and potential, provides a signal to principals on the quality of the agent's services, and thereby helps to distinguish the superior agent from the inferior. In the absence of such authenticated discriminatory information there is a tendency for only the services of inferior agents to be traded (Akerlof, 1970).

THE CASE FOR ACCOUNTING REGULATION

Reliance on unregulated markets for the allocation of resources raises problems in two respects. First, there may be circumstances where the conditions necessary for the achievement of Pareto efficient allocations are not met and markets fail. Second, a means must be found of selecting between efficient alternatives, that is, of exercising social choice on matters affecting equity and distribution.

Market Failure

Markets may fail to produce efficient allocations of resources for several reasons.

Lack of rules governing market behaviour. A market system can only operate where there is a set of clearly defined rules to govern the way in which market transactions take place. These rules must state the nature of property rights which persons may have, the ways in which commodities may be allocated, the form of contracts for market transactions, and the methods for settling disputes and enforcing rules. Governments typically provide a framework of such rules and the associated institutions necessary to regulate market transactions. Rules and institutions impinge on accounting in numerous ways. UK company law, which is the subject of chapter 3, regulates the relationship between the management of companies and shareholders, including the provision of information to shareholders, and certain accounting issues such as the measurement of distributable profit. Company law also establishes a requirement for accounting statements to be audited, and this monitoring mechanism is discussed in chapter 8. In addition, laws relating to the prevention of fraud have accounting implications as does legislation on insider trading on the Stock Exchange. More generally, government legislation has established institutions responsible for encouraging the fair operation of markets. For example, the Fair Trading Act of 1973 established the office of the Director-General of Fair Trading with wide-ranging responsibilities in this sphere. As well as direct intervention to regulate markets, governments accept or encourage the regulation of markets by private bodies as an alternative or complement to their own activities. This type of regulation has been prominent in the field of investor protection in the UK and recent proposals for new legislation encouraged its expansion. The characteristics of self-regulation are discussed more fully later in this chapter and in chapter 2.

The supply of information in markets. The achievement of an efficient allocation of resources requires a series of market exchanges and this implies a process of negotiation between individuals. In economic theory this is typically assumed to occur without cost. The achievement of equilibrium in markets can be viewed as the result of the making and breaking of successive contracts. This recontracting process provides a means by which information about market conditions and the preferences of others can be freely obtained by individuals. In practice, however, transactions costs do exist and they may prevent the attainment of equilibrium since it may be too expensive to seek a better position. Individuals do not have the initial endowments of information necessary to make optimum allocations, and transactions costs and other obstacles to recontracting mean that information is costly to obtain but, as we have noted, there may be private incentives to incur the costs of obtaining information. However, whilst there may be very significant private returns to information production through insider trading, there may be zero or negative social returns to the resource costs invested in information production (Hirshleifer, 1971). This provides a case for the provision of publicly available information as an alternative to privately produced information. The costs of information may mean that individuals are imperfectly informed about present conditions or the outcomes of their decisions. Different decisions may be made with imperfect information than if more or different information were available. A number of areas where accounting information impinges on economic decisions made in markets may be identified, and hence accounting information may give rise to economic consequences (Zeff, 1978). The economic consequences of accounting information are discussed in detail in chapters 6 and 7.

At a general level, accounting information may affect the aggregate level of risks in the economy and the distribution of risks among individuals, since risk is a reflection of the supply of information. We have already noted the relevance of accounting information for the agent–principal relationship. Accounting information may alter the distribution of risks between agent and principal by modifying incentive contracts. In our earlier discussion we considered only managers and shareholders, but other agent–principal relationships exist, for example those between managers and creditors and debenture holders. Accounting information may affect the level and distribution of risks (and hence decisions) through the terms of lending agreements, debt convenants and dividend restrictions.

Accounting information may affect aggregate consumption and production. The provision of information on enterprise profitability can influence decisions on the attractiveness of consumption, saving and investment, and thereby interest rates and the rate of capital accumulation. Many other economic effects follow from such changes, for example, the rate of economic growth may change as may productivity, costs and product prices. Moreover, accounting information can cause the reallocation of resources between alternative uses. Investment may be reallocated between enterprises as accounting information affects investors' expectations of risk and return associated with investment opportunities. If capital is reallocated, there will be an impact on the demands for other factors of production, and output, costs and prices.

Recognition of economic consequences does not lend automatic support to the case for accounting regulation. It could be argued that regulations directed towards increasing the quantity and improving the quality of accounting disclosures and widening access to them would improve assessments of risk and return and the relationships between them. Similarly, institutions which reduce risks, such as limited liability companies and capital markets may be created. Normally, such institutions are regulated to ensure that they fulfil their objectives, and hence accounting regulation may be introduced indirectly. However, a counter-argument is that regulations on public disclosure may create competitive disadvantage (Beaver, 1981) if the returns to innovation or research and development are adversely affected.

Market distortions. An optimal allocation of resources requires all producers and consumers to respond to the same set of prices. If this occurs, then decisions on production and consumption are consistent, but if prices facing producers and consumers are different, optimality may not be achieved. A divergence of prices could occur if the supply of a commodity is restricted by monopoly. A monopolist is able to restrict the flow of resources into an industry and thereby maintain price differentials. The supply of accounting information is monopolized by reporting enterprises which are under legal obligations to disclose information to certain groups of users. In the absence of a normal pricing system, demands for additional information cannot be made effective by consumers who are dissatisfied with the level of supply of accounting information (Gonedes and Dopuch, 1974), and additional resources are not allocated to information production. Certain groups such as investment analysts or institutional investors could be expected to have access to more than the legal or conventional minimum amount of information, indicating greater market power than individual shareholders (Bromwich, 1981). The costs of supplying accounting information are borne either by the supplying enterprise or some other economic units to whom costs are passed via the process of production or exchange. This weakens the connection between costs and incentives to produce or consume accounting information.

If information is not publicly available, some transactors will be less informed than others about market opportunities. In the case of the capital market this will mean that investments which have different characteristics may sell at the same price (the equivalent of different prices for the same commodity). This can lead to the phenomenon of adverse selection (Akerlof, 1970) whereby only poor quality commodities find their way on to markets. In the case of investments, only those of low quality may be offered for sale. This will cause investors to bear greater risks, or if they anticipate the presence of poor quality investments, to reduce their investment. As a result, the holders of good quality investments (enterprises issuing relatively low risk or high return securities) may voluntarily disclose information, which will allow their quality to be assessed. If this information is authenticated, and if the authentication is accepted, it may alleviate some of the adverse effects on risk taking and investment. However, unless all enterprises make voluntary disclosures of audited information, market distortions will remain. A requirement to make such disclosures, either by law or by the rules of the capital market, may be a more effective solution.

A special problem of market distortion arises where the cost of providing an incremental unit of a commodity is very low. Such cases are normally associated with long-run declining average costs, spare capacity in production or jointness in supply. In each case, prices which reflect marginal costs would be so low that the total costs of production could not be covered. The problem is whether to charge prices unrelated to marginal costs (and distort market allocations) or to charge prices related to marginal cost (with no guarantee of profitable provision through the market). Accounting information appears to exhibit declining unit costs of production and is supplied jointly to users at a very low incremental cost. According to this analysis, without regulation accounting, information would either be priced above marginal cost by monopoly suppliers, thereby distorting the market, or not be provided at all. Accounting regulations requiring minimum disclosures may be the only means of guaranteeing the provision of information.

Externalities and public goods. In order for markets to create efficient allocations of resources, it is necessary for all goods and services to be exchanged and priced in markets. If certain commodities are not exchanged in markets, they go unpriced and consumers and producers may receive resources for which they do not pay. Thus, private and social costs may diverge if extra-market transactions take place. Social costs and benefits include both private costs and benefits priced in markets and unpriced externalities. If externalities are present, the market may fail to yield a socially optimal allocation of resources.

Public goods are a special case of externality and another source of market failure. Private goods are characterized by rivalry and exclusion in consumption, and exclusion is typically ensured by price. Hence, preferences may be expressed for private goods in markets. Public goods exhibit non-exclusion and non-rivalry since, if provided for one person, they are available for all without any discrimination. Consequently, there are great difficulties involved in revealing preferences for public goods and ensuring their provision by markets. Individuals have an incentive to conceal their true preferences and to become free riders on the demands of others. Thus, the true demand for a public good tends to be understated and underprovision occurs. The problems posed by public goods leads to the conclusion that non-market means of allocation are necessary to ensure supply.

Accounting information can be thought of as giving rise to externalities and having public good characteristics. If accounting information is publicly disclosed all may share in its consumption and it is thereby a public good in the sense of jointness of consumption. Rational persons would not buy information unless exclusion could be applied to its consumption. Exclusion might be practiced by allowing full property rights over accounting information, and in the absence of free riders and with perfect competition, market mechanisms can be demonstrated to produce efficient allocations of accounting information (Gonedes and Dopuch, 1974). An example of the exercise of property rights over accounting information is insider trading. When exclusive property rights to accounting information do not exist, or, in the case of insider trading, are prohibited, Pareto optimal allocations of resources in accounting information production are not possible.

However, even if exclusion is possible in the consumption of accounting information, externalities are likely to be present in the exercise of consumption rights. An individual who has acquired additional accounting information may use it to make trading decisions which will affect market prices for securities or other commodities. Others, observing either the actions of the owner of accounting information or the behaviour of prices, may draw inferences about the unknown information. In this manner information may leak into the market. This has a number of implications. It may reduce the value of the information (Grossman, 1977) and weaken the incentive to purchase it, and it may generate externalities (Foster, 1980). As we have already noted, externalities cause private and social costs to diverge and non-optimal allocation results.

Merit and demerit goods. Whilst public goods involve very large elements of externality, less extreme but none the less significant elements of market failure may be associated with merit and demerit goods. Merit goods exhibit significant external benefits in consumption such that there may be an important demand for a commodity which is not given expression in the market, as in the cases of education or health care. Similarly, in the case of demerit goods, there may be significant preferences against the consumption of certain commodities felt by those who do not directly consume, as in the case of cigarettes. Publicly available accounting information supplied to minimum levels of quantity and quality by all enterprises may be thought of as a merit good in that non-users' welfare is improved by their knowing that stock market investment represents a 'fair game'. By the same token, insider trading would be a demerit good, as would fraud or financial scandals. Recognition of merit and demerit goods may be seen as reflecting a difference between individual preferences and those of society. In cases where regulators intervene in the free operation of markets in which merit or demerit goods are traded, society may be seen as attempting to impose its preferences on individuals by claiming to know better than them what is good for them.

Distribution Considerations

If an unregulated market for accounting information succeeded in ensuring efficient allocations of resources which satisfied the criterion of Pareto optimality there would remain the problem of choosing between alternatives on distributional grounds. Likewise, non-Pareto optimal allocations of resources have associated distributions of resources, and policy makers may need to evaluate them and make good inefficiencies.

There are two related distributional issues to consider. First, the distribution of accounting information between economic units, and second, the distribution of income and wealth which results from the operation of markets. The latter is of course influenced by the level of supply and distribution of accounting information, as we noted above when considering the existence of economic consequences of accounting information.

Government may apply taxation and transfer policies directly to redistribute income and wealth. In this regard, distributions of income and wealth resulting from inequitable endowments of accounting information are no different from those resulting from, say, the inequities in endowments of skills or ownership of property. Thus, governments may not be led to regulate the supply and distribution of accounting information but may deal directly with the results of an unregulated market allocation. Alternatively, government might adopt policies to alter endowments of accounting information in order to remove a cause of an inequitable distribution of income and wealth. Under this approach, the need for accounting regulation arises in response to distributional considerations. Viewed in this way company law, which requires enterprises to supply financial reports of a prescribed form and content at zero cost to all shareholders, is analogous to the state providing free compulsory primary and secondary education. Notionally at least, each endows all members of particular socio-economic groups with a basic allocation of a resource. Distributional policies with respect to accounting information cannot generally operate in precisely the same manner as other policies do in redistributing resources. For example, the conventional wisdom regarding taxation policy holds progressive taxes and regressive benefits to be equitable, but accounting information cannot be redistributed in a directly analogous fashion. The nearest equivalent is the removal of asymmetries in information endowments (Beaver, 1981) by the outlawing insider trading or by the provision of information to employees for the purpose of collective bargaining (Cooper and Essex, 1977).

SOCIAL CHOICE AND ACCOUNTING REGULATIONS

Distribution considerations, as we have already noted, require the application of social rather than economic criteria of choice. The existence of economic consequences following from the use of accounting information means that users of accounting information will have preferences (as shown in figure 1.1) for accounting alternatives, and for alternative accounting regulations. Selection between such alternatives requires the application of a social choice rule by regulatory bodies. The prospects for exercising social choice were investigated by Arrow who presented his impossibility theorem to the effect that:

> There is no method of selecting among social alternatives that is not dictatorial, but is Pareto optimal, independent of irrelevant alternatives and provides a complete, transitive and reflexive ranking of social alternatives. (Arrow, 1963)

This theorem was applied by Demski (1973) to the question of choice between accounting regulations, and he concluded that even if all individual preferences for accounting regulations were known, generally acceptable accounting regulations are impossible. Similarly, Marshall (1972) found that optimal accounting regulations were impossible if individual preferences were unknown.

The work on which these conclusions is based has been criticized and developed by other writers with interesting implications for accounting regulation. For example, Cushing (1977) has criticized Demski and Marshall on several grounds. He points out that their assumption of heterogeneous tastes and beliefs may be inappropriate. On the contrary, it is likely that there will be significant degrees of homogeneity in the preferences of groups of users, for example shareholders, and there may even be sufficient homogeneity overall to allow a consensus to be identified. More pragmatic concerns for accounting regulators than achieving completely unambiguous decisions may thus be the identification of the degree of homogeneity of preferences which is present and the degree of heterogeneity which can be tolerated. In short, these involve identifiying politically feasible solutions. Cushing develops this theme by arguing that a potentially important element in achieving acceptable regulatory decisions may be the creation of an approved framework for making those decisions. If there is general agreement amongst interested parties that the mechanism for selecting accounting regulations is suitable, this may be seen as a surrogate for general agreement on the regulations themselves. In this respect there is a parallel with political decision making in a democracy: people on the whole are prepared to accept decisions with which they disagree if democratic methods have been used to arrive at the decisions. Unfortunately, it is perhaps not a very close parallel, since preferences for mechanisms of accounting regulation are more likely to collect around mechanisms to be avoided (e.g. legally enforced accounting standards) than mechanisms to be sought.

In democratic political systems, voting is a substitute for collective choice and regulatory bodies are able to use similar mechanisms to derive their decisions from the preferences of their constituencies. These constituencies will be numerous and widespread if the reporting of accounting information affects decision making and has economic consequences. For example, *The Corporate Report* (Accounting Standards Committee, 1975) identified a wide variety of users of accounting information, in terms of those individuals and groups whose interests are affected by the reporting entity. Thus, social choice by the regulator could require an explicit and careful consideration of the preferences of all those who are affected by policy alternatives. In such circumstances the regulator may be seen as merely a coordinator of preferences. Although the means at the disposal of private sector bodies such as the Accounting Standards Committee in the UK or the Financial Accounting Standards Board (FASB) in the USA, for canvassing opinions and considering them, may fall far short of those necessary to meet generally accepted standards of political democracy, they can go some way in that direction. The long-standing emphasis in accounting standard setting on 'due process' (discussed in chapter 4) in the USA and its more recent acceptance in the UK reflects this type of consideration. Consultation between the regulators and interest groups is an important element in 'due process', but it carries with it the danger that undue emphasis may be put upon the views of certain groups to the detriment of others. It is also possible that informal means may be used to exert influence over regulators. The history of regulatory activity (and indeed of policy making more generally) contains many examples of lobbying by interested parties and such behaviour has come to be recognized as important in accounting policy making. These issues are discussed more fully in chapters 5 and 7.

Whether regulatory bodies derive their decisions from the preferences of their constituencies or impose their own preferences upon those whose activities they regulate, there remains the fundamental problem of determining the objectives of regulation, and hence of the regulators. May and Sundem (1976) argue that the regulator should act so as to maximize social welfare by behaving in the public interest. However, although governments have the authority for such behaviour, the position of private accounting regulatory bodies such as the ASC or FASB is less clear. As the FASB (1978, p. viii) expressed it:

> Should accounting standard setters deliberately mandate what they believe to be an inferior accounting method in order to better achieve [sic] the public policy objectives (a) they perceive or (b) someone else perceives?

This quotation neatly summarizes the problem faced by private accounting regulatory bodies and no generally acceptable answer has been found by either those bodies themselves or commentators on accounting regulation. The problem is related to other issues, such as the relationship between private sector regulation and public sector regulation. The importance of public interest considerations to private sector bodies, and indeed perceptions of what constitutes the public interest, depends in part upon the nature of public sector bodies. The public interest is more explicitly relevant and clearly defined for the FASB in the USA, given the presence of a powerful federal government agency in the form of the SEC, than for the ASC, operating as it does in a less formal institutional framework of legal regulation. These issues are discussed more fully in chapter 2 and other international comparisons are drawn in chapter 10. The prospects for changes in the position regarding public and private regulation in the UK are examined in chapter 11.

SUMMARY

This chapter has considered the cases for and against the regulation of accounting and in the process a number of characteristics of accounting regulation have emerged as well as a series of problems associated with it. In order to evaluate the need for and nature of regulations governing accounting statements we analysed accounting information from the point of view of an economic good and saw that, for a variety of reasons, unregulated markets could not be relied on to satisfy all needs for information disclosure. This discussion has also provided a context for consideration of the role that can be fulfilled by regulations in general and by specific public sector and private sector regulatory bodies. The rest of this book is devoted to more detailed considerations of issues raised in this chapter, with reference to the particular framework of regulation which currently applies in the UK and the different sources of regulation within it. A brief outline of the contents of the other chapters is provided below.

Chapter 2 considers the relationships which may exist between public and private sector regulation, and the use of both in the UK. Chapter 3 examines in more detail the ways in which legal regulation has been applied, whilst chapter 4 outlines the structure of the main private sector body, the ASC. Influences on the ASC's activities are considered in chapter 5. Chapters 6 and 7 explore an important theme in financial reporting namely the economic effects which may result from changes in decisions following from disclosures in accounting statements. As we have noted above, the existence of such economic effects is potentially important for accounting regulation. The mechanisms used in the UK for monitoring disclosure are examined in chapter 8. Chapters 9 and 10 broaden the discussion to consider regulation in an international context. Chapter 9 reviews the growing international character of accounting regulation and the implications of this for the UK, whilst chapter 10 describes comparative systems of accounting regulation existing in a number of countries. Finally, chapter 11 looks forward to possible future developments in the UK system of regulation.

REFERENCES

Accounting Standards Committee 1975: *The Corporate Report.*
Akerlof, G.A. 1970: 'The markets for "Lemons": qualitative uncertainty and the market mechanism'. *Quarterly Journal of Economics*, Vol. 84.
Arrow, K.J. 1963: *Social Choice and Individual Values*, Yale University Press.
Beaver, W.H. 1981: *Financial Reporting – An Accounting Revolution*, Prentice Hall.
Benston, G.J. 1969: 'The value of the SEC's accounting disclosure requirements'. *The Accounting Review*, Vol. 44.
Benston, G.J. 1973: 'Required disclosure and the stock market: an evaluation of the Securities and Exchanges Act of 1934'. *American Economic Reviews*, Vol. 63.
Bromwich, M. 1981: 'The setting of accounting standards, the contribution of research'. In M. Bromwich and A.G. Hopwood (eds), *Essays in British Accounting Research*, Pitman.
Bromwich, M. 1985: *The Economics of Accounting Standard Setting*, Prentice Hall International in association with the Institute of Chartered Accountants. in England and Wales.
Cooper, D.J. and Essex, S. 1977: 'Accounting information and employee decision making'. *Accounting, Organisations and Society*, Vol. 2.
Cushing, B. 1977: 'On the possibility of optimal accounting principles'. *The Accounting Review*, Vol. 52.
Demski, J.S. 1973: 'The general impossibility of normative accounting standards'. *The Accounting Review*, Vol. 48.

Financial Accounting Standards Board 1978: *Economic Consequences of Financial Accounting Standards – Selected Papers*, Stamford.

Flint, D. 1982: *A True and Fair View in Company Accounts*, Gee.

Foster, G. 1980: 'Accounting policy decisions and capital market research'. *Journal of Accounting and Economics*, Vol. 2

Gonedes, N.J. and Dopuch, N. 1974: 'Capital market equilibrium, information production and selective accounting techniques: theoretical framework and review of empirical work'. *Journal of Accounting Research*, Supplement, Vol. 12.

Grossman, S.J. 1977: 'The existence of future markets, noisy rational expectations and information externalities'. *Review of Economic Studies*, Vol. 44.

Hirshleifer, J. 1971: 'The private and social value of information and the reward to inventive activity'. *American Economic Review*, Vol. 61.

Jensen, M.C. and Meckling, W.H. 1976: 'Theory of the firm: managerial behaviour, agency costs and ownership structure'. *Journal of Financial Economics*, Vol. 4.

Leftwich, R. 1978: 'Accounting information in private markets: evidence from private lending agreements'. *The Accounting Review*, Vol. 53.

Marshall, R.M. 1972: 'Determining an optimal accounting information system for an unidentified user'. *Journal of Accounting Research*, Vol. 10.

May, R.G. and Sundem, G.L. 1976: 'Research for accounting policy: an overview'. *The Accounting Review*, Vol. 51.

Watts, R.L. 1977: 'Corporate financial statements: a product of the market and political process'. *Australian Journal of Management*, April.

Watts, R.L. and Zimmerman, J. L. 1978: 'Towards a positive theory of the determination of accounting standards'. *The Accounting Review*, Vol. 53.

Watts, R.L. and Zimmerman, J.L. 1985: *Positive Accounting Theory*, Prentice Hall.

Zeff, S. 1978: 'The Rise of Economic Consequences'. *Journal of Accountancy*, December.

2

Public and Private Regulation of Accounting Disclosure

Financial reporting in the UK has traditionally relied on two main elements, a general framework prescribed by law and the professional judgement, recommendations and conventions of accountants, auditors and others involved in the reporting environment. Prior to 1970, when accounting standards were first introduced, the responsibility for published financial reports rested upon the judgement of directors and auditors to a much greater degree than subsequently. This is not to say that no private sector regulatory activity existed before the establishment of an accounting standard setting body but such activity was less formal. At its most informal it involved the gradual building of an ethical framework for the accounting profession. At its most formal it entailed the issuing of recommendations reflecting the evolution of a body of practice which represented the conventional wisdom on how best to conform to the general framework prescribed by law. Some formal regulation was also applied by the Stock Exchange and the Bank of England through policies directed at regulating the financial system.

In this chapter we examine the development of the system of accounting regulation in the UK, and discuss the relationship which has existed between public sector regulation, through legal statute, and private sector regulation, through accepted convention and the rules and recommendations of professional institutions. Two main sources of private sector regulation that have existed alongside company law are examined: the accounting profession and the securities industry. The development of legal requirements on accounting will be looked at in some detail in the following chapter.

THE DEVELOPMENT OF ACCOUNTING REGULATION

The development of accounting regulation is closely bound up with that of accounting itself, and each has been greatly shaped by broad social and economic forces. Before the Industrial Revolution, the predominant source of finance for business enterprise was internal and consequently financial statements served only the needs of the proprietor/manager. As the Industrial Revolution progressed, and as internal sources of finance proved insufficient to meet the needs of increasingly large-scale industrial enterprises subject to rapid technological change, external financing became more important. With the development of the joint stock company, a new group of people having an interest in the affairs of the enterprises emerged, namely shareholders. Management and ownership were divorced and financial statements became important vehicles for the provision of information to actual and potential shareholders. More recently, the position of, for example, members of an enterprise's workforce has been recognized as more akin to that of stakeholders than employees. As well as new classes of user of financial information, new categories of transaction have emerged and with them new accounting problems. For example, mergers of companies became extremely popular once the limited liability form of company organization became widespread (Prais, 1976), and brought with it the need for methods of group accounting.

The foregoing suggests that developments in accounting may be associated with two influences: namely, the general philosophy prevailing in society and the growth of business enterprises. These influences may also be associated with the development of accounting regulations (Underdown and Taylor, 1985, pp. 25–7). In the nineteenth century, the prevailing attitude was for *laissez-faire* and this implied that financial affairs were a private matter. The corollary is that financial reporting was also a private matter. Public disclosure further offended against prevailing opinion by promising to give competitive advantages to other enterprises. Private interest and public interest were viewed as converging in the matter of the rate of capital accumulation. The needs of society for financial reporting were seen as being satisfied if accounting reports provided for the needs of investors and ensured the efficient allocation of capital. Thus, legal disclosure requirements sought to meet society's needs by attempting to satisfy those of creditors and investors. As interest shifted to social aims in addition to capital accumulation, legal disclosure requirements were altered and extended, as, for example, with the requirements to disclose data on exports and charitable and political contributions.

Developments in regulation have also come about in response to shocks experienced in the financial reporting environment. These shocks have largely come in the form of scandals or important business failures (Rose, 1965). For example, the failure of the Royal British

Bank in 1856 led to the enactment of the Prevention of Fraud Act of 1857 and the Joint Stock Banking Act of 1858, and the failure of the City of Glasgow Bank in 1878 stimulated the Companies Act, 1879. More recently, the establishment of the Accounting Standards Steering Committee (ASSC) in 1970 came as a direct response to extensive public criticism of accounting practices following a succession of notorious take-over bids (see chapter 4).

REGULATION BY THE ACCOUNTANCY PROFESSION

The accountancy profession has exerted considerable influence on the development of financial reporting and regulation. This influence has been exerted in three ways. First, accountancy bodies have laid down codes of practice governing the behaviour of their members and have applied rules controlling entry to the profession. Second, accounting principles and practices have been developed which provide a framework to guide practising accountants and auditors. This has sometimes entailed the provision of formal guidance to members on practical matters of accounting or auditing. Finally, the accountancy profession, through individuals and professional bodies, has exerted an influence on legislation.

Professionalization

Professional bodies have a history spanning over 100 years in the UK. The Institute of Chartered Accountants in Scotland was founded in 1854 under the title of the Society of Accountants in Edinburgh and the Institute of Chartered Accountants in England and Wales (ICAEW) was established in 1880, bringing together professional bodies which already existed in London and elsewhere. According to Johnson (1980), the ICAEW very rapidly created barriers to entry through the costs of obligatory articles and the severity of professional examinations. These barriers stimulated the growth of other bodies, notably the Society of Incorporated Accountants and Auditors in 1885 and the London Association of Accountants in 1904. From an early date, the development of legal regulation tended to enhance the position of the professional bodies and strengthen the controls which they were able to exercise. The Companies Act, 1844, which made the joint-stock form of organization more readily available required compulsory audits, although it did not specify their nature or require that they be carried out by accountants. The Companies Act, 1855, made limited liability generally available for joint-stock companies and in the following year an act included a specimen set of articles of association, including voluntary disclosure and audit provisions (Nobes and Parker, 1979). This legislation, whilst not compelling the involvement of members of the accountancy profession, had the practical effect of doing so (Edey and Panitpakdi, 1956). An annual audit was made compulsory in 1900 for all limited liability companies and from an early date the Board of Trade recognized members of the chartered accountancy bodies for the purpose of company audits. Edey (1979) points out that in the period preceding the Companies Act, 1900, support had been expressed for the introduction of a compulsory requirement for a company audit by a professional accountant. It was not until 1948 that the law required that auditors should be professionally qualified, and specified the qualifications of persons permitted to be auditors.

The position of the professional bodies was enhanced in other ways. The Winding-Up Act, 1948, for example, served to give public accountants an effective monopoly over the conduct of bankruptcies (Jones, 1981). More general government policies also had a similar effect. For example, during the First World War, government policies directed to the control of profiteering in war-time industries involved limiting prices to cost of production plus reasonable profit margins. The task of establishing reasonable cost-plus prices fell to accountants who were appointed to the civil service (Crawford, 1984).

Development of Accounting Principles and Standards

Interest in the development of accounting principles by professional accountancy bodies began in the 1930s with the activities of research bodies associated with academic and professional accountants (Zeff, 1972), but it was not until the 1940s that any significant activity was undertaken. The quickening of institutional interest in the 1940s was a result of the setting up of the Cohen Committee on company law. The committee was established in 1941 to examine the Companies Acts with a view to their reform. The ICAEW formed the view that the committee was likely to recommend a significant increase in legal control over financial reporting unless the accountancy profession acted to make improvements. This, coupled with internal pressures for reform, led the ICAEW in 1942 to establish a Taxation and Financial Relations Committee (TFRC) (subsequently named the Taxation and Research Committee). Shortly afterwards the TFRC sought and received permission to prepare drafts of pronouncements on accounting principles for consideration by the Council of the ICAEW. The significance of those decisions is well illustrated by the observation of Zeff (1972):

Historically, the Institute's 45-man Council had stood aloof from its members' accounting and auditing activities, never having published a booklet or guidance statement in the technical field.

Between December 1942 and November 1969, a series of 29 *Recommendations* was produced. Although there is evidence that the *Recommendations* succeeded in improving practice they were not mandatory upon ICAEW members, and it remained 'a matter for each individual member to consider his responsibility in regard to accounts presented by directors' (Zeff, 1972).

The next major development in professional regulation of accounting practice was the announcement, in December 1969, of the creation of the ASSC. The move followed widespread criticism of accounting practice in a number of well-publicized take-overs, and concern over the flexibility permitted by the *Recommendations* series. The intention was that the ASSC would provide a definitive approach to regulation of practice, and thus divert the potential threat of increased legislative control. The history, role and activities of the Accounting Standards Committee (ASC), as the ASSC subsequently became known, is described in detail in chapter 4, but a few summary points may be stated here.

The ASSC first met in March 1970 and put together a list of subjects considered suitable for accounting standards, some of which were taken over from the *Recommendations* series (Leach, 1981). The first Statement of Standard Accounting Practice (SSAP) appeared in 1971. Although the ASSC was the initiative of the ICAEW, its membership was soon extended as other professional accountancy bodies became involved. Since 1976, the ASC has been a committee of the Consultative Committee of Accountancy Bodies (CCAB) and is financed by and responsible to the six professional bodies which make up the CCAB. Whilst the ASC prepares SSAPs they are approved and issued by the member bodies of the CCAB and it is these bodies which are responsible for compliance. The disciplinary mechanisms of the CCAB bodies provide sanctions for non-compliance by accountants and auditors, and the qualification of the audit report is a sanction against the reporting company. Accounting standards have been adopted as part of the accounting requirements of the Stock Exchange Listing Agreement, although in individual cases the Stock Exchange has found compliance difficult to enforce. As SSAPs are intended to apply to all accounts required to show a true and fair view, they may also have a legal sanction if the courts choose to adopt standards as generally accepted accounting principles in judging whether accounts are true and fair.

The Accountancy Profession and Legal Regulation

As noted above, the professional accountancy bodies have been the beneficiaries of many of the changes and extensions which have taken place in accounting regulation. Naturally, they have long recognized their interest in influencing legislation related to financial reporting. By 1890, ten years after its founding, the ICAEW had reached the conclusion that it was 'imperative to keep watch over legislation affecting commercial interests' (Howitt, 1966). Such an opinion led logically to lobbying, an activity made easier by the importance and esteem in which the ICAEW was held by government officials, although lobbying was not confined only to the ICAEW. In the case of the ICAEW, it did not lobby for an extension of disclosure until the 1940s and the Cohen Committee. Prior to that, the ICAEW's position had been consistently against extension of disclosure (Aranya, 1979). Some other professional bodies were less conservative. In the wake of the Royal Mail Case, the Society of Incorporated Accountants and Auditors recommended that company law be reformed to require the profit and loss account to show the true balance for the period. That the government made no revision to the law may be a reflection of their view that matters of accounting might best be left to the accountancy profession (Edwards, 1976).

Since 1942 and the introduction of the Recommendations series, and more recently with accounting standards, the profession has provided pronouncements which have sought to complement and extend the regulation contained in statute. The professional bodies have also continued their lobbying activities individually and collectively through the CCAB and the Accountancy Bodies Joint Parlimentary Committee on Company Law and Taxation, although the latter committee was disbanded in 1984 in favour of the separate institutes making their own submissions to government. With membership of the EEC came another forum where political influence might usefully be applied. The UK professional bodies have been able to express their views to the EEC institutions through their membership of the Groupe d'Etudes, a group comprising representatives of the principal accountancy bodies of the EEC.

REGULATION BY THE SECURITIES INDUSTRY

The main sources of regulation affecting the generality of companies are the law and the accounting profession. In the more limited sector of listed companies, those involved in the securities industry have also had a role in helping to regulate financial disclosure, both through issuing their own rules and by promoting rules issued by the accounting profession.

Regulation by the Stock Exchange

For some considerable time, the Stock Exchange has exercised an influence over companies' financial reporting in the context of the issue of and trading in company securities. The definitive regulations of the Stock Exchange regarding companies and their securities are set out in the *Admission of Shares to Listing*. This document, introduced in 1972, contains rules regarding the procedures to be followed by a company seeking a listing for its share capital, or if already listed, for a new issue of securities. With respect to company financial reporting and disclosure, there are rules regarding the provision of information on a company's trading record for five years prior to the application for listing, and rules governing the prospectus which must be published in conjunction with an issue of securities and the accountant's report on information contained in a prospectus.

Companies must also enter into the *Listing Agreement* on the admission of their securities for listing. The *Listing Agreement* is perhaps the most influential aspect of Stock Exchange regulation as far as financial reporting is concerned. It aims to secure a regular supply of information to investors and others and specifies the information which must be supplied by a company. The major disclosure requirements may be grouped under three headings. First, the *Listing Agreement* requires companies to disclose certain types of information to the quotations department of the Stock Exchange. Second, it requires that the published financial reports of listed companies contain certain types of information. Third, it provides for the publication of information in the press. The main disclosure requirements are summarized in appendix 3.

There are a number of interesting relationships between the *Listing Agreement* and regulations from other sources. The *Listing Agreement* requires the disclosure of some information not legally required, for example, interim reports. There have been examples in the past where Stock Exchange requirements have led to subsequent legislation. For example the Stock Exchange introduced a requirement for companies seeking listing to publish consolidated accounts in 1939, whilst legal provisions for group accounts appeared in the Companies Act, 1948. Similarly, the disclosure of turnover was required by the Stock Exchange one year before it was introduced in the Companies Act, 1967. The *Listing Agreement* also assumes consistency of company financial reporting with accounting standards by requiring the disclosure of reasons for departures from standards.

In recent years a number of important developments have occurred which have implications for financial reporting. In November 1980 the Stock Exchange set up the Unlisted Securities Market (USM). Listing on the USM has broadly the same functions as full listing on the Stock Exchange, namely allowing companies access to a capital market for the raising of new capital and allowing a company's owners to realize their investment. However, the USM involves lower outside involvement in the ownership of a company (only 10 per cent of the share capital need be marketed as opposed to 25 per cent with a full listing), less stringent standards of investigation of trading record and marginally less stringent reporting requirements compared with a listing.

The year 1983 marked the beginning of a period during which significant changes in the regulation of the Stock Exchange are likely. The Office of Fair Trading commenced legal action against the Stock Exchange on the grounds that it operated restrictive trade practices, in particular the strict demarcation between jobbers and brokers, the system of fixed commissions on transactions and the restriction of trading to members only. In July 1983 the Stock Exchange came to an agreement with the government to abandon fixed commissions and to allow non-members to become part-owners of brokerage and jobbing firms, and in return the Office of Fair Trading ceased the legal action. These changes are likely to have very significant effects on the structure and operation of the Stock Exchange (Peasnell and Ward, 1985). Other changes in the overall framework of regulation for investor protection have been proposed (Department of Trade and Industry, 1985) and are discussed in a later section. The proposals continue to place emphasis on a system which is largely self-regulated but with the addition of statutory backing for the main regulatory agency. Whilst having no direct implications for financial reporting, they suggest that the regulatory climate, within which financial reporting is conducted, is changing in important ways.

The City Code on Take-overs and Mergers

The establishment of the City Panel on Take-overs and Mergers in 1968, and the publication by it of the *City Code on Take-overs and Mergers* (Council for the Securities Industry, various dates) was the direct result of a series of acrimonious and dramatic take-over bids which occurred in the 1950s and 1960s (recounted by Stamp and Marley, 1970). In a previous attempt to control this area of business activity, in 1959, a working party set up by the Governor of the Bank of England had produced *Notes on Amalgamations of British Business*. These *Notes* were vague as to principles and permissive on procedures and were insufficient to prevent a recurrence of public concern over the conduct of take-overs and mergers. The Governor of the Bank of England reconvened the working party and while it was drafting new rules, a new body, the City Panel, was established to supervise the application of the rules when they emerged. On this development Stamp and Marley (1970) observed: 'The working party knew its rules would have no force and they demanded that the Governor of the Bank of England produce the requisite moral authority by appointing a new watchdog body to do the voluntary policing.' The panel has shown the extent to which statutory regulation and self-regulation may be subtly intertwined. The first chairman was a former Deputy Governor of the Bank of England and the panel's secretariat consisted of Bank officials on secondment. The Governor has the power to appoint the panel's chairman and three lay members. The purpose of the *Code* is to maintain high standards of business morality, and it consists of general principles and specific procedures to be followed in particular circumstances involving take-overs and mergers. It has no legal status, and observance relies upon the powers of the Stock Exchange to discipline stockbrokers or suspend security listings, and of the Issuing Houses Association to discipline merchant banks.

THE ROLES OF PUBLIC AND PRIVATE SECTOR REGULATION

The regulation of accounting disclosure has involved a combination of statutory requirements and rules produced by private sector agencies. In this section we discuss the different roles of, and the relationship between, these two spheres of regulatory activity. The underlying approach which allows legal and professional rules to exist side by side and also the interdependence between them in practice are considered.

The Structure of Financial Reporting Regulations

One way of identifying the relationship between legal and professional regulations is by looking at the nature of the regulations issued. These regulations may be classified according to different types:

(1) requirements for disclosure of an accounting statement;
(2) requirements for disclosure of specific items of information;
(3) specification of the format in which information is to be disclosed in an accounting statement;

(4) specification of the rules by which individual items of information may be measured.

The progression from (1) to (4) above reflects an increasing amount of standardization regarding accounting disclosure. Type (4) rules have perhaps the greatest impact on the flexibility which companies have in producing accounting information. Broadly it may be said that in the UK the traditional framework of regulation has been that the law has been largely confined to type (1) and (2) regulations and the accounting profession has been responsible for governing the areas covered by types (3) and (4). For example, the Companies Acts have required disclosure of a balance sheet and profit and loss account, and particular items of information such as turnover, depreciation and directors emoluments. The role of the accounting profession has been mainly in influencing the manner in which this information is disclosed, i.e. the format and measurement rules, both through the informal rules implied by convention and the more formal accounting standards.

This complementarity of role has undergone some changes in recent years and cannot be applied rigidly to all the regulations contained in law and professional statements. For example accounting standards require disclosure of a source and application of funds statement and earnings per share figures, which would fall in types (1) and (2) respectively. More significantly, the Companies Act, 1981, introduced specific formats for the presentation of the profit and loss account and balance sheet and specified certain measurement principles which should govern the preparation of accounts.

However, to a large extent the increasing statutory control present in the Companies Act, 1981, was forced on the UK through membership of the EEC and the duty to enact the Fourth Directive on Company Law. The Directive was in fact introduced in a way which disturbed the existing reporting structure as little as possible. The underlying philosophy which characterizes the approach to accounting regulation in the UK remains that the law should establish the broad framework and the accounting profession should develop detailed procedures and rules which assist in the practical implementation of that framework in a business environment which is constantly changing.

The Relationship between Self-regulation and Legal Regulation

Private groups in many areas of activity have long exercised an important role in the determination of standards of behaviour. Examples of such groups are professional bodies, trades unions, trade associations and other representative bodies. As Page (1980) points out, government attitudes towards regulation by private bodies of the behaviour of their members has varied from passive acceptance to active encouragement. Self-regulation may be seen as a means by which government policies may be more effectively implemented, as a complement to legal regulation or as an alternative. Government frequently delegates authority for regulation to private bodies. For example the legal and medical professional bodies have statutory authority to regulate entry to their professions.

The most frequently encountered form of self-regulation is the 'code of conduct'. Although most codes of conduct do not carry the force of statute, legislative provision has been made for their existence in certain spheres, for example consumer protection, where the Fair Trading Act, 1973, requires the Director General of Fair Trading to encourage the formulation and dissemination of codes of conduct. Investor protection has been an important area for self-regulation. Codes of conduct protecting investors have been developed, in response to criticism of the adequacy of existing regulation, in an attempt to reconcile the public interest to the interests of private bodies.

The essence of self-regulation is the protection of non-members of the group being regulated but this is not to say that the introduction of self-regulation does not have important elements of self-protection. The responses of the ICAEW, first to the Cohen Committee and second to public criticism in the late 1960s, are cases in point. Similarly, the introduction of the first *City Code on Take-overs and Mergers* in March 1968 and the formation of the City Panel to administer it was a response to a crisis of confidence and the threat of legal regulation. The first edition of the *City Code* stated the alternatives baldly as either 'a system of voluntary self-discipline, based on the Code and administered by the City's own representatives or legislation by law enforced by officials appointed by Government.' On this occasion government, through the agency of the Bank of England, was instrumental in setting the wheels of self-regulation in motion. Government encouragement of self-regulation seems to show that it is perceived as an alternative to statutory regulation. Page (1980) argues that this represents a functional incapacity of government to intervene in certain spheres of business activity: government's preference for self-regulation over statutory legislation being a reflection of the greater comparative costs and difficulties involved in devising and implementing statutory controls. From government's point of view, self-regulation may possess the merit of flexibility and may be more accurately focused than would be the case with statutory regulation. In addition, it may overcome the resistance of interest groups to regulation. Private bodies are used as the agents of government and, because of their knowledge and standing with regard to those who are to be regulated, are able to defuse opposition and engender a greater degree of voluntary compliance.

Mention of this agency role of self-regulation bodies implies that government views such activity as being in the public interest. However, there may be circumstances where self-regulation is otherwise. For example, private regulatory bodies may restrict access to their service or may discriminate against certain of their members. Also, their regulatory power may be used to exploit the public for private interest. This factor introduces the issue of the supervision and control of self-regulatory bodies by government. Supervision and control may be exercised in five ways:

(1) by specific statutory controls directed towards the regulatory body, for example the Independent Broadcasting Authority Act, 1973;
(2) by more general legislation, for example the Fair Trading Act, 1973, and the Unfair Contract Terms Act, 1977;
(3) by arguments before the Court that self-regulatory bodies' activities are contrary to the rules of natural justice;
(4) by government involvement in the formulation of the rules of self-regulatory bodies;
(5) by government monitoring of their activities, and by the threat of intervention.

By its nature self-regulation involves private bodies in the implementation of regulatory activity. A crucial element in implementation is enforcement, and this aspect of self-regulation contains important potential weaknesses. In the case of accounting standards, implementation is indirect: standards are prepared by the ASC, but responsibility for their implementation lies with the individual member bodies of the CCAB. The ASC has no enforcement powers and relies upon the member insitutions of the CCAB for such powers.

The effectiveness of self-regulation may be assessed in terms of its costs and benefits relative to statutory regulation. Self-regulation requires voluntary general adherence and is thus prey to the paradox that those most in need of regulation are least likely to conform to regulations. Where significant powers of enforcement exist, they may be inappropriate for particular regulations since they may have been designed for other purposes. Also, the severity of the powers, as in the case of suspension of dealing in a security, may be a deterrent to their use. However, statutory regulation may be inflexible and difficult to apply, so that imperfect self-regulation may be more effective than statutory regulation.

Whilst the rules of self-regulatory bodies may not themselves be legally enforceable, they may carry indirect legal force. Such rules may form the basis of a contract and thus be enforceable. In the case of accounting, the statutory requirement that financial statements give a true and fair view does not carry with it any legal definition and has no absolute meaning. In this context, accounting standards may be taken as authoritative statements of the policies and practices which will produce a true and fair view, and thus may carry indirect legal force.

The Framework for Investor Protection

In 1981 the government commissioned Professor L.C.B. Gower to review investor protection in the UK. His report was published in January 1984 and twelve months later the government published plans for legislation (DTI, 1985). Although concerned with the control of investment business, the plans contain a number of points relevant to our consideration of the structure of regulation in accounting.

The basic approach adopted in the government proposals is that investor protection can best be achieved by a system which relies on self-regulation within a legal framework. It is proposed that new legislation to control investment business will be introduced in 1986, and will place reliance on two levels of self-regulation, as illustrated in figure 2.1.

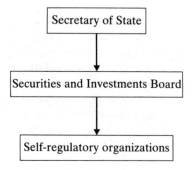

Figure 2.1   The new framework for investor protection

The first level is a new body, referred to as the Securities and Investments Board (SIB).[1] The legislation will give the Secretary of State regulatory powers and also enable him to delegate those powers to a body such as SIB. As a result SIB will have statutory backing. The chairman and members of SIB will be appointed by the Secretary of State and the Governor of the Bank of England. The SIB is therefore a body drawn from the private sector but mandated by the state. One

---

[1] Originally a second body, the Marketing of Investments Board (MIB), was envisaged, to regulate the marketing of pre-packaged investments, for example unit trusts.

effect of the creation of SIB has been the dissolution, in October 1985, of the Council for the Securities Industry. The Council had been set up in 1978 at the instigation of the Bank of England and financial and investment institutions, and between 1978 and 1985 acted as the main supervisory and coordinating body for the existing machinery of self-regulation. The SIB effectively replaces the Council, although with greater potential powers.

The second level of self-regulation is the self-regulatory organizations (SROs), for example the Stock Exchange and the National Association of Security Dealers and Investment Managers, which will be recognized by the SIB. Recognition will depend on the SROs' ability to regulate the conduct of its members, and the SIB will have authority over its rules and procedures. Members of an SRO will be authorized to engage in 'investment business'. As far as accountants are concerned, it is proposed that the accounting bodies should be exempted from the requirement to register as self-regulatory organizations, on the grounds that investment business does not represent a significant part of their members' activities.

The creation of the SIB as the key regulatory agency in the framework is a significant development in the traditional UK approach of blending a mixture of self-regulation and legal regulation. It is an attempt to maintain reliance upon self-regulation but to give it the effective backing of statutory powers. This development could have significant parallels in other areas of regulation, such as accounting, in the future.

Professor Gower, in his report, not only commented on investment business, but also expressed concern about accounting and made some proposals regarding the status of accounting standards.

> We now have a confusing mixture of statutory principles, statutory rules, statutory references to generally accepted accounting principles and non-statutory standards which sometimes obtain statutory backing by a sidewind.

> If the non-statutory standards were merely recommendations by the ASC on the best way to comply with the statutory rules, they would present no problem. But they now go way beyond that. In effect they (or many of them) are principles or rules differing only from those in the companies acts in the way in which they are expressed and in the fact that no one is legally compelled to enforce them. (Gower, 1984)

The solution he proposed to this situation is for the DTI to require financial disclosure to be made in accordance with the standards prescribed by the SROs. Gower envisaged that the accountancy bodies would become SROs and this proposal was really a proposal to ensure that they could enforce observance of ASC standards. As the government now plan that the accountancy bodies will not be required to register as SROs, it would appear that this opportunity for legal backing for standards will not be taken.

SUMMARY

This chapter has been concerned with the relationship which exists between the principal sources of regulation of accounting practice in the UK. The sources of regulation which have been identified have been categorized into 'public sector' (the legal regulation of statute) and private sector (the self-regulation of the accounting profession and the securities industry). The involvement of the private sector bodies in accounting regulation has been outlined and the use of the law to control financial disclosure will be discussed in detail in the following chapter.

It is not possible to conclude the discussion of the relationship between public and private sector regulatory bodies by making rigid definitive statements as to the nature of the relationship, other than to say that it is a complex one. Rather we have considered a number of facets of the relationship and have seen that it includes areas of overlap as well as complementarities, and involves many interdependencies. Government may rely on the flexibility of self-regulation to ensure rules are developed quickly to cope with changes in the business environment. In turn, professional bodies rely on government recognition of their status and role in regulation, and on the possibility of their rules having indirect legal effect.

The structure of regulation which has traditionally characterized the UK business environment has involved a mixture of legal control and self-regulation, and this continues to be the dominant underlying approach: self-regulation within a legal framework. However, it may be that changes in the environment, particularly with respect to compliance with regulations, will mean that this structure will become increasingly formalized, for example in statutory recognition of the status of accounting standards. The boundaries between legal control and self-regulation may also become less clear cut, as in the case of the SIB which is part of a structure of self-regulation but will possess statutory backing.

REFERENCES

Aranya, N. 1979: 'The influence of pressure groups on financial statements in Britain'. In T.A. Lee and R.H. Parker (eds), *The Evolution of Corporate Financial Reporting*, Nelson.

Council for the Securities Industry, *City Code on Take-overs and Mergers*, various dates.

Crawford, A. 1984: 'Cost accounting, work control and the development of cost accounting in Britain, 1914–25'. Paper presented at the European Accounting Association, St. Gallen, Switzerland.

Department of Trade and Industry 1985: 'Financial services in the United Kingdom – a new framework for investor protection'. Cmnd. 9432, HMSO, London, January.

Edey, H. 1979: 'Company accounting in the nineteenth and twentieth centuries'. In T.A. Lee and R.H. Parker (eds), *The Evolution of Corporate Financial Reporting*, Nelson.

Edey, H. and Panitpakdi, P. 1956: 'British company accounting and the law, 1844–1900'. In A.C. Littleton and B.S. Yamey (eds), *Studies in the History of Accounting*, Sweet and Maxwell.

Edwards, J.R. 1976: 'The accounting profession and disclosure in published accounts, 1925–1935'. *Accounting and Business Research*, Vol. 6.

Gower, L.C.B. 1984: *Review of Investor Protection*, Cmnd. 9125, HMSO.

Howitt, H. 1966: *The History of the Institute of Chartered Accountants in England and Wales, 1880–1965*, ICAEW.

Johnson, T. 1980: 'Work and Power'. In G. Esland and G. Salaman (eds), *The Politics of Work and Occupations*, Oxford University Press.

Jones, E. 1981: *Accountancy and the British Economy 1840–1980: The Evolution of Ernst and Whinney*. Batsford.

Leach, R. 1981: 'The birth of British accounting standards'. In R. Leach and E. Stamp (eds), *British Accounting Standards*, Sweet and Maxwell.

Nobes, C. and Parker R.H., 1979: 'Chronology: the development of company financial reporting in Great Britain, 1844–1977'. In T.A. Lee and R.H. Parker (eds), *The Evolution of Corporate Financial Reporting*, Nelson.

Page, A.C. 1980: 'Self-regulation and codes of practice', *The Journal of Business Law*.

Peasnell K.V. and Ward C.W.R. 1985: *British Financial Institutions and Markets*, Prentice Hall.

Prais, S.J. 1976: *The Evolution of Giant Firms in Britain*, Cambridge University Press.

Rose, H. 1965: *Disclosure in Company Accounts*, 2nd edn, Institute of Economic Affairs.

Stamp, E. and Marley, M., 1970: *Accounting Principles and the City Code*, Butterworths.

Underdown B. and Taylor, P.J., 1985: *Accounting Theory and Policy Making*, Heinemann.

Zeff, S., 1972: *Forging Accounting Principles in Five Countries*, Stripes Publishing.

3

The Legal Framework

The history of legal regulation of accounting in the UK contains regular changes and developments not only in the content of accounts required by law but also in the emphasis and objectives of the statutes. Since the first Joint Stock Companies Act in 1844, numerous companies acts have introduced varying amounts of change in the legal requirements for accounting disclosure. The current framework is the result of legislation over a period of almost four decades, starting with the Companies Act 1948. The 1948 Act has been added to by further Acts of Parliament in 1967, 1976, 1980 and 1981 and most recently the Companies Act 1985 was introduced with the primary objective of consolidating these different statutes into a unified piece of legislation.

In this chapter we look at the way in which the law has been used to regulate accounting practice. An appreciation of the approach to regulation reflected in the law is as important to an understanding of accounting disclosure as is a knowledge of the detailed contents of individual statutes. Therefore, company law with respect to accounting is discussed in terms of the pressures and influences which provided the impetus for particular changes in the law and the underlying philosophy represented in legislation. To begin with, the historical background of the early development of legal rules on accounting, covering the period 1844 to 1929, is presented. Next, the individual statues introduced between 1948 and 1981 are reviewed with respect to their main emphasis and principal provisions, and the current framework contained in the Companies Act 1985, is outlined. The pattern of changing objectives of companies legislation which can be identified in these statutes is also considered.

THE EARLY DEVELOPMENT OF LEGAL REGULATION

Central to the framework of accounting regulation has been the development of legal statutes as part of company law. Although joint-stock companies existed in Britain from the sixteenth century their incorporation depended upon acts of parliament or royal charters. The communication of financial information by such companies was both rare and relatively unimportant since ownership and control were combined (Aranya, 1979). The accelerating growth of companies in the early nineteenth century and increasing demands from shareholders and creditors led to the passing of the Joint-Stock Companies Act 1844. This Act made incorporation by registration possible for the first time but only with unlimited liability (Nobes and Parker, 1979). In addition, the Act required companies to maintain accounts, present a balance sheet showing a full and fair position to shareholders and to appoint auditors who were to report on the balance sheet. However, the Registrar of Companies had no control over the information contained in the balance sheet nor powers to require compliance with the Act.

In 1855 a further Joint-Stock Companies Act introduced general limited liability by registration. Despite the evident widespread evasion of the accounting provisions of the 1844 Act (Edey, 1979), when legislation consolidating the Acts of 1844 and 1855 was introduced in 1856, the compulsory accounting and auditing requirements were removed from the statute book. They were replaced by model sets of optional company articles which included more advanced accounting and auditing clauses.

The period from 1855 to 1900 has been described as being marked by a complete absence of statutory regulation under the general company law in matters of accounting and audit. This permissiveness did not extend to certain special categories of companies whose corporate status and limited liability derived from special legislation. These categories included railways, banks and insurance companies, and gas and electric companies. Each was required to prepare, have audited and publish detailed accounting statements. This difference of treatment from the generality of companies reflected, respectively, the importance of railway company shares on the Stock Exchange, the potentially serious social problems of failure of financial companies (insurance companies and banks) and the economic and social significance of public utilities (electric and gas companies). Banks were subject to a statutory requirement for compulsory annual audit.

In 1929, legislation introduced four extensions to the regulation of company financial reporting (Edey, 1979). First, the regulations applying to prospectuses for new issues of securities were extended to include an auditor's report on the profits and dividends of the issuing company. Second, some acknowledgement was made of the increasing significance of holding companies by defining them and requiring some general disclosures of the methods by which subsidiaries' profits had been accounted for. Third, an annual profit and loss account was required to be presented to shareholders, although there was no requirement to file it with the Registar of Companies. No regulations were imposed on the contents of the profit and loss account nor was it required to be audited. Finally, more detailed and extensive regulations were applied to the content and form of the balance sheet.

Throughout the period covered by the above review, the dominant objective in accounting regulation was the desire to ensure proper stewardship of the owners' business by the managers. Concern for the protection of shareholders was evident in the creation of limited liability status and this emphasis also influenced the accounting requirements. Company accounts were seen as providing a historical account of the managers' stewardship of the company's assets and as a control against potential fraud or misappropriation of the shareholders' and creditors' funds.

THE COMPANIES ACT 1948

Almost 20 years elapsed after the 1929 Act before the next major piece of companies legislation in 1948. However, the absence of legislation does not mean that no concern was expressed over the adequacy of accounting disclosure during this period. The modifications which had been made to company law from 1900 had significantly extended the regulations applied to company financial reports. In 1931 the relevance of these extensions was called into question by the Royal Mail Case (Edwards, 1976). It had become a frequent practice of companies to build up secret reserves which were used to increase profits in subsequent years of poor trading. The Royal Mail Steam Packet Company had followed this practice and its auditor was tried on a charge of aiding and abetting the publication of false accounts. Although the auditor was acquitted, and despite the absence of any further companies legislation until 1947, the criticism which the case brought down upon current accounting practice, particularly in regard to the adequacy of the profit and loss account as an indicator of investment performance, stimulated many companies to improve their reporting practices (Edwards, 1976).

The introduction of the Companies Act 1948, marked a radical departure from the approach adopted in previous legislation. For the first time emphasis was placed upon the importance of the provision of information in financial statements to assist in investment decisions. The Act, which was based in a large part upon the recommendations of the

Cohen Committee on Company Law Reform which had reported in 1945, established the framework and approach to accounting disclosure which still applies today.

Disclosure requirements were introduced in a number of areas which had not been subject to legislation previously. Amongst the major provisions contained in the Act were the following:

(1) Every company was required to present annually to the shareholders in general meeting a set of accounts, which should comprise a balance sheet and profit and loss account, together with a directors report and the auditor's report on the accounts. The profit and loss account was to be subject to audit for the first time, reflecting a concern for the quality of information on investment performance rather than simply the stewardship of assets.

(2) Group accounts were also required for the first time. Where one company had a controlling interest in another company, then the former was to present consolidated financial statements reflecting the aggregate profitability and position of the companies.

(3) Both individual company accounts and group accounts were subject to greatly extended requirements regarding the individual items of information which should be disclosed in the financial statements and supporting notes. These items of information were specified in the Eighth Schedule to the Act, which provided the statutory minimum disclosure requirements. Some exemptions from disclosure were permitted for certain special classes of companies, banking, discount, insurance and shipping companies, but apart from these exemptions all companies were required to comply with the disclosure provisions.

(4) A different approach to the criteria that the accounting information should satisfy was also reflected in the requirement placed upon auditors to report whether the financial statements, i.e. balance sheet, profit and loss account and notes thereto, provided a 'true and fair view' of the company's financial position at the end of the period and profitability during that period. The equivalent requirement prior to 1948, which had applied to the balance sheet only, referred to the accounts being 'true and correct'.

The 1948 Act represented a radical change both in the approach to and the structure of companies legislation regarding accounting. The emphasis moved from stewardship of assets towards appraisal of investment performance, from numerical accuracy and a correctness towards the fairness of the overall picture of the company represented in the accounts, and from limited to more extensive disclosure of information.

In 1967 a further Companies Act revised and extended the requirements of the 1948 Act. Again the Act was partly the result of a government appointed commission on company law, the Jenkins Committee, which had reported in 1962. The 1967 Act can be described primarily as a disclosure statute. No major changes were made in the structure of reporting, but disclosure requirements were extended.

For example requirements were introduced for disclosure, in the profit and loss account or notes, of the turnover for the year and its method of computation, income from investments, auditors' renumeration, interest payable and the amount charged in respect of hire of plant and machinery. The 1948 requirement for disclosure of the aggregate amount of directors' emoluments was extended to require details of the breakdown of this figure between the chairman and directors at various levels of emoluments. With respect to the balance sheet and related notes, examples of new disclosure requirements were: the aggregate of loans not repayable within five years, the amount of fixed asset acquisitions and disposals in the year and details on investments. The information required in group accounts regarding subsidiary companies was expanded to include details of the name of the subsidiary, its country of incorporation, the class of shares held and the proportionate holding.

The information to be included in the directors' report was also considerably extended with respect to both general business information, such as turnover from exports and from each major class of business, and information on the directors' interests in the company, such as business contracts in which a director has an interest and amounts of shareholdings. In addition, the audit report was simplified and companies were obliged to appoint a suitably qualified professional accountant as auditor.

When the disclosure requirements in the 1948 and 1967 Acts are looked at together, it is interesting to consider the rationale behind many of the individual items. We have already seen that the early Companies Acts reflected a stewardship objective and this influence is also present in the 1948 and 1967 legislation, for example, the disclosure of the amount of fixed assets and current assets, the movements on reserves and provisions and the details of the remuneration of directors and higher paid employees. The protection of creditors and measurement of liquidity can also be seen as an influence in the provisions relating to for example, details of liabilities and interest payable. However, it is also possible to view some of the information requirements as being relevant to the assessment of the future performance of the company rather than past stewardship. Examples in this category would be details on interest payable, the breakdown between loans payable within and beyond five years, and the details of capital expenditure authorized but not contracted and contracted but not provided for in the accounts, all of which could be relevant to an assessment of the future cash flows of the company. Thus a trend towards providing information relevant to investment decisions can be seen. This trend is also reflected in the requirements for disclosure of certain accounting policies or measurement bases, such as the computation of turnover and the valuation of fixed assets, and in the overall intention expressed in the audit requirement for a 'true and fair view'. These provisions indicate an approach concerned more with the quality of information as a basis for forming an overall picture of the financial performance and position of a company than with the numerical accuracy of each item of information.

THE COMPANIES ACT 1976

The principal objective of the Companies Act 1976, was to amend the law relating to certain aspects of company administration and the registration of business names. In the area of accounting regulation, the main changes introduced in the Act can be summarized as follows:

(1) The introduction of an 'accounting reference date' for each company in order to provide a more precise definition of the reporting periods to be covered by the financial statements. The regulations for the maximum time following the end of the reporting period within which the company must report were also tightened.

(2) New requirements were introduced regarding the nature of accounting records that would constitute proper books of account. The accounting records must be sufficient to show and explain the company's transactions and also to disclose at any time with reasonable accuracy the financial position of the company, as well as providing the basis for true and fair accounts, which had been the definition of proper books implied in the 1948 Act.

(3) A number of new provisions were specified with respect to the appointment, removal, resignation, remuneration and qualification of auditors.

Overall the 1976 Act involved changes of administration and definition to deal with certain weaknesses and ambiquities in the existing legislation. It did not reflect any significant new trends in financial reporting or change the fundamental nature of the 1948 framework.

The Companies Act 1980, provided the first main impact in companies legislation of a new influence, namely that of the European Economic Community (EEC). The Act was partly the result of the need to implement the EEC Second Directive which dealt with the formation and maintenance of capital of public companies. Provisions were also introduced to deal with abuses highlighted in some Department of Trade investigations involving share dealings and directors' conflicts of interest.

Few of the requirements of the 1980 Act had direct implications for company accounting. New rules were introduced for classification of companies. Previously, all companies were public unless they met the definition of a private company. Now, all companies are private unless they satisfy the conditions contained in the Act defining public limited companies. The Act also introduced new provisions in connection with the issue of, payment for and maintenance of capital of public companies, provided new definitions of distributable profits and specified additional disclosure requirements regarding transactions involving directors.

The European influence continued in the Companies Act 1981, which implemented in the UK the EEC Fourth Directive on Company Law. The Fourth Directive was concerned specifically with requirements for company accounts, and involved a compromise between the approach to reporting followed in the UK and that present in some of the other EEC member states. This compromise inevitably meant that the approach to accounting regulation present in UK legislation would change somewhat and, as a result, the 1981 Act involved a more major revision of the structure of the Companies Act 1948, than any of the intervening statutes. The significance of the Act can be seen by looking at the main elements of its provisions.

(1) Format of accounts: The Act prescribed a limited number of specified formats for presentation of financial statements. There are two possible balance sheet formats and four profit and loss account formats. This requirement is due to the influence of some EEC countries such as France and Germany where rigid formats have been prescribed in law for many years, and contrasts with the previous flexibility in the UK.

However, the effect of the formats should not be overrated, as even in the absence of legal formats most UK companies tended to follow by convention a similar pattern of reporting. Also the Companies Act 1981, included as much flexibility as was permitted under the Directive, in terms of allowing disclosures in the notes to the accounts rather than in the main statements.

(2) Accounting principles: The second main area of departure from the previous UK approach was the inclusion of accounting principles in legal statute. While the inclusion of principles in law was new in the UK, the set of principles to be included owed much to the influence of the UK negotiators in the drafting of the Directive. The general principles to be followed in preparation of accounts are the going concern, consistency, prudence and accruals principles, which were already effective in the UK through their inclusion in SSAP2. Thus, while the potential significance of legal regulation in the field of accounting principles is great, the practical significance of the Fourth Directive and the Companies Act 1981, was limited. However, the inclusion of these principles in statute could lead to some inflexibility in the future development of professional recommendations on principles.

(3) True and fair view: The influence of the UK in the development of the Directive was also evident in the provision that accounts should show a true and fair view. While this approach had been present in the UK since 1948, the Companies Act 1981, did specify the requirement in slightly different terms. It was stated as an overriding consideration, which should not be jeopardized by strict adherence to the other requirements of the Act, and can be used to justify departure from those requirements.

(4) Disclosure requirements: The trend towards increased disclosure which we have seen in earlier Companies Acts continued in the 1981 Act. The most notable new disclosure requirement was for details of cost of sales information to be given in the profit and loss account.

(5) Classification of companies: Since 1967 when the status of 'exempt private company' was abolished, all companies, irrespective of size were subject to the same disclosure requirements, apart from a few minor reliefs. The Companies Act 1981, introduced classification of companies into three tiers: small, medium-sized and large. Modified disclosure requirements were introduced for small and medium-sized companies. These modifications apply only to public disclosure through filing accounts with the registrar of companies; the accounts presented to shareholders must still meet the full requirements. However, the classification of companies may provide a basis for differential standards of disclosure in the future and the government is looking at ways of moving in this direction.

(6) The directors' report: A final area of reporting to be changed was the directors' report. The content of the report was expanded, for example to include a statement of future prospects, and for the first time it was made subject to audit in that the auditor must report on any inconsistencies between information in the directors' report and related information in the accounts.

Overall, it can be seen that the Companies Act 1981, involved a number of major changes in UK law. However, these changes can best be described as modifications in the UK approach to statutory regulation of accounting disclosure rather than as presenting a fundamental change of approach. The modifications were the result of EEC membership and the necessity of implementing an EEC directive, but the UK negotiators ensured that the content of the directive was as far as possible consistent with UK practice. Thus, the impact of the 1981 Act on the regulatory framework was greater than its impact on actual accounting practice. However, the precedent that has been established of having accounting principles included in a statute law could be important in the future development of accounting regulations.

THE CURRENT FRAMEWORK: THE COMPANIES ACT 1985

While the 1948, 1967 and 1981 Companies Acts have been the main statutes which have shaped the disclosure requirements in the UK, the overall legal framework is now contained in the Companies Act 1985, which was introduced purely with the objective of consolidating existing legislation. The need for consolidation had long been felt by those involved in interpreting and applying company legislation. Five separate Companies Acts were on the statute book, some of them involving a considerable amount of cross-referencing to previous legislation, together with statutory instruments and provisions relating to companies in other legislation.

The objective of consolidation, as stated by the Government was, thus, to provide a 'thorough reorganisation' which would allow shareholders to 'more readily identify and more easily understand their rights', and assist companies to 'more efficiently and effectively discharge their legal responsibilities and obligations'. Whether the Act satisfies this objective is debatable, but it does provide a considerable improvement on the previous situation. In fact, the process of consolidation has led not only to the Companies Act, 1985, but also to three minor supporting Acts, the Companies Consolidation (Consequential

Provisions) Act: the Business Names Act and the Companies Securities (Insider Dealing) Act, the latter two covering subjects which stand on their own.

The main section dealing with accounting and audit requirements is Part VII of the Companies Act 1985. No significant new requirements are introduced and the provisions contained in previous legislation have been reorganized in the following structure:

(1) accounting records;
(2) accounting reference periods, i.e. determining the financial year;
(3) the form and content of individual company and group accounts;
(4) the requirements for directors' and auditors' reports; and
(5) the presentation of the annual accounts to members and filing of accounts with the Registrar of Companies (including provisions regarding modified accounts for small and medium-sized companies).

The detailed disclosure requirements regarding the format and contents of the accounts and directors' and auditors' reports are now contained in a series of schedules (numbers 4 to 10) rather than in the main body of the Act.

Given that the Act involves the rearrangement of existing legislation rather than the introduction of new requirements, it does not contain significant provisions which have not been commented on earlier, or reflect any change of emphasis in the approach to company accounts. A summary of the detailed requirements of company law with respect to accounting disclosure and audit is contained in appendix 1.

The powers of the Secretary of State to modify the legislation are set out in Section 256 of the 1985 Act. By use of a statutory instrument the Secretary of State may add to the classes of document to be included in company or group accounts, and amend the disclosure requirements regarding the contents of those documents.

CHANGING OBJECTIVES IN COMPANY LAW

The requirements of successive Companies Acts have reflected a changing pattern of objectives and influences in the development of accounting regulation. In the nineteenth century and early twentieth century the principal concerns were the possibility of business failure and protection against fraud or misappropriation of funds. The changing nature of companies as economic entities was also an influence as directors became increasingly separated from shareholders. Thus the

The Legal Framework

emphasis was placed on the directors' stewardship of assets and funds, and the protection of investors and creditors. The continued development of the business entity has led to emphasis being placed on the use of information in investment decisions, and the disclosure of an increasing amount of information, as well as the fact that that information should be publicly available. Table 3.1 provides a summary of the main developments in company law and the associated influences and objectives which have been discussed in the foregoing sections.

Table 3.1 The development of statutory regulation of accounting disclosure

Statute	Principal provisions	Objectives and influences
Joint Stock Companies Acts (JSCA)		
1844 JSCA	Allowed registered companies	Growth in business
	Required full and fair annual balance sheet	Desire to ensure solvency and honesty of directors
1856 JSCA	Limited liability established	Growth in business
	Publication of accounting information voluntary	Accounting information viewed as internal
1862 JSCA	Dividends only allowed out of profits	Maintenance of capital and protection of creditors
Companies Acts (CA)		
1900 CA	Compulsory audit	Separation of management from shareholding
1908 CA	Accounts of public companies to be filed with registrar	Public access to information given changing nature of companies

1929 CA	Increased accounting regulations; profit statement required, though unaudited Details on assets and valuation; balance sheet to be 'true and correct'	Concern over secret reserves Measurement of performance over time recognized as important as well as periodic valuation for stewardship
1948 CA	Balance sheet and profit and loss account to be true and fair Detailed provisions on content of accounts established Group accounts required	Appraisal of investment performance Truth and fairness of overall picture rather than numerical accuracy Extending disclosure
1967 CA	Additional disclosure requirements	Increasing disclosure of information
1976 CA	Accounting reference periods Accounting records	Clarification of existing statutes
1980 CA	Public companies defined	EEC Second Directive
1981 CA	Specified format for accounts Included accounting principles in law Classification of companies Extended disclosure requirements	Compliance with requirements of EEC Fourth Directive Overriding importance of 'true and fair' reasserted
1985 CA	Consolidating 1948–81 CAs	Consolidation of various statutes

During much of the period covered by our review, a clear tendency may be discerned for legislation either to be framed in the immediate aftermath of a financial scandal or to lag behind an apparent need for change. Two reasons may be offered for this legislative lag. First, the type of market forces which we discussed in chapter 1 may, whilst not being dominant, none the less exert some influence over financial accounting practice. In response to perceptions of need, some companies' financial reporting practices may move ahead not only of those of other companies, but of legal requirements. Edwards (1976) shows that some companies were producing directors' reports and profit and loss accounts many years before they were statutorily required. Second, changes in legislation require a consensus. Even without disparities in practice, this may take some considerable time to achieve; with them, the achievement of consensus may be long delayed. One means of achieving a consensus is by the development of a body of acceptable accounting knowledge. Edwards (1976) concludes that the apparent failure to legislate after the Royal Mail Case may be explained by the lack of a body of acceptable accounting knowledge. Extension in disclosure requirements and audit requirements, and the application of the concept of true and fair, have depended on the development of the accounting profession and its ability to formulate principles and practices which provide the body of knowledge to implement legislation. Thus, the interdependence between statutory and professional control of accounting practice, which was discussed in the previous chapter, has been important as companies legislation has developed.

SUMMARY

In this chapter we have examined various aspects of the legal framework for the regulation of accounting in the UK. We have seen that there have been not only regular changes and developments in the content of accounts prescribed by law, but also changes in the emphasis and objectives of the statutes. We noted that the central pillar of the legal framework of accounting regulation, the statutes, has been modified by various influences. These include the changing nature of companies and their financial characteristics, changes in the emphasis placed upon stewardship and decision making as objectives of financial reporting, and, latterly, the influence of the European Economic Community.

The Companies Act 1948, is notable as representing a radical change in the approach to legal regulation of accounting. That Act shifted emphasis away from stewardship as the function of disclosure to one of appraising investment performance. Also, the 1948 Act introduced the criterion that financial statements should present a true and fair view. The framework established in 1948 was subjected to a major revision by the Companies Act 1981. This act, although containing major changes in UK company law, none the less served to modify the basic approach rather than introduce a fundamental change of emphasis. However, the precedent which was set of including accounting in statute law may in the future prove to be an extremely important development.

REFERENCES

Aranya, N. 1979: 'The influence of pressure groups on financial statements in Britain'. In T.A. Lee and R.H. Parker (eds), *The Evolution of Corporate Financial Reporting*, Nelson.

Edey, H.C. 1979: 'Company accounting in the nineteenth and twentieth centuries'. In T.A. Lee and R.H. Parker (eds), *The Evolution of Corporate Financial Reporting*, Nelson.

Edwards, J.R. 1976: 'The accounting profession and disclosure in published accounts, 1925–1935'. *Accounting and Business Research*, Vol. 6.

Nobes, C. and Parker, R.H. 1979: 'Chronology: the development of company financial reporting in Great Britain, 1844–1977'. In T.A. Lee and R.H. Parker (eds), *The Evolution of Corporate Financial Reporting*, Nelson.

4

The Accounting Standards Committee

In addition to the legal framework for controlling accounting practice, regulations are produced by the accounting profession. In particular, the ASC is responsible for developing SSAPs and Statements of Recommended Practice (SORPs) on behalf of the professional accounting bodies. The first SSAP was issued in 1971 and by the end of December 1985 a total of 23 standards had been developed, 21 of which were still effective.

Previous chapters have emphasized the need to look at regulations in the context of the pressures which have led to their introduction, how the choice of regulations is made and how compliance is ensured or enforced, as well as the particular practices that are required. Consequently, this chapter discusses the manner in which SSAPs are determined, rather than the contents of individual standards. The chapter starts by looking at the creation of the ASC. Subsequent sections describe the role of accounting standards and the structure and procedures of the ASC. Finally, the work of the ASC in its sixteen-year existence is outlined and evaluated. A brief description of the main contents of published SSAPs is provided in appendix 2.

THE CREATION OF THE ACCOUNTING STANDARDS COMMITTEE

Professional statements on accounting practice had existed for much longer than the ASC. From 1945 to 1969 the ICAEW produced a series of *Recommendations on Accounting Principles*. However, as authoritative statements on best accounting practice, these recommendations suffered from a number of deficiencies. Adherence to the recommendations was not mandatory, they took a long time to produce, they often included alternative approaches and there were no procedures for consultation with interested parties.

The need for change in this system was highlighted by a number of 'scandals' in the 1960s when flexibility of accounting practice led to strong criticism of the accounting profession (see Stamp, 1969; Stamp and Marley 1970). The issue which led to most criticism was that of profit forecasts in the context of take-over bids, the most famous case being the GEC–AEI take-over. Three months before the end of the financial year the AEI directors, who were opposing a take-over bid by GEC announced a profit of £10 million for the financial year. Following the take-over the published accounts revealed a £4.5 million loss. While £5 million of the total £14.5 million difference could be attributed to matters of fact, £9.5 million was due to judgement regarding accounting principles and bases.

Action to increase the standardization of accounting was needed, both to deal with the real problem of too much flexibility in the choice of accounting policies and also to divert criticism that the accounting profession was complacent about the apparent deficiencies in accounting practice. Without action by the profession, it is possible that the government might have established a regulatory agency to give a lead in the development of consistent accounting principles. In December 1969, the Council of the ICAEW took the initiative and published a *Statement of Intent on Accounting Standards in the 1970's* (ICAEW, 1969). The main intentions outlined in the statement were:

(1) narrowing the areas of difference and variety in accounting practice by publishing authoritative statements on best accounting practice;
(2) recommending disclosure of accounting bases when accounts include significant items which depend on judgement or estimates;
(3) recommending disclosure of departures from established definitive accounting standards;
(4) providing an opportunity for wider exposure of draft proposals on accounting standards.

The option for some flexibility in the new procedures was preserved in that while the *Statement of Intent* suggested that, where possible, accounting standards would be 'definitive', it also referred to the 'impracticability of rigid uniformity'.

The following month, January 1970, saw the creation of the ASSC, to carry out the above proposals by developing definitive standards of financial reporting. To begin with the ASSC was a committee of the ICAEW alone, but its representativeness as a professional body grew quickly. Representatives from the Institute of Chartered Accountants of Scotland (ICAS) and the Institute of Chartered Accountants in Ireland

(ICAI) were added later in 1970, and in the following year from the Institute of Cost and Management Accountants (ICMA) and the Chartered Association of Certified Accountants (CACA). The sixth body to join the ASSC, the Chartered Institute of Public Finance and Accountancy (CIPFA), joined in 1976. These six governing bodies work together through the Consultative Committee of Accountancy Bodies (CCAB), formed in 1974, and in February 1976 the ASSC was reconstituted as a joint committee of the CCAB. The word 'steering' was dropped from the title to leave the Accounting Standards Committee, and we will use this title to refer to the body throughout its existence.

THE ROLE OF THE ACCOUNTING STANDARDS COMMITTEE

In common with similar bodies in other countries, the ASC can be seen to have two main functions. First, it has a production function: to develop standards and decide on best accounting practice. Second, it has a marketing function: to ensure that the standards produced are accepted within and outside the profession and complied with, thus maintaining the accounting profession's power and influence in the regulation of practice. The relative importance of these two functions, which can be seen as related to the two original pressures of the need to reduce flexibility in practice and the need to divert the related criticism of the profession, may vary over time and between different issues. It is probably true that the ASC's awareness of its marketing role has grown throughout its existence.

The ASC's Constitution

The ASC's production function is recognized and specified in some detail in the objects and terms of reference laid down in its constitution. These are as given below:

Objects. The Committee's objects shall be to define accounting concepts, to narrow differences of financial accounting and reporting treatment and to codify generally accepted best practice in the public interest. These objects encompass:

(a) fundamentals of financial accounting and the application of financial statements;
(b) definition of terms used;
(c) questions of measurement of reported results and financial position; and
(d) the content and form of financial statements.

Terms of reference. The Committee's terms of reference are: bearing in mind the intention of the governing bodies to advance accounting standards and to narrow the areas of difference and variety in accounting practice by publishing authoritative statements in the public interest on best accounting practice which will wherever possible be definitive, the Committee shall:

(a) keep under review standards of financial accounting and reporting;
(b) propose to the councils of the governing bodies statements of standard accounting practice and interpretations of such statements;
(c) publish consultative documents, discussion papers and exposure drafts and submit to the governing bodies non-mandatory guidance notes with the object of maintaining and advancing accounting standards;
(d) consult as appropriate with representatives of finance, commerce, industry and government, and other bodies and persons concerned with financial reporting; and
(e) maintain close links with the International Accounting Standards Committee and the accountancy profession in Europe and throughout the world.

The above, which is taken from the Constitution of the ASC, paras 2 and 3, raises a number of interesting points concerning the role of the ASC and the purpose and scope of accounting standards. First it is stated that the ASC is to work in 'the public interest'. This is a necessary condition if SSAPs produced by a private sector professional body are to have general application. However, while the ASC's recommendations may affect a wide spectrum of interests or groups, it is likely that in practice the ASC will have direct contact with only an incomplete representation of those affected. The ASC's interpretation of the public interest is likely to be influenced most strongly by the views of those who will have to implement a standard and those who comment in the exposure period. The need to make choices in the public interest thus presents the standard setters with considerable problems as to how they define public interest and measure the effect of alternative policies upon it. This problem of social choice is discussed in more detail in chapter 6.

Second, related to the above point, emphasis is placed on the importance of consultation, through invitation to comment on proposals and through direct contact between the ASC and other bodies concerned with financial reporting. The ASC has no legal power to enforce compliance with SSAPs and must rely on acceptance both of its authority to regulate practice and of its recommendations on particular issues. If a standard is not adhered to, then the credibility of the whole standard setting process may be threatened. Consequently, it is necessary, as far as possible, to ensure in advance of a standard being issued that its contents will be acceptable. The objects paragraph above refers to 'generally accepted best practice'. The need to produce acceptable standards may limit the scope of the ASC to introduce innovations into accounting practices. It may also mean that the ASC is open to influence from those groups with power to influence the implementation of a standard.

Third, the ASC's constitution refers to different types of standards. Some standards involve definition of concepts, some will be intended to lead to uniform accounting treatment and some will simply involve a codification of established existing practice.

Fourth, the objects clause outlines the possible scope of accounting standards. They may cover fundamental accounting principles, measurement issues, disclosure of information (content of financial statements) and the manner in which disclosure is made (form of financial statements).

Finally, the ASC's terms of reference indicate that its role is to propose SSAPs and interpretations of those statements. While the ASC can publish proposals for standards and consultative documents, the authority to issue SSAPs is retained by the professional institutes. For a standard to come into effect, it much have the support of the Councils of all the governing bodies of the ASC. This position contrasts with that of the FASB in the US, which has the power not only to develop but also issue standards. In the case of SORPs, which are non-mandatory, the ASC can issue statements on its own authority.

Accounting Standards and the True and Fair View

Accounting standards in themselves have no formal legal status, but it would be wrong to conclude from that, that they have no authority. Members of the governing bodies are required to try to ensure adherence to standards. SSAPs will therefore be a major influence on professional accountants as they advise clients, prepare accounts and audit the financial statements of companies. Non-compliance with an accounting standard is likely to be noted in the audit report and may lead to a qualified report. The threat of audit qualification may encourage companies to comply with the requirements of SSAPs, if they fear an adverse market reaction to qualification.

To begin with it was stated that standards would provide 'a definitive approach to . . . a true and fair view'. More recently, the ASC has defined standards as applying to all accounts intended to show a true and fair view (ASC, 1983). On this basis, accounts which do not comply with accounting standards will not satisfy the legal requirement to show a true and fair view. In 1983 the ASC obtained and published a written opinion from counsel on the status of SSAPs with respect to the true and fair view and the position if the provisions of a standard conflict in some way with the detailed requirements of company law (Hoffman and Arden, 1983).

The opinion expressed by counsel was that although SSAPs had no direct legal effect they could have an indirect effect on the interpretation that the court will give to the concept of true and fair. Accounting standards have this role for two reasons. First, they represent statements of accepted practice regarding the preparation of financial statements. Second, the existence of standards creates an expectation on the part of readers that accounts will comply with standards, and the expectation of readers could be important in deciding whether accounts provide a true and fair view. While the courts are not bound to endorse the requirements of an SSAP, compliance with accepted accounting practices will provide prima-facie evidence that accounts are true and fair and non-compliance will suggest prima-facie that they are not. The notion of 'true and fair' is a legal concept, at a high level of abstraction. As such, the *meaning* remains unchanged, but the *content* which the courts will give to the concept can change. Therefore developments in accounting standards, which may differ from and go further than the statutory provisions, need not conflict with the unchanging legal requirement for truth and fairness.

There are no reported cases in which the courts have defined true and fair specifically, although in the unreported case of Argyll Foods in 1981, non-compliance with SSAP14 on group accounts was used as contributory evidence of a breach of the law in this respect (Bird, 1982). The counsel opinion to the ASC suggests that accounting standards have a significant role in relation to the true and fair view. The presumption that compliance with an SSAP is necessary to give a true and fair view will be strengthened by the extent to which the standard is accepted and applied, and this fact emphasizes again the need for the ASC to develop standards which are acceptable to producers of accounts.

The question of the relationship between accounting standards and the true and fair view has been most clearly illustrated by the issue of inflation accounting. In developing a pronouncement to follow SSAP16, the ASC was faced with the dilemma that if it stated that accounting for the effects of inflation is necessary for a true and fair view, then any standard should really apply to all companies, and be rigidly enforced, but if the position was adopted that inflation accounting was not essential to a true and fair view then could they reasonably issue a standard and expect companies to comply? Further, auditors could be faced with major problems if they were required to enforce a standard as true and fair given the high level of non-compliance with SSAP16.

The formal structure of the ASC has changed and developed since it was first created. The original ICAEW body consisted of 11 members, but that number grew with the involvement of the other professional institutes. Also, during the first years of its existence, the ASC was drawn exclusively from the membership of the governing bodies, but that is no longer the case, although members of the institutes still provide the large majority of the ASC. The following points set out the composition of the ASC (ASC Constitution, paras 7–14):

(1) The committee shall have not more than 20 members. They are appointed (not elected) *annually* from 1st July. Up to five of these places may be reserved for users of financial statements, who need not be members of the governing bodies. There must be at least one member from each of the governing bodies.
(2) Two additional non-voting representatives of government may be co-opted.
(3) Members are appointed for a three year term initially, with the possibility of reappointment for a further three years, but no longer.
(4) The power of appointment is vested in the CCAB.
(5) The chairman is also appointed by the CCAB, for a period of up to three years, with the possibility of reappointment.

Members of the ASC are part-time and unpaid, and the committee normally meets monthly. It is supported by a small full-time secretariat. This position contrasts sharply with that of the ASC's US counterpart, the Financial Accounting Standards Board (FASB) which has seven full-time members, appointed irrespective of background, plus a large supplementary staff and research establishment, and with an annual budget of several million dollars.

The structure and membership of the ASC are important because they help to establish its legitimacy as a body to regulate accounting practice. Legitimacy comes first of all from the technical expertise of members of the profession to form judgements about accounting issues. However, the choices that are made by the standard setters have wider implications than the selection of technically best practice. A wide variety of interest groups may be affected by accounting standards, and, as outlined earlier, the ASC should not act on behalf of any particular sectional interest but in the public interest. The kind of social legitimacy which this role requires means that there should be adequate representation in the standard setting process of the interests of all those who are likely to be affected by standards. It is extremely difficult for a private professional body to achieve this in practice. However, sufficient legitimacy to make the system work is achieved if the standard setting body provides for representation of, and acts in a way which is acceptable to, those groups that are most influential in determining the acceptance and implementation of standards.

The possibility of up to five members of the ASC being users of accounts, who need not be members of the governing bodies is one step to ensure that the composition of the ASC is regarded as sufficiently representative. Additionally, all members are required to regard themselves not as delegates of particular interests but rather to be guided by the need to act 'in the general interest of the community' (ASC Constitution, para 11). The organizational backgrounds of current members of the ASC are shown in table 4.1.

Table 4.1 Backgrounds of ASC members at
31 December 1985

In practice	7
In private and public industry and commerce	6
Users	4
Non-trading public sector	2
Academic	1
	20

It can be seen that professional interests and those of the preparers of accounts (industry and commerce) are well represented on the ASC but certain other groups have no direct representation. Those classified as 'users' are concerned either with investment in shares or debt finance, and those in industry and commerce all come from very large organizations. There are no members from the trade unions, consumer groups or small businesses, and although representatives from government departments are present as observers, they have no voting rights.

It is possible to argue that the membership of the ASC is not representative of as wide a spectrum of opinion as it might be, given that its recommendations apply to all companies (and some public sector organizations) and may have consequences affecting a wide variety of interests. On the other hand, it can also be argued that complete representation of all groups that might possibly be affected by accounting standards is not practicable, and that membership of the ASC is drawn from those most involved with financial reporting. Further, the case can be made that if the ASC behaved in a manner which was against the public interest, the government would act, either to stop a particular standard or to replace the ASC with its own agency. Some evidence for this view is provided by the case of inflation accounting where, in 1975, the government action in setting up the Sandilands Committee effectively stopped the ASC proposals for general price level accounting and set the ASC on course for some form of current cost accounting.

THE STANDARD SETTING PROCESS

The process by which accounting standards are set by the ASC has been changed in some significant respects in recent years. In this section we will concentrate on the nature of the process as it stands after these changes.

In January 1978 the ASC initiated a review of the standard setting process. The first stage of the review involved a consultative exercise and resulted in *Setting Accounting Standards* (the Watts Report, ASC, 1981), published in January, 1981. Although no radical changes to the status quo were proposed, a number of areas of possible improvement were noted. The main conclusions were that: standards should be definitive, not benchmarks against which departures should be disclosed; there should be no more standards than necessary; the job of producing and issuing standards should be retained by the profession; standards should be set only after extensive and open consultation; supervision of compliance with standards is needed, but should also be maintained in the private sector; and more resources should be made available for the standard setting process.

Having identified possible areas for change, the ASC then appointed a working party to develop practical procedures which would improve the existing process. The working party's findings provided the basis for publication in July 1983 of *Review of the Standard Setting Process* (ASC, 1983), which introduced a number of innovations and revisions in the ASC's procedures. The main points contained in the review were:

(1) increased emphasis on effective consultation and communication;
(2) SSAPs will only be issued on matters of major and fundamental importance affecting the generality of companies; they will be few in number and apply to all accounts intended to give a true and fair view;

(3) a new form of consultative document, the Statement of Intent, was introduced;
(4) a new category of pronouncement, the Statement of Recommended Practice, was also created, to cover topics which do not meet the criteria for an accounting standard;
(5) A further category, of 'franked' SORP's, where recommendations are prepared outside the ASC on topics of limited application and then endorsed or 'franked' by the ASC, was also introduced.

The Stages of the Process

The revised process for setting accounting standards involves a number of stages, some of which were important in the previous process but have now been made explicit. The following outline refers to the development of SSAPs but the process is largely similar for SORPs.

Identification of topics. Individual standards have always been set within a long range programme of work approved by the ASC. However, there has been some criticism of the informal way in which topics find their way onto the ASC's agenda. The revised arrangements seek to formalize matters by making the planning sub-committee of the ASC responsible for monitoring the programme of future work and advising on priorities. In identifying suitable topics it is suggested that particular regard should be given to the requirements of users of accounts, subject to consideration of costs and practicability (ASC, 1983, para. 4. 8).

Research. The ASC may initiate and undertake or sponsor research on a topic, in order to define issues, specify alternative courses of action and survey current practice.

Formation of a working party. Following initial research, a decision is taken on whether to proceed towards a published pronouncement on the topic. A working party is appointed to undertake the technical drafting of consultative documents and draft statements. The working party also suggests to the ASC a consultation plan (see below).

The consultative process. As we have seen already, acceptance is essential to successful accounting standards. The ASC sees effective consultations as important in achieving acceptance and places considerable emphasis on wide consultation.

The ASC has three types of discussion documents. A Discussion Paper is an exploratory document intended to stimulate debate. It might contain tentative conclusions on a subject, but will not set out proposed standard practice. Indeed a standard (or SORP) need not follow automatically from a discussion document. A Statement of Intent (SOI) is a new form of consultative document introduced in the 1983 review. It summarizes how the ASC intends to proceed with a topic and is intended to help reduce problems at the exposure draft stage. The Exposure Draft (ED) is a document setting out the full text of a proposed standard and inviting comment on the proposals. An accounting standard will always be preceded by an ED, unlike a discussion document and SOI, which are optional. Apart from public consultation through consultative documents, the working party may also propose a 'consultative plan'. This plan identifies particular groups with whom meetings and consultations should be held, coordinates consultation with the governing bodies and advises on press coverage, and the possibility of public hearings.

Exposure period. Publication of an exposure draft is followed by a period during which any commentator can submit written opinions to the ASC. Any public hearings take place during this period.

Reconsideration, finalization and issue of a standard. Comments received during the exposure period are reviewed and a decision taken on how to proceed. For example, in the case of research and development a new exposure draft was necessary (ED 14 and ED 17). More recently, the ASC followed ED 31 on acquisitions and mergers with an SOI outlining how the intentions for a standard differed from the ED. Normally, however, an SSAP will be drafted, on the basis of the ED and the comments received. The final draft standard adopted by the ASC is sent to the six governing bodies for approval. If this approval is forthcoming the standard is then issued by the bodies. Associated Guidance Notes and a Technical Release may be issued by the ASC at the same time.

The above revised procedures are set out in much greater detail than was previously the case. There is increased emphasis upon formality and planning, suggesting a desire on the part of the ASC to demonstrate that SSAPs result from a 'due process' rather than *ex machina*. In particular, consultation has been given increased formal attention. The emphasis on consultation is partly the result of the ASC moving to more controversial topics where a consensus view may be more difficult to obtain (e.g. deferred tax, inflation accounting and accounting for leases) and partly related to the problems of ensuring compliance with SSAPs.

The Planning Sub-committee

The role of the ASC planning sub-committee should be noted. This sub-committee has responsibilities for advising the ASC on the choice of topics for the ASC programme, the selection of priorities among those topics and the need for research. It also recommends the membership of working parties, reviews documents and proposals before they are presented to the ASC and generally oversees the progress of projects. Consequently, the planning sub-committee is potentially an influential element in the standard setting process.

Statement of Recommended Practice

SORPs differ from SSAPs in both nature and status. While SSAPs deal with issues of major and fundamental importance, SORPs cover matters which are either of widespread applicability but limited importance, when the ASC will develop the SORP itself, or limited applicability, when the SORP may be developed by, for example, representatives of a particular industry, and then 'franked' by the ASC.

Where the ASC undertakes the development of an SORP itself, the procedures followed will be largely the same as outlined above. However, an ED is not essential, an SOI may be issued instead. In the situation where development of proposals has taken place outside the ASC, the ASC will have to be satisfied of both the technical quality of the proposals and also the adequacy of the process by which they have been prepared before awarding the status of 'franked SORP'.

One of the most significant factors about SORPs and franked SORPs is that they are not mandatory. The ASC hopes that their 'quality and status' will ensure respect and compliance, but there is no requirement to disclose departure from an SORP in company accounts. SORPs are issued by the ASC itself, rather than by the governing bodies. The creation of a new category of pronouncement, with which compliance is not considered essential, can be seen as a reaction to the problem of acceptance of accounting standards. The ASC now has more scope to issue statements without the fear that conflict arising from non-compliance will threaten the credibility and acceptance of the ASC itself.

THE WORK OF THE ACCOUNTING STANDARDS COMMITTEE

So far our discussion has considered the framework and procedures for setting accounting standards. In this section we review the output of the process, the actual standards produced, concentrating on the nature of

Table 4.2 EDs, SSAPs and SORPs issued July 1970 to December 1985

Subject	Exposure Drafts		Standards		Period ED–SSAP (months)[a]
	ED No.	Date	SSAP No.	Date	
Associated companies	1	Jul 1970	1	Jan 1971	7
	25	Oct 1979	1 (revised)	Apr 1982	30
Disclosure of accounting policies	2	Feb 1971	2	Nov 1971	9
Acquisitions and mergers	3	Feb 1971	b		—
	31	Oct 1982	23	Apr 1985	30
Earnings per share	4	Mar 1971	3	Feb 1972	11
Extraordinary items and prior year adjustments	5	Sep 1971	b		
	7	Jul 1972	6	Apr 1974	
	16	Sep 1975	e		
	36	Jan 1985			—
Stock and work in progress	6	May 1972	9	May 1975	36
Inflation	8	Feb 1973	7 (P)	May 1974	15
	18	Dec 1976	b		
	24	May 1979	16	Mar 1980	39
	35	Jul 1984	d		
Government grants	9	Mar 1973	4	Apr 1974	13
Value added tax	10	May 1973	5	Apr 1974	11
Deferred taxation	11	May 1973	11	Aug 1975	27
	19	Jun 1977	15	Oct 1978	16
	33	Jun 1983	15 (revised)	May 1985	23

Taxation under the imputation system	12	Jun 1973	8	Aug	14
Source and application of funds	13	May 1974	10	Jul 1975	14
Research and development	14	Feb 1975	b		—
	17	Apr 1976	13	Dec 1977	34
Depreciation	15	Feb 1975	12	Dec 1977	34
	37	Mar 1985	c		—
Groups of companies	20	Aug 1977	14	Sep 1978	13
Foreign currency translation	21	Oct 1977	b		—
	27	Oct 1980	20	Apr 1983	66
Post balance sheet events	22	Mar 1978	17	Aug 1980	29
Contingencies	23	Mar 1978	18	Aug 1980	29
Investment properties	26	Sep 1980	19	Nov 1981	14
Petroleum revenue tax	28	Mar 1981	d		—
Leasing and hire purchase	29	Oct 1981	21	Aug 1984	34
Goodwill	30	Oct 1982	22	Jan 1985	27
Pension information	32	May 1983	c		—
Pension schemes	34	Apr 1984	SORP1	approved in 1985	20
Accounting by charities	f38	Nov 1985	c	issued in 1986	

[a] where an ED has been superseded by a second ED, the period from the date of the first ED is shown
[b] superseded by a subsequent ED
[c] extant, awaiting development of a statement
[d] ED withdrawn without a standard being issued
[e] ED 16 was partly covered by SSAP 20 on foreign currency
[f] ED for a SORP.

the work undertaken and range to topics considered by the ASC since its creation in 1970, rather than the detailed requirements and mechanics of individual standards. Up to December, 1985, 38 exposure drafts had been issued, and had led to 23 standards (21 still in force). The subjects considered by the ASC and the related EDs and statements are listed in table 4.2. A brief outline of the main contents of each standard is included in Appendix 2.

Types of Accounting Standards

It is not possible to present a classification scheme which partitions standards into totally distinct groupings. Many standards contain a combination of recommendations and could be allocated to more than one grouping. Nevertheless, it is useful to classify the different types of regulations standards may contain. The classification used below is based on Edey (1977) and its application to extant standards is set-out in table 4.3. The first three types in this classification are concerned with various aspects of disclosure, the fourth with measurement.

Description. Some standards are concerned with disclosure of information concerning accounting policies and methods, or the inclusion of a descriptive narrative to accompany the figures in the accounts. The main standard in this group is SSAP2, but many other standards include specific requirements for disclosure of accounting policy, in addition to the general requirement to this effect in SSAP2. For example, the standards on foreign currency translation (SSAP20) and leasing (SSAP21) require disclosure of accounting methods.

Disclosure. A second group of standards specify the disclosure of some specific information, which may not be covered by legal requirements. For example SSAP3 requires disclosure of the earnings per share figure, SSAP10 requires disclosure of a statement showing sources and applications of funds, and SSAP21 requires disclosure of, amongst other things, operating lease rentals charged to the profit and loss account.

Presentation. The requirements of some standards relate to the manner of disclosure and are intended to lead to uniformity in the presentation of accounts. This grouping would include SSAP6 on the treatment of extraordinary items and prior year adjustments and SSAP1 which includes rules concerning the way in which information on associated companies is presented in consolidated accounts.

Table 4.3 Classification of principal requirements of SSAPs

SSAP No.	Type of requirement			
	Description	Disclosure	Presentation	Measurement
1				*
2	*			*
3		*		
4				*
5			*	
6			*	
8			*	
9	*			*
10		*		
12	*	*		*
13	*			*
14		*	*	
15		*		
16		*	*	*
17		*		
18		*		
19				*
20	*	*		*
21	*	*		*
22	*			*
23	*	*		*

Measurement. Perhaps the largest grouping of standards is those concerned with measurement. They relate to the valuation of balance sheet items and the measurement of periodic profit or loss. Examples are SSAP9 on stocks and work in progress, SSAP13 on research and development and SSAP22 on accounting for goodwill.

Subjects Considered by the ASC

Inspection of table 4.2 reveals the variety of topics which have been considered by the ASC. Indeed, the range of subjects is wider than that shown in the table, as a number of subjects have been included on the ASC agenda but have never led to an ED or SSAP. One-quarter of the topics on the original five-year work programme established in 1970 were subsequently deleted (Tweedie, 1981). The nature of the subjects covered by SSAPs varies considerably. Some standards are on issues which affect the entire financial statements, for example SSAP16 and SSAP20. Others relate to very specific issues some of which may not affect all companies, for example SSAP13 and SSAP19. Also some standards are very closely related, for example SSAPs 1, 14, 22 and 23 all deal with different aspects of consolidated group accounts, and a case could be made for putting them together in one standard, to ensure consistency between the practices recommended.

It is also apparent from table 4.2 that the order in which topics have been considered does not follow any particular pattern. Why should associated companies have been the subject for the first ever standard? Why should extraordinary items and prior year adjustments have been considered seven years before post balance sheet events and contingencies which are in some ways similar? It is not clear how the need for a standard is perceived by the ASC, but the answer probably has as much to do with reaction to outside pressures or changes in the reporting environment as to the pursuit of a coherent well-ordered programme. The kind of influences which may affect the work programme of the ASC and the outcome of that work are discussed in chapter 5.

The work programme most recently published (March 1986) is reproduced as table 4.4. This programme was published with an invitation to comment on the scope and nature of its contents. It contains a number of projects which were added as a result of comments received during a previous consultation in 1984. One noticeable feature of the current programme is the number of projects concerned with reviewing existing standards. Review of the operation of standards is likely to become an increasing part of the ASC's work, and may limit the development of new standards.

Production of Standards

The development of an accounting standard can take a considerable length of time. The publication dates of EDs and SSAPs, and the length of time between ED and SSAP, are shown in table 4.2. Production of a standard is a much longer process now than when the ASC first began operations. The first 11 SSAPs were produced in the five years 1971–5. The average period between ED and SSAP was 17 months, but only three subjects involved periods over 15 months. In the period 1976–80,

Table 4.4 Accounting Standards Committee – work programme March 1986

Project	Status
Review of SSAP6: extra-ordinary items and prior year adjustments	Revised standard, based on ED36, approved by ASC for submission to CCAB councils
Accounting for pension costs	Publication of ED planned for 1986, and a standard in 1987
Review of SSAP9: stock and WIP	Review of long-term contract work in progress. ED expected in 1986 and a revised standard in 1987
Materiality	Joint ASC/APC project. ED expected 1986 and final statement 1987
Review of SSAP2: disclosure of accounting policies	Project recently commenced. Includes consideration of realized profits and substance over form. ED expected 1986
Pension scheme accounts	SORP1 approved, to be issued May 1986
Review of SSAP12: accounting for depreciation	Revised standard being finalized. Publication expected mid 1986
Review of SSAP 13: research and development	To be reconsidered in 1986
Charities	ED 38 issued, SORP expected early 1987
Review of explanatory foreword	Revised EF, approved by ASC, with CCAB councils for approval
Related party transactions	Joint ASC-APC project; working party is preparing ED
Fair value	ED expected in 1986
Segmental reporting	ED expected in 1986
Interim reporting	Work scheduled to start in 1986
Review of SSAP5: accounting for value added tax	Work scheduled to start in 1986

seven standards were issued, with an average period ED to SSAP of 28 months, and in only one case was the period less than 15 months. The years 1981–5 have seen a further eight statements produced (five standards, two revised standards and one SORP, approved in 1985 although not issued until 1986), taking on average 30 months between ED and statement. In addition, these figures do not reflect the period of development before an ED is issued. For example, accounting for leases was on the ASC agenda for some five years before ED29 was published!

The increasing time taken to produce standards may be caused by a number of factors. When the ASC was first created there was an immediate need to produce some standards quickly, to be seen to be doing something to answer the criticism of the profession. Greater development time has been needed as the ASC has moved into more controversial areas where a consensus is harder to achieve, such an inflation accounting, research and development and foreign currency translation. The need to take account of international developments has also slowed the process on some issues. Finally, as the demands on companies from accounting standards have increased through the existence of more and more standards, and as the novelty of this form of regulation has worn off, compliance with standards has become increasingly uncertain. Consequently more care in the development of an SSAP may now be necessary than when the ASC began operations.

Criticism of the Accounting Standards Committee

A number of criticisms have been levelled at the way the ASC has set about the development of accounting standards. Disregarding criticism relating to individual standards and practices, a few points of a more general nature should be mentioned. It has been argued that the ASC has considered individual standards largely in isolation one from another. As stated earlier, there has been no apparent plan to the ASC's agenda. As a consequence of this approach, it is possible for there to be inconsistencies between standards. For example, the conflict between the accruals and prudence concepts, discussed in SSAP2, is apparent in standards such as SSAP9 and SSAP13.

In a number of cases, with the notable exception of inflation accounting, the ASC has tended to induce standards from existing practices. This approach can mean that some standards simply involve codification of a number of alternatives, or leave considerable discretion over the application of recommended practice, rather than requiring complete uniformity of practice. The ASC has thus been criticized for seeking to ensure the acceptability of standards at a cost to the rigour of their content.

In line with the above point, some have argued for the need for a complete theoretical framework for accounting, and criticized the ASC for devoting too little time to the development of such a framework. The validity of this criticism is discussed more fully in chapter 5.

SUMMARY

In this chapter we have looked at various aspects of the process by which accounting standards are developed including the objectives, structure and procedures of the ASC and the work it has undertaken. A major theme which has recurred throughout our discussion of these aspects is the increasing importance of an emphasis upon procedures to ensure compliance with accounting standards. In the absence of powerful enforcement measures the ASC seeks to substitute the self enforcement of a consensus, based on the confidence of preparers and users of accounts in the mechanisms by which regulations have been set and upon their agreement with the content of those regulations.

The ASC's concern over acceptance of its legitimacy to regulate accounting practice and compliance with standards is evident in the statement of objectives of acting in the public interest, the emphasis on consultation and due process in the revised standard setting process and in the increasing care taken in the development of standards. A similar motivation is apparent in the introduction of the additional category of pronouncement, the SORP.

REFERENCES

Accounting Standards Committee 1970: *Constitution*, June.
Accounting Standards Committee 1981: *Setting Accounting Standards, Final Report*.
Accounting Standards Committee 1983: *Review of the Standard Setting Process*.
Bird, P. 1982: 'After Argyll Foods what is a "true and fair view"? *Accountancy*, June.
Edey, H.C. 1977: 'Accounting standards in the British Isles'. In W.T. Baxter and S. Davidson (eds), *Studies in Accounting Theory*, Sweet and Maxwell.
Hoffman, L. and Arden, M.H. 1983: 'Legal opinion on "true and fair"'. *Accountancy*, November.
Institute of Chartered Accountants in England and Wales, 1969: *Statement of Intent on Accounting Standards in the 1970's*.
Stamp, E. 1969: 'Auditing the auditor'. *The Times*, 11 September.
Stamp, E. and Marley, M. 1970: *Accounting Principles and the City Code*, Butterworths.
Tweedie, D. P. 1981: 'Standards and objectives and the Corporate Report'. In R. Leach and E. Stamp (eds), *British Accounting Standards*, Sweet and Maxwell.

5

Influences on the Standard
Setting Process

The determination of statements of standard accounting practice
requires not only the creation of a structure and set of procedures for
developing standards, but also the application of some criteria for
choice between competing alternatives. The procedures of the ASC
provide a framework within which the choice of accounting standards
can be made but they do not in themselves provide the basis for that
choice. When individual issues are considered for regulation, the result
will depend on the influence of a number of factors, and it is sometimes
difficult to identify the precise reasons for the adoption of a particular
practice as standard.

The nature of accounting policy choice in standard setting may be
viewed in two contrasting ways, which we will call the 'technical' view
and the 'political' view. The technical view sees the problem of choice as
essentially one of identifying 'best' accounting practice, and which can
therefore be solved by the development and application of technical
rules or concepts of accounting. Accounting policy choices are seen as
capable of solution by reference to accounting theory. In contrast the
political view sees accounting standards in terms of choice between
conflicting interests which might be served better by different practices.
These political conflicts are regarded not as constraints on what would
otherwise be a technical process but rather as fundamental to the nature
of regulation and choice. While the process of standard setting may
involve reference to technical considerations the output of the process
will be determined by political factors.

When accounting standards were first established, they were seen
primarily as technical pronouncements. Those involved in the standard
setting process may wish to retain this view, because their authority to
regulate practice is drawn from technical expertise rather than from a
mandate to make choices between competing interests. However,

analysis and research of the activities of standard setting bodies has established the political explanation of choice as the prevailing view. The issue is not whether the standard setting is a technical or a political process, but rather to what extent the political considerations should be explicitly recognized and debated when individual standards are being developed.

In common with standard setting bodies in other countries, the ASC actively seeks outside influence in the development of standards by inviting submissions on proposals and consulting with various interest groups. The ASC's procedures and the concern for 'due process' reflect the political nature of its activities. Standardization involves debate, lobbying, consideration of the likely reaction to and compliance with different alternatives as well as their technical merits. In this chapter we discuss the principal sources of influence that may affect the work of the ASC by, firstly, looking at the environment in which the ASC operates, secondly, describing the extent to which the ASC has sought to develop a theoretical approach to accounting choice and, finally, considering evidence of actual influence in some specific standards.

THE STANDARD SETTING ENVIRONMENT

Many possible factors may influence the eventual choice of an accounting standard. Some may be personal to individual members of

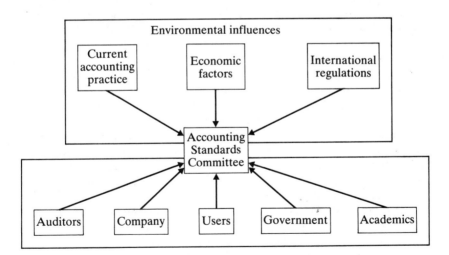

Figure 5.1   Influences on the standard setting process

the ASC, for example experience in a particular area of reporting or personal views on the objectives of accounts. At a more general level, however, a number of broad categories of influence can be identified. Figure 5.1 lists eight sources of potential influence on the ASC's decisions.

Three of these sources can be regarded as general environmental influences (current accounting practice, the economic environment and international regulations), and the remaining five represent particular interest groups who could be expected to try to influence the choices made by the ASC. The individual sources of influence should not be regarded as entirely independent, there will be overlaps between different sources. For example, the economic environment may influence the views of management, government and users of accounts, and auditors will have the opportunity to influence and be influenced by the views of the management in their client companies. The ways in which the various sources of influence affect the standard setting process may also be difficult to observe and will vary between different standards. Some attempts at influence will be direct and observable but much will be indirect, informal and extremely difficult to identify. The eight sources of influence noted in figure 5.1 are discussed in more detail in the following sections.

Current Accounting Practice

Existing practice obviously provides an input and influence on the standard setting process. What is currently done in practice is likely to represent a large part of the experience and knowledge base of the standard setters concerning a particular issue on which standard practice is being considered.

In developing a standard the ASC will probably look first at current practice and some have criticized the ASC for inducing standards from existing dominant practices and also for the fact that some standards appear to be simply a codification of alternatives already found in practice. In this sense, current accounting practice may act as a constraint on the development of accounting standards, regarding both the ASC's ability to innovate and introduce new practices and also the likelihood of adoption of rigid standards which do not allow alternative treatments. The ASC might also be expected to try and ensure consistency between the way in which different accounting standards are resolved. Thus the types of practices permitted in existing standards would influence the development of new standards. However, it should be noted that some inconsistencies do exist between the policies which have been adopted by the ASC on different issues.

Economic Factors

Accounting statements are intended to measure and report economic variables and events. As a result, changes in economic factors and developments in business practices may lead to changes in the structure and content of accounting reports. For example, in the 1970s high levels of inflation can be linked to the priority placed by the ASC on the development of a standard on accounting for the effects of changing prices and the move from fixed to fluctuating exchange rates had implications for the need for a standard on foreign currency translation.

As well as giving rise to or emphasizing issues which the ASC might consider, economic factors may also be relevant to the assessment of the appropriate choice for an accounting standard. Certainly, possible economic effects which would follow from an accounting standard are likely to influence the attitudes and lobbying behaviour of interested parties such as management and government. As yet the ASC has given little explicit recognition to the economic impact of accounting standards although it is difficult to assess the extent to which members of the ASC consider possible economic effects informally. It should also be noted that there is a considerable gulf between the idea that, because accounting standards involve implicit choices between possible economic effects, more explicit consideration should be given to them and to the development of methods which deal with the considerable practical and political difficulties of doing so. The issue of the economic consequences of accounting standards is taken up and discussed more fully in chapter 6.

International Regulations

International accounting practice can exercise an influence on standard setting in the UK in a number of ways. The diversity of accounting systems internationally provides a source of information on alternative practices and regulations and experiences with their use and application. Comparison of the position in the UK with developments in other countries can lead to new topics being considered for inclusion on the ASC's work programme. In this role, the influence of international considerations is indirect, providing information as an input to the ASC's procedures.

International factors may also be important as a more direct influence through the existence of regulations which, although developed internationally, are intended to apply in the UK. The two most authoritative sources of international regulations are the European Economic Community (EEC) and the International Accounting Standards Committee (IASC).

As we have already seen when considering developments in legal regulation of accounting, the EEC adopts directives which member countries are obliged to implement through national legislation. As well as affecting the law, the EEC directives on accounting have influenced the work of the ASC. Implementation of the Fourth Directive prompted the ASC to undertake reviews of a number of standards, including those dealing with stock and work in progress and extraordinary items. Changes in the law have also constrained to some extent the flexibility available to the ASC in choosing standard accounting practice.

Through membership of the IASC, the UK profession is expected to promote the application of Interntional Accounting Standards. The existence of international standards thus provides another consideration when a UK standard is being developed, and SSAPs usually include some paragraphs referring to the consistency between the ASC's requirements and those of any relevant international standard.

The nature of the international aspects of regulation of accounting and their effect on the UK provide the subject of chapter 10.

Auditors

Auditors have an important role in the implementation and enforcement of accounting standards. Members of the professional institutes who are involved in auditing are expected to encourage management to accept standards and to qualify their audit report if they disagree with management's decision not to follow a standard. Traditionally, the auditing firms have provided one of the main elements in the power base of the ASC. It is in the interests of the audit firms to seek to maintain the status of the ASC's standards in order to preserve the regulatory role of the accounting profession, and, in one sense, accounting standards could be viewed as a form of collective action by auditors as a means of increasing the power of individual auditors *vis-à-vis* management in the production of accounting statements.

The corollary of this situation is that the audit firms can also be expected to have a significant voice in the development and approval of standards which they will be obliged to enforce. Individuals in professional practice comprise the largest single grouping of members of the ASC, and all its five chairmen since it was formed have come from large accounting firms. The major firms will submit opinions on proposals for all accounting standards and, to this extent at least, are involved in lobbying for a particular outcome. There is, however, a danger in regarding all audit firms as a single homogeneous grouping. This is not necessarily the case and on many issues the interests and desires of the larger firms may be in conflict with the views of smaller practitioners. Indeed, the ASC has sometimes been criticized for being dominated by what are known as the 'Big Eight' accounting firms.

The nature of auditors relationships with company management is important in assessing their influence on accounting standards. To some extent, auditors have an advisory role, which may mean they are able to influence mangement views on an accounting policy, but equally this position can put auditors under pressure to see things from a management point of view. Although the auditor is appointed to act on behalf of and report to shareholders, he may have certain common interests with management. For example, with respect to regulations which extend disclosure, management may not wish to disclose more information and auditors may feel that the extension is not in their own interests because it could increase the possibility of an audit error leading to litigation.

Company Management

The second largest grouping of members on the ASC is those 'in private and public industry and commerce', that is company management. Management has the legal responsibility for production of accounting statements and will have an interest in the type of standards the ASC requires for those statements, because of possible reactions to the information they contain. For example if management believe that disclosure of a new piece of information will affect competitive decisions by other firms, or if they feel that the effect of the application of a measurement technique on reported profit will influence shareholders' assessment of the returns associated with their investment, then these beliefs will determine the position adopted by management regarding possible accounting standards.

In general it might be expected that management would have a natural reluctance to support increased disclosure and more rigid regulation of accounting practices. More disclosure implies management revealing more about the way in which they operate the enterprise and rigid regulations reduce the amount of discretion management has over the reporting methods used in the accounts.

Management are likely to seek to influence the ASC in their choice of accounting standards, and will constitute a very important potential influence because of their control over the production of accounts. The fact that standards are not legally binding means that the ASC is largely dependent on their acceptance by management to ensure their success. The possibility of non-compliance gives management a very significant and powerful role in standard setting. The lobbying behaviour of management has been subject to a growing amount of research (Kelly Newton, 1980) and some examples of management influence on the ASC are provided in a later section of this chapter.

Users of Accounts

The category of users of accounts covers a number of groupings whose interests in accounting information are quite diverse, for example shareholders, creditors, employees and those involved in trading relationships with a company. The views of these different groupings on individual standardization issues may conflict to a considerable extent.

It might be expected that the interests of users, or some limited user groups, would be the most important influence on the ASC. The users are the recipients of accounting statements and the ASC has expressed the view that accounting statements should satisfy the needs of users for information to assist in decision making. However, this approach has not been developed to specify which users and which decisions and so has not dealt with the issue of conflicting interests between different groups. The ASC does include four members described as users, but all of these individuals come from a background concerned with the supply of finance to companies, i.e. the investment and banking business, and they are very much in the minority in comparison to the members involved in the production of accounts, management and auditors.

When the submissions to the ASC on individual accounting issues are analysed, it is noticeable that relatively few come from accounts users. Those that do again tend to represent the suppliers of capital. Other potential users of accounting information, for example trade unions, do not appear to have become involved in the standard setting process in any major way.

Government

The role and influence of the government in accounting standard setting is difficult to observe and measure. Formally, the ASC is a professional body, and has no specific statutory mandate from government. However, that is not to say that government will not take an active interest in accounting standards. The ASC seeks to regulate in 'the public interest' and its activities are bound to be reviewed by government.

Two representatives of government departments attend ASC meetings as observers. While they do not have the power to vote, they can speak in debates and so have the ability to indicate, explicitly or implicitly, a government attitude on specific matters. Such an indication is likely to carry considerable weight in the minds of the ASC members when deciding an issue. Also, while a standard is being developed, there may be communications between representatives of the ASC and officials from government departments, for example to discuss interpretation of relevant legislation.

The government is clearly in a position to influence the choice of standard accounting practice in informal ways, but it can also do so by more explicit formal action. The most often quoted example of such action is the setting up of the Sandilands Committee in 1973, which effectively reversed the ASC's plans to introduce an inflation accounting standard based on current purchasing power accounting.

Academics

A final group who may influence accounting standard setting are those involved in the academic accounting community. The ASC has one member drawn from a university accounting department, and individual academics sometimes make submissions to the ASC on particular accounting standards.

The academic community could also have a role in the supply of theories or of empirical research as inputs to the choice of standard practice. However, the ASC does not have a consistent approach regarding referring to or commissioning research when a new issue is being considered. It is also true that much of the direction of academic research in recent years has been towards investigating and understanding the nature of the process of choice in standard setting rather than seeking to provide information to guide the ASC's decisions on particular issues.

THE ROLE OF THEORY

One of the criticisms that has repeatedly been directed at the ASC is that it has treated individual standardization issues in too independent a fashion and reacted too much to political pressures from vested interests when deciding issues, rather than applying a consistent theoretical framework as its basis for choice. Grinyer (1985), for example, criticizes the ASC for rejecting a theoretical approach in favour of pragmatism.

The outcome of this (the ASC's) process is statements which sometimes lack internal coherence, are often mutually inconsistent and seem to reflect political pressures to a greater extent than logic. In my view the fundamental reason for the difficulties I have identified is the ASC's failure to adopt a clearly articulated theory for accounting.

It is possible to point to various statements in ASC publications which refer to the need to set standards 'in the public interest' or with reference to 'the needs of users of accounts'. However, these very general statements lack definition and do not provide an operational basis for choice on individual issues. Indeed, it could not be assumed that 'the public interest' and 'users' needs' would lead to the same choices.

While it can be argued that accounting standards have not been developed on the basis of a theoretical framework, this does not mean that the ASC has not considered the need for a theoretical approach to standard setting. Three areas of the ASC's work could be said to have something to do with the development of a general theoretical approach to standard setting, namely SSAP2 Disclosure of Accounting Policies, the Corporate Report and the Conceptual Framework project.

SSAP2

SSAP2 was not intended to provide a basic theory of accounting, and this is acknowledged in the standard (ASC, 1971). However, in laying down a number of 'fundamental accounting concepts' which should apply in the preparation of accounts, it does represent an attempt to approach accounting policy choices in a conceptual way. By establishing four concepts which preparers of accounts should apply in drawing up accounting statements, the ASC also created a set of rules which could be applied to its own decisions. The four fundamental concepts which are stated in SSAP2 are:

(1) going concern – the business will continue in operational existence in the foreseeable future;
(2) accruals – revenues and costs are recognized as they are earned or incurred, not as cash is received or paid, and matched with one another as far as a relationship can be established;
(3) consistency – there should be consistency of treatment of like items within each period and over time;
(4) prudence – revenues and profits are not anticipated, but recognized when realized; provision is made for all known liabilities, even if there is uncertainty over their amount. Where prudence and accruals conflict, prudence prevails.

This set of concepts in fact represents a mixture of principle, convention and assumption, and in practice the ASC has not found it easy to follow these rules when setting standards. The conflict between the prudence and accruals concepts has often arisen in the context of new standards but, contrary to SSAP2, the ASC has not always allowed prudence to prevail, for example the valuation of long-term contract work in progress (SSAP9) and the capitalization of development expenditure (SSAP13).

In addition the ASC has made use of a number of other concepts or 'practical rules' to decide on standard practice, for example the idea that accounts should reflect economic substance rather than legal form is applied in accounting for leases (SSAP21), and the concept of materiality is referred to in a number of standards. Other conceptual considerations such as the universality of application of accounting standards and cost-benefit factors have also influenced the ASC's work. While SSAP2 stated that the four concepts should be 'capable of variation and evolution as accounting theory and practice develop', it has taken from 1971 to 1986 before a review of the standard has been set in train.

The Corporate Report

SSAP2 failed to address the fundamental issues of the purposes and meaning of accounting statements, but in 1975 the ASC issued a discussion document, *The Corporate Report* (ASC, 1975) which gave a much more careful consideration of these matters.

The Corporate Report adopted a user decision oriented view of accounting, that is that the purpose of accounting statements is to provide information useful to users in decision making.

> In our view the fundamental objective of corporate reports is to communicate economic measurements of and information about the resources and performance of the reporting entity useful to those having reasonable rights to such information. (ASC, 1975, S3.16)

This statement leads logically to the question of which groups have a legitimate right to information and what their information needs are. *The Corporate Report* identified a variety of interest groups as having a legitimate right to information: the equity investor group, the loan creditor group, the employee group, the analyst-advisor group, the business contact group, the government and public. The report then went on to consider the use of information, concluding that it should assist decisions concerning the performance, efficiency, vulnerability, stability and future prospects of the enterprise. New types of statements were suggested: a value added statement, an employment report, a statement of exchanges with government, a statement of foreign currency transactions, a statement of future prospects and a statement of corporate objectives. The report also recommended research into the idea of multicolumn reporting.

The above brief summary indicates that *The Corporate Report* provided a more fundamental consideration of the purpose of financial reporting and was potentially more far reaching in its conclusions than any other document issued by the ASC. The report was, however, issued as a discussion document and the foreword by the then chairman of the ASC emphasized that it did 'not necessarily represent the views of the ASC nor of any individual accounting body', although an ASC press release did accept the main conclusions of the report and promise follow-up research. Some research was carried out on some of the suggested statements but no work was undertaken on the fundamental issues of users and their information needs nor on the more radical suggestions such as social reporting. The impact of *The Corporate Report* on accounting standard setting bore little relation to the seriousness of the issues it raised and, in the words of one commentator, 'the study was stillborn' (Tweedie, 1981). This may in part have been due to the ASC's continuing preoccupation with the single issue of inflation accounting.

A Conceptual Framework

When the ASC reviewed its operations in 1978 a consultative document was issued which, as well as evaluating the ASC's procedures and structure, also raised the question of a conceptual framework for accounting on which the choice of standard accounting practices could be based (ASC, 1978). There is often considerable confusion regarding what a conceptual framework is and what it can achieve.

> In essence, a conceptual framework comprises a set of basic principles that command general support and can be used to help with detailed decisions by increasing the likelihood of consistency and reducing the costs of analysis. (Carsberg, 1984)

At the time of the ASC's review there was considerable enthusiasm for the idea of developing a conceptual framework. The six UK accountancy bodies called for research, as did 14 of the 20 regional committees who commented on the ASC's consultative document and nine of the top ten accounting firms (Tweedie, 1981). This enthusiasm was largely confined to the accounting profession, which appeared to see the conceptual framework as a mechanism which would provide the answers to questions of choice over accounting standards, and would stand as an authoritative point of reference which government, preparers of accounts and others would accept. It was seen as a means of removing controversy from accounting standard setting.

Even advocates of a conceptual framework would not go this far. Carsberg (1984) states that the purposes of a conceptual framework are to facilitate decisions on controversial issues, to avoid wasted effort in standard setting, and to lessen the need for a large number of detailed standards, but also points out that it cannot eliminate the room for dispute. What a conceptual framework may do, in fact, is focus attention on the underlying conflicts of interest which lead to disputes on individual standards. In other words the issues involved in the development of a conceptual framework highlight the controversies in accounting standard setting, rather than remove them (Peasnell, 1982). 1982).

In the United States, the FASB has devoted considerable resources to a conceptual framework project and has developed a number of 'concepts statements' on such things as the objectives of financial statements and the qualitative characteristics of accounting information. However, these statements have been criticized for being framed in a very broad way, such that many positions on individual issues can be justified from them and they are of little assistance in resolving difficult issues.

The ASC's own research, involving a review of existing efforts towards developing a conceptual framework (Macve, 1981), concluded that while agreement on broad statements would be possible, for example that accounting statements should be useful, there was little prospect of obtaining agreement on more detailed objectives for accounts and how they should be pursued, due to the variety of users' needs, conflicts of interest and the fact that 'good' or 'better' accounting practice remains a subjective matter. It is interesting to note that when the ASC research was published, only nine responses were received to the invitation to comment on its conclusions, mainly from academics.

The choice of the various components for any theoretical or conceptual framework to guide accounting standard setting are equally as controversial as the choice of standard practice on individual issues, if not more so. This problem of agreement leads Bromwich (1985) to conclude that 'the attainment of such a framework may be regarded as impossible in the present state of knowledge'.

The ASC and Accounting Theory

In summary, while the ASC has not ignored theory altogether, it remains true that it has not approached standard setting from the point of view of a coherent theoretical framework. No statement of what the ASC sees as the purpose and nature of financial reporting has ever been produced. While a generally agreed conceptual framework may be regarded as unlikely, a statement of the ASC's own approach to accounting statements would at least focus attention on its basis for choosing standards, rather than on individual practices.

The American Accounting Association (AAA) has categorized approaches to accounting theory into three main types (AAA, 1977):

(1) the classical approach, divided into:
   (a) the inductive approach – rationalizing existing practice;
   (b) the normative–deductive approach – attempts to 'improve' existing practice;
(2) the decision–usefulness approach – looking at users' needs
(3) information economics – looking at information as an economic good and analysing the demand for accounting regulations.

While the ASC has made reference to user needs, it is probably true to say that most of its work reflects a normative–deductive approach (Tweedie, 1981). This is reflected in the notion of establishing standards of 'best practice' without specifying the subjective choices that this approach implies.

IDENTIFYING INFLUENCE IN INDIVIDUAL ACCOUNTING STANDARDS

While the political nature of the accounting standard setting process in general has become increasingly recognized over the last decade, relatively few attempts have been made to analyse and explain the development and choice of individual standards in these terms. One reason why this is so is that it is extremely difficult to observe or measure the behaviour of interested parties in an accounting issue, and thus to establish a link between that behaviour and the choice made by the ASC. In other words, it is difficult to identify the source of power and influence in practice.

The amount of lobbying behaviour that is observable is restricted principally to the formal written submissions on exposure drafts that are made to the ASC and press coverage of the position adopted by different parties. Other key elements in the process are not observable, for example meetings between significant parties and opinions expressed by officials from government departments in informal contact. Even in the United States, where meetings of the FASB are public and it is possible to observe the voting on individual standards, it is not clear that the exercise of power in standard setting can be located. Also the development of standards on individual issues is only one point in the process at which influence may be exerted. Other issues, such as how it is decided whether or not a topic will be included on the ASC's work programme, are more difficult to investigate.

The ASC publishes the written submissions received on exposure drafts and when a standard is issued, it is usually accompanied by a technical release which includes some analysis of those submissions. Table 5.1 documents the number and source of comment received on individual exposure drafts. The number of submissions provides an indication of relative interest of different parties in the various issues which have been considered by the ASC. For example, with the notable exception of inflation accounting, the number of submissions from practising firms and from associations, representative bodies and district societies shows a much higher degree of consistency between different issues than the number received from limited companies. It may be that the larger practising firms will tend to submit comments on all exposure drafts while company management will only comment on those which are likely to affect their reporting function in significant ways.

In the remainder of this section we report some examples of how the ASC appears to have been influenced on particular standards. These examples are based partly on studies which have analysed the submissions on exposure drafts, but the limitations of this approach as a means of identifying influence noted above should be borne in mind.

We have already commented on the difficulties involved in identifying who has the power to influence the outcome of the standard setting process. The examples quoted below are not intended to represent a complete explanation of the ASC's choice on individual standards and all the influences which affected their devolopment, but rather to provide illustrations of the effect of some of the sources of influence discussed earlier in the chapter.

Research and Development Expenditure

The development of an accounting standard on accounting for research and development (R&D) expenditure has been analysed by Hope and Gray (1982). The R&D issue involved three main elements. (1) definition of R&D expenditures, (2) the accounting treatment, whether such expenditure should be expensed as incurred, or whether some

Table 5.1 Sources of comments received on Exposure Drafts

ED Number	Subject	Total	Practising Firms	Companies	Representative bodies and groups of accountants	Other representative bodies	Individuals
1	Associated companies	152	22	51		26	53
2	Accounting policies	69	13	16		22	18
3	Acquisitions & mergers	88	28	17		32	11
4	Earnings per share	66	18	9		24	15
5	Extraordinary items	83	17	25		30	11
6	Stocks	153	21	72		32	28
7	Extraordinary items	77	13	19		29	16
8	Inflation accounting	113	13	27		36	37
9	Industry grants	76	14	24		26	12
10	Value added tax	52	9	11		27	5
11	Deferred taxation	118	25	44		33	16
12	Taxation	67	18	14		27	8
13	Funds statements	98	22	29		32	15
14	Research & development	66	15	15	23	8	5
15	Depreciation	101	21	36	22	9	13
16	Extraordinary items (supplement)	79	19	27	19	7	7

17	Research & development	49	9	8	19		9	4
18	Current cost accounting	746	83	336	30	123	13	204
19	Deferred taxation	115	26	29	23		10	17
20	Group accounts	85	18	28	25		9	6
21	Foreign currency translations	119	24	45				16
22	Post balance sheet events	91	23	29	20		11	8
23	Contingencies	81	21	19	26		9	6
24	Current cost accounting	248	34	75	64		10	65
25	Associated companies	109	24	31	29		17	8
26	Investment properties	107	21	47	9		16	14
27	Foreign currency	107	20	46	12		13	16
28	Petroleum revenue tax	30	8	18	1		3	
29	Leasing & hire purchase	137	23	59	8		22	25
30	Goodwill	97	24	25	28		9	11
31	Acquisitions & mergers	86	22	17	28		11	8
32	Pension information	99	22	16	40		17	4
33	Deferred taxation	77	24	25	5		10	13
34	Pension scheme accounts	72	17	8	27		12	8
35	Current cost accounting	143	17	41	32		14	39
36	Extraordinary items	82	16	14	32		8	12
37	Depreciation	88	20	27	28		8	5

should be carried forward for matching with future revenues, and (3) whether or not companies should disclose the total amount of R&D expenditure. The main events and factors influencing the development of the standard, as identified by Hope and Gray are as follows:

(1) The ASC's first proposals for an accounting standard on R&D (ED13, Jan. 1975) recommended immediate write-off of R&D expenditure in the year incurred, and disclosure of the amount written off. Immediate write-off was largely consistent with current practice, as 93 per cent of companies adopted this policy in 1973/4.

(2) In the submissions on ED13, a majority of commentators supported the policy of no deferral of R&D expenditure. Eight responses from industry, nine from practising firms and twenty-two from other groups and individuals (including two from government departments) favoured write-off, compared with five, four and two respectively who argued for some deferral. On the question of disclosure, 14 submissions were against the ED13 proposal, mainly from industry.

(3) A second exposure draft (ED17, April 1976) was issued by the ASC and provided the basis for an accounting standard (SSAP13, Dec. 1977). The ASC's approach in these documents is very different from that in ED13. The standard requires immediate write-off of research expenditure but permits carry forward of development expenditure, if certain criteria are met; disclosure is required of details of expenditure carried forward, but not amounts written off.

Hope and Gray attribute the ASC's change of approach on accounting treatment of R&D largely to four submissions on ED13 from the aerospace industry. These submissions argued that deferral should be permitted because the profit percentage allowed in government contracts was calculated on capital employed, which was defined as including development expenditure included in the balance sheet. Immediate write-off therefore would have reduced the profit calculation. In other words, the aerospace industry was worried about the possible economic effects of an accounting standard. Hope and Gray also trace the change in the disclosure requirement to the submissions of a number of industrial companies.

Accounting for R&D expenditure provides an example of an occasion when the ASC changed its mind. The issue involved considerations of current practice, the conflict between the prudence and accruals concepts and formal submissions from industry, practising firms and government, but the most notable feature of the standard's development is the apparent influence of a single industrial grouping concerned with the effect of accounting practice on economic factors.

Deferred Taxation

The contentious nature of the issue of deferred taxation is indicated by the fact that the ASC has issued three exposure drafts, two standards and a revision of a standard on the subject. Briefly, deferred taxation is a means of accounting for the effects of differences between accounting profits and taxable profits. There are two main elements to this issue: the choice between alternative methods of calculation, knows as the 'liability' method and the 'deferral' method; and the extent of the differences between accounting and taxable profits which should be recognized in the calculation. Hope and Briggs (1982) have documented a number of influences on the ASC's consideration of this subject.

(1) The first exposure draft (ED11, May 1973) recommended the deferral method. Hope and Briggs attribute this choice to the influence of existing recommendations in America and from the Accountants International Study Group.

(2) Submissions on the exposure draft from both industry and professional practice criticized its insistence on one method. As a result, the standard that was introduced (SSAP11, Aug. 1975) called for the comprehensive provision for deferred taxation, but allowed companies to choose the method of calculation.

(3) In the presence of high inflation and with the use of capital allowances and stock appreciation relief in calculating taxable profits, application of the standard resulted in the creation of large deferred taxation balances in companies' accounts. In the manufacturing and distribution industry between 1971 and 1976, deferred taxation balances rose from 4.4 per cent to 21.6 per cent of shareholders funds and the annual charge rose from 13.3 per cent to 39.8 per cent of the total taxation charge. The significance of deferred taxation in companies accounts shifted the debate from the choice of method to the question of the extent to which it should be provided.

(4) Faced with growing industrial opposition, the ASC agreed to review the standard, and issued a new exposure draft (ED19, May 1977). This reversed much of the approach of SSAP11; it restricted the extent to which deferred taxation should be provided and recommended the liability method.

(5) Out of 29 submissions on ED19 from industry, 25 supported its recommendations. Professional opinion, however, was more divided, between those who agreed with the ED as a workable practical solution and those who criticized it for trading 'theoretical rigour for pure expediency', for its subjectivity and for departing from the fundamental concepts in SSAP2. When the second standard was introduced

(SSAP15), it included most of the controversial elements of ED19, but again did not specify the method of calculation to be used.

(6) A further exposure draft (ED33, Aug. 1983) led to a revision of SSAP15 (May 1985). This revision specified the liability method and further clarified the extent to which provision should be made for deferred taxation.

The history of the deferred taxation debate thus illustrates a number of aspects of influence in standard setting: international considerations, economic factors and their effect on management attitudes, the formal position adopted by management and auditors in submissions to the ASC and the conflict between a conceptual approach and the production of practical solutions acceptable to management. Overall it would appear that management views prevailed and were mainly responsible for the ASC's change of direction.

Accounting for Effects of Changing Prices

The most controversial issue that the ASC has attempted to regulate, and the one that has occupied more of its time than any other, is undoubtedly the development of an inflation accounting standard. The inflation accounting debate has been on the ASC's agenda throughout its existence, but also has a much longer history than the ASC. It is a contentious issue because of the fundamental judgements that are required on basic concepts concerning income, asset valuation and capital maintenance. It would be inappropriate to attempt to give a complete description or explanation of the development of an inflation accounting standard here (for such reviews see Mumford, 1979; Westwick, 1980; Whittington, 1981; and Sutton, 1984). Rather, we shall point to just a few events in the ASC's consideration of the subject, as illustrations of influence.

(1) The ASC's first publication on inflation account (ED8, Jan. 1983) advocated a system of current purchasing power (CPP) accounting. This approach reflected the prevailing view in the profession, in both the UK and the United States, and in industry. In 1968 the Research Committee of the ICAEW had published a report advocating supplementary CPP statements, and in 1972 the Confederation of British Industry expressed support for this method.

(2) In July 1973 the government announced that it was establishing a committee of inquiry on inflation accounting (the Sandilands Committee). This move effectively restricted the ASC's power to introduce a standard, and so ED8 was followed by only a 'provisional' standard (SSAP7, May 1974). The most common explanation of the govern-

ment's action is a fear of the possible economic effects of general indexation, in other words that CPP could institutionalize inflation.

(3) The next ASC document was not produced for a further three years (ED18, Nov. 1976). The ED effectively adopted the position of the Sandilands Committee, which had reported in 1975, and recommended a form of current cost accounting (CCA). The implementation of ED18 as a standard was prevented by action within the profession. Two small practitioners (Messrs Keymer and Haslam) forced a special meeting of the ICAEW at which a resolution was passed against making CCA compulsory. Their concern was partly that ED18 suggested that CCA would apply to all companies, irrespective of size.

(4) When a standard was introduced (SSAP16, Mar. 1980) following another exposure draft (ED24, Apr. 1979) it included two additional adjustments, for monetary working capital and gearing, to those in ED18, the depreciation and cost of sales adjustments. These new adjustments may reflect the interests of some parts of industry and commerce, for example, companies such as banks and supermarkets, which have significant monetary working capital considerations.

(5) SSAP16 was introduced for an experimental period of three years, after which it would be reviewed. During this period, however, the level of compliance from companies fell continuously. The effect was infectious, once a number of companies had departed from the standard without any sanction from the Stock Exchange, others were unwilling to incur the costs of preparing CCA statements. Significantly this trend also affected the position of practising firms. Faced with the fact that their clients were unwilling to follow the standard, a number of audit firms decided that, if SSAP16 remained in force, they would no longer qualify their audit reports for non-compliance. This threat effectively removed the main power base that the ASC had for enforcing CCA and consequently its attempts to develop a new standard were dropped. The follow-up exposure draft (ED35, 1984) was abandoned in March 1985 and SSAP16 was made non-mandatory in July 1985, thus satisfying the audit firms' position.

The above discussion provides only brief comments on a number of points in the long and complicated history of inflation accounting in the UK. It is interesting to note that this subject, which perhaps involves more fundamental theoretical considerations than any other subject considered by the ASC, has also provided the most politically controversial debate faced by the ASC. We have noted evidence of the influence of government, industry and practising firms at different stages in the debate, as well as significant interrelationships between the positions adopted by these groups.

SUMMARY

The reasons which lie behind the choices made by the ASC are extremely difficult to identify. While a number of possible influences on the ASC can be specified, it is less easy to make conclusive statements about the impact of these influences, on either the general approach of the ASC or its decisions on individual standards. Much influence may be impossible to observe and the significance of different sources of influence will vary on different issues. What is clear is that setting accounting standards is not a neutral activity where choices are derived from some explicit set of objectives or concepts. The process of standard setting involves consideration of conflicting interests and the ASC will be subject to pressure from different interest groups. Issues will be resolved through a mixture of technical or theoretical considerations and political pressures. We have looked at a few examples which illustrate the conflict between technical and political factors and the ways in which some interest groups become involved in standard setting. Of particular note is the role of industrial management, who appear to have considerable power because of the fact that accounting standards are not legally enforceable and the ASC therefore depends to a large extent on management support for the success of its pronouncement.

REFERENCES

Accounting Standards Committee 1971: *Disclosure of Accounting Policies, SSAP2*.
Accounting Standards Committee 1975: *The Corporate Report – A discussion paper*.
Accounting Standards Committee 1978: *Setting Accounting Standards — A consultative document*.
American Accounting Association, 1977: *A Statement of Basic Accounting Theory*.
Bromwich, M. 1985: *The Economics of Accounting Standard Setting*, Prentice-Hall International in association with the Institute of Chartered Accountants in England and Wales, Hemel Hempstead.
Carsberg, B.V. 1984: 'The quest for a conceptual framework for financial reporting'. In B.V. Carsberg and S. Dev (eds), *External Financial Reporting*, Prentice-Hall International, Hemel Hempstead.
Grinyer, J. 1985: 'ED37 – a house built on sand?' *Accountancy*, July, 14–15.
Hope, A. and Briggs, J. 1982: 'Accounting policy making – some lessons from the deferred taxation debate'. *Accounting and Business Research*, Vol 12, 83–96.

Hope, A. and Gray, R. 1982: 'Power and policy making – the development of an R and D standard'. *Journal of Business Finance and Accounting*, Vol. 9, 531–58.

Kelly-Newton, L. 1980: *Accounting and Policy Formulation: The Role of Corporate Management*, Addison-Wesley.

Macve, R. 1981: *A Conceptual Framework for Financial Accounting and Reporting – The Possibilities of an Agreed Structure*, Institute of Chartered Accountants in England and Wales, London.

Mumford, M. 1979: 'The end of a familiar inflation accounting cycle'. *Accounting and Business Research*. Vol. 9, 98–104.

Peasnell, K.V. 1982: 'The function of a conceptual framework for corporate financial reporting'. *Accounting and Business Research*, Vol. 12, 243–56.

Sutton, T.G. 1984: 'Lobbying of accounting standards setting bodies in the UK and the USA: a deconsian analysis'. *Accounting, Organisations and Society*, Vol. 9.

Tweedie, D.P. 1981: 'Standards, objectives and the Corporate Report'. In R. Leech and E. Stamp (eds), *British Accounting Standards – The First Ten Years*, Woodhead Faulkner, Cambridge.

Westwick, C.A. 1980: 'The lessons to be learned from the development of inflation accounting in the UK'. *Accounting and Business Research*, Vol. 10, 353–74.

Whittington, G.A. 1983: *Inflation Accounting: an Introduction to the Debate*, Cambridge University Press.

6

The Effects of Accounting
Standards

Since the 1960s there has been a growing interest in the economic and
social effects of accounting regulations, particularly accounting
standards. Formerly, it was generally held that accounting was neutral
in its influence on economic variables. However, according to the
American Accounting Association Committee on the Social
Consequences of Accounting Information, the issue of economic and
social consequences has become the central contemporary issue in
accounting (AAA, 1978). This concern emerged first in the USA and
has remained strongest there, but latterly has become important in the
UK and other countries. Increasingly, accounting standards setting
bodies such as the ASC and FASB have been confronted with
arguments that particular proposals for accounting standards, or
existing standards, give rise to economic consequences. The issue of
whether, and how, consequences might be incorporated within the
standard setting process has attracted a good deal of attention. In this
chapter we examine three issues, namely, the reasons for interest in the
economic consquences of accounting standards, the possible sources of
economic consequences, and the problems involved in incorporating
consideration of economic consequences in the setting of accounting
standards. In the following chapter we review the literature devoted to
the investigation of possible economic consequences associated with
particular accounting policy choices.

INTEREST IN ECONOMIC CONSEQUENCES

The idea that accounting information may give rise to economic effects
is not in itself controversial or novel. The justification for the provision
of external financial reports is to a large degree provided by the need to

make economic decisions. Such a justification may be implicit, as in the case of the stewardship function of financial reporting, or explicit, as in the case of the AAA's celebrated definition of accounting:

> the process of identifying, measuring and communicating economic information to permit informed judgements and decisions by the users of the information. (AAA, 1966, p. 1)

This definition typifies user or decision orientated approaches to accounting. These approaches derive criteria for judging the desirability of accounting alternatives from considerations of usefulness or relevance to decision making. There is great variety inherent in user or decision orientation. For example, *The Corporate Report* (ASC, 1975) identifies those groups possessing a right to receive financial reports as being those whose interests are 'impinged' upon by business activity and decisions, whilst the Trueblood Report (American Institute of Certified Public Accountants, 1973) recognizes the need to make decisions as conferring the right to receive information. It is possible to adopt either a normative approach to accounting choices, by specifying normative decision models (AAA, 1969; Revsine, 1973), or a positive approach, based on the uses made of accounting information by different users (Arnold and Moizer, 1984; Sherer, Southworth and Turley, 1981).

Despite this variety, a clear common theme is discernible: that accounting information is used for decision making. From this premise follows the notion of economic consequences. To the extent that external financial reports provide information which is used in making economic decisions, such information may be said to have economic consequences. As Zeff (1978) puts it:

> By 'economic consequences' is meant the impact of accounting reports on the decision making behaviour of business, government unions, investors and creditors.

A related, but separate issue is whether accounting regulations such as accounting standards give rise to economic consequences. If financial reports based upon standardized accounting practices lead to decisions which are different from those that would have been taken if the standard were not applied, then accounting regulations can be said to have potential economic consequences. Even though an accounting regulation cannot change the underlying economic reality of a set of transactions, it may affect the way in which the results of those transactions are reported, and this may in turn affect subsequent decisions. Expressed thus, interest in the economic consequences of accounting regulation is merely an extension of the decision usefulness approach.

There are also other grounds for considering the economic consequences of accounting regulations. First, evidence has been collected suggesting that economic consequences have followed from certain accounting standards. Such evidence is discussed at length in chapter 7. Second, there has been an increasing amount of intervention and lobbying in the process of accounting standard setting. Of particular interest is the increased frequency with which arguments couched in the language of economic consequences have been put forward in favour of or against alternative proposals for accounting standards. Formerly, debates were most frequently conducted with reference to technical criteria. In the USA a number of accounting issues have generated vigorous debate involving economic consequences. Cases in point are foreign currency translation, accounting for exploration costs in the oil and gas industry, accounting for leases and inflation accounting (Wyatt, 1977; Rappaport, 1977; Sweringa, 1977). Moreover, the FASB and SEC have demonstrated an active interest in economic consequences (FASB, 1978) and FASB officials have acknowledged that accounting regulations give rise to consequences. However, this is not to say that economic consequences have only recently become important. It is probably more realistic to conclude that the earlier tendency to discuss accounting regulations in terms of technical criteria obscured a continuing concern with economic effects which has only recently emerged explicitly.

Zeff (1978) has suggested a number of explanations for the recent increase in interest in economic consequences in the USA. These include the change in general social attitudes which seeks to hold institutions responsible for the effects of their actions, the intractability of many of the accounting problems examined by accounting standard setters, and the scale of the impact of accounting standards. Claims that accounting rules give rise to economic consequences are especially popular with non-accountant critics of accounting standards (Sutton, 1984). While the FASB (or ASC) may rebuff criticisms of accounting standards on technical grounds, economic arguments lie outside its competence and authority. In the USA critics of rules imposed by the FASB may address their criticisms on economic consequences to the SEC, as occurred in the debate on a proposed accounting standard on accounting for oil exploration costs (Collins and Dent, 1979).

There has not been the same degree of interest expressed in the economic consequences of accounting standards set by the ASC in the UK. This may be explained by the nature of the institutional arrangements for accounting standard setting in this country. The lack of even a delegated legal authority on the part of the ASC reduces the costs of non-compliance with accounting standards and makes non-compliance a feasible alternative to actual lobbying on economic grounds (Sutton, 1984). However, instances of intervention stimulated by concern over economic consequences can be cited, as in the case of the formulation of an accounting standard on research and development (Hope and Gray, 1982) and, in the case of accounting for leases, the ASC explicitly requested submissions from interested parties on the potential economic consequences associated with lease capitalization (ASC, 1981).

SOURCES OF ECONOMIC CONSEQUENCES

Economic consequences can be classified in terms of effects on the distribution of income and wealth, and effects on resource allocation, either between enterprises or within the firm (Beaver, 1981; Selto and Neumann, 1981).

The possible sources of economic consequences can be identified as changes in (1) the behaviour of the intended recipients of an accounting report, (2) the behaviour of 'free riders', and (3) the behaviour of the reporting entity (Rappaport, 1977). 'Free riders' are individuals or groups of users other than the intended recipients of the accounting reports. Whether intended recipients or free riders, the decisions of users of financial reports may be changed because the information contained in the reports changes their evaluations of certain economic factors such as the risk or return associated with a corporate security. The behaviour of the reporting company may change because management alters its decisions, perhaps because management remuneration is linked to accounting variables, or because managers believe that users will react to accounting information in a certain way. This impact on management decisions has been termed 'information inductance' (Prakash and Rappaport, 1977; Selto, 1982).

A similar analysis of the effects of accounting disclosure has been used by Staubus (1977), who has summarized the costs and benefits resulting from the provision of any particular type of accounting information under the following general headings.

Potential Benefits from an Accounting Method

(1) Direct benefits to parties associated with the reporting entities, that is present and prospective owners, creditors, suppliers, customers, employees and government and regulatory bodies. These occur through:

   (a) improvements in their own decisions, using information provided by the entity and produced with the accounting alternative in question;
   (b) higher direct compensation from the entity due to its more effective management and greater profitability with the aid of the accounting alternative in question.
(2) Benefits to competitors through more useful information about the reporting entity activities.
(3) Diffused benefits through the better functioning of the economy, for example through the allocation of resources, reduction of variations in the level of economic activity, and the distribution of income between consumption and investment.

Potential Costs of an Accounting Method

(1) Reductions in the profitability of competitors (and in distributions to their constituents) as a result of better decisions by the reporting entity.
(2) Reductions in the profitability of the reporting entity through better decisions by its competitors, creditors, suppliers, customers and employees who bargain with the reporting entities.
(3) Reductions in the profitability of the reporting entity due to the effects upon management decisions of reporting to shareholders and others by means of the accounting method.
(4) The costs of producing and verifying information by the accounting method.
(5) The costs of analysing and using the information produced by the accounting method.

The economic consequences which Staubus lists as costs and benefits are derived from the decisions of users of accounts, and a more detailed consideration of the nature of economic consequences commences with those groups who have an interest in companies and who may use the information contained in financial reports as an input into their decisions. These may be identified as:

   Management
   Shareholders
   Suppliers of resources, both short- and long-term
   Employeees
   Consumers
   Government bodies

Each of these groups will have decisions to make concerning companies which make financial reports. The decision makers and their possible decisions are set out in table 6.1.

Some of these decisions will be related directly to economic variables on which information is provided in financial reports. If such decisions are taken, their effects may be termed direct. Included in direct effects are those resulting from information inductance. The behaviour of management may be influenced by their beliefs regarding the uses to which recipients of information may put it. Consequently, management decisions may be different in the presence of certain financial reporting alternatives than they would have been in their absence due to expectations of the users' responses to that information.

Other decisions will be made in response to direct decisions and their effects, and contribute to the economic consequences of accounting information. Such decisions and effects may be termed indirect. Most of the studies which have been undertaken into economic consequences have concentrated upon the direct effects. However, there is a strong case for the inclusion of indirect effects (Taylor and Turley, 1986).

An analogy can be drawn between the economic consequences following from accounting standards and the economic effects of taxes. Taxes and accounting standards are both imposed by institutions on economic units and both may alter economic behaviour. All explicit taxes have clearly defined bases and the burden of a tax may be initially associated with the base upon which it is designed to fall. Thus, one may say that corporation tax, since it falls on company profits, affects the income and wealth of a company's shareholders. This intitial burden is termed the impact of a tax. However, economic units may adjust their economic behaviour to try to mitigate impact. The impact of a tax may be passed to other economic units through market transactions, resulting in 'tax shifting'. For example the burden of corporation tax may be shifted to employees if wages are reduced to make good profits paid in tax. The ultimate burden of a tax, after shifting has taken place, is termed incidence.

The decisions listed in table 6.1 would give rise to economic consequences similar to the impact of a tax, but if indirect effects occur, this will generate other economic consequences which modify impact into incidence. If concern is with the overall economic consequences of an accounting standard, both the direct and indirect effects should be considered, and the incidence of an accounting standard rather than its impact, evaluated.

Table 6.1 The decisions of users of accounting information

Management	Shareholders	Short-term suppliers of resources	Long-term suppliers of resources	Employees	Consumers	Government
Investment	Share purchase, holding or selling	Whether to supply resources	Whether to supply resources	Supply of labour	Purchase of goods or services	Taxation and subsidies
Acquisition and divestment		Choice of terms for supply	Choice of terms for supply	Employment contract, wages and conditions	After sales service	Regulation
Research and development		Foreclosure	Foreclosure			Demand for goods and services
Financing policy and financial structure	Purchase, holding or sale of securities		Purchase, holding or sale of securities			
Divident policy						Supply of goods and services
Funds management						

Table 6.1 continued

Management	Shareholders	Short-term suppliers of resources	Long-term suppliers of resources	Employees	Consumers	Government
Choice of technology						Macro-economic policies
Choice of inputs						
Bargaining on input costs and terms						
Pricing and output						
Stock holding						
Debtors and creditors management						
Choice of suppliers of resources						

MANAGEMENT PREFERENCES FOR ACCOUNTING POLICIES

The above discussion indicates that a wide range of potential economic consequences may be associated with the decisions of various interest groups. It can be argued that management is the most important interest group from the point of view of economic consequences analysis. Management has the greatest influence over economic variables associated with firms, and also has the primary role in selecting the accounting policies adopted by firms. It is these policies, as well as changes in them, which provide the stimuli for the decisions which give rise to economic consequences.

Ball and Foster (1982) have identified the following as explanations of the firm's choice of accounting policy:

(1) The accounting model view. This view holds that accounting choices are made using accepted models of accounting, for example matching and conservatism.
(2) The economic reality view. This argues that accounting methods are chosen in order to report the underlying economic reality of a firm's operations.
(3) The comparability view. This holds that the overriding criterion of choice is to facilitate inter-firm and inter-period comparisons.
(4) The economic consequences to the shareholders view. This holds that mangement chooses accounting policies in the same way as it is assumed to make other resource allocation decisions, that is to benefit shareholders.
(5) The economic consequences view. This holds that managements choose accounting policies which maximize their own utility or welfare. A number of variants of this view have been propounded and are considered in more detail below.
(6) The regulatory compliance view. When a new accounting regulation is prescribed by a regulatory body, management must decide whether or not to comply. Managements' decision may depend on the means which are available for enforcing compliance and managements' preceptions of related costs and benefits. Hence, this review is related to views (4) and (5).
(7) The innovation diffusion view. This treats the decision to adopt an accounting policy as equivalent to that to adopt productive technologies.
(8) The dominant personality view. This view is frequently cited in anecdotal evidence of accounting policy choice and holds that strong personal preferences may be the determining factor.

Two of the explanations of accounting choice cited above ((4) and (5)) explicitly refer to econonic consequences and others (notably (2), (3) and (6)) imply economic effects. This indicates that the relationship between accounting policies and economic effects is two-way. As we shall see in the following chapter, the main emphasis of research activity has been upon the search for economic effects following from accounting changes. However, the choice of accounting policies in anticipation of their economic effects has long been recognized as of considerable importance.

> The criterion a corporate management uses in selecting among accounting principles is the maximisation of its utility or welfare. (Gordon, 1964)

Recently, the philosophy underlying this idea has been used to develop a formal theory of the choice of accounting policy, based upon the principles of agency theory (Watts, 1977; Watts and Zimmerman, 1978). As Holthausen and Leftwich (1983) observe:

> theories of economic consequences are driven by contracting and monitoring costs associated with firms' contractual agreements, such as management compensation contracts and lending agreements, and with firms' political visibility.

Contracting costs refer to the costs of evaluating, negotiating, writing and renegotiating the terms of contracts. Monitoring costs cover the costs of interested parties becoming informed about a firm's performance under contracts and of evaluating compliance with the terms of contracts. Contracting and monitoring costs, economic consequences and accounting policies are generally associated via four causal links. These may be explained as follows:

(1) Management compensation: Schemes which allow managers a share of a firm's profits are frequently stated in terms of accounting profit or rate of return on book value of assets. Hence, management compensation may be affected by voluntary or compulsory changes in accounting policy and managers may be motivated to choose accounting policies which have the most favourable effect on accounting variables related to their compensation. In addition, management may vary operating or financing decisions to counteract the effects of mandatory accounting policies which might adversely affect their compensation through effects on accounting numbers.

(2) Government regulatory behaviour: In the US many firms, for instance privately owned utility companies and banks, are subject to regulation by government agencies. This involves control over prices

and wages, and decisions on permissible increases in these variables are based upon accounting numbers. Hence, changes in accounting policies may alter accounting numbers and provide a justification for price or wage increases. Such policy changes may be in the interest of the managers of regulated companies or in the interest of regulators themselves. Regulation of this type is emerging in the UK with the privatization of publicly owned enterprises, and with it one may presume the motivations noted above.

(3) Lending agreements: Agreements by which companies obtain borrowed funds may contain restrictions, for example on the payment of dividends, the issuance of new debt or merger activity. The terms of these restrictions are often stated in accounting numbers and hence are susceptible to variation through accounting policy changes. Such agreements are common in the US (for evidence see Leftwich, 1983) but from the limited evidence available, seem to be rarer in the UK (Cadle and Theobald, 1985). It may be that accounting numbers (and hence accounting policies) have a less formal relevance in this context in the UK, since accounting statements are widely used by lenders in the appraisal of lending decisions. Management may wish to take decisions which would violate lending agreements (or which might preclude lending if their results appear in financial statements) and as a consequence may be motivated to choose accounting policies which disguise such effects.

(4) Political visibility: Accounting numbers which are made public may affect the extent to which a company is criticized or supported by outside groups such as trades unions, consumers and, particularly, government. High reported profits may encourage demands for large wage increases or price controls, or may be used to justify increases in taxation. On the other hand, low profits (or losses) may encourage support for subsidies or protection. All firms will be affected by their political visibility, but some firms and industries will possess greater potential or actual visibility, for example oil companies and banks. Management of firms with significant political visibility may be motivated to select accounting policies which optimize that visibility.

In summary, management's choice of accounting policies may be based upon an anticipation of economic consequences: either in order to avoid undesirable consequences (on their remuneration or their firms' operations for example), or in order to achieve desirable consequences (for example a subsidy from government).

AN EXAMPLE OF ECONOMIC CONSEQUENCES ANALYSIS:
ACCOUNTING FOR LEASES

The groups making direct and indirect decisions, and the decisions which they make, will vary with different accounting regulations. Take, for example, the case of an accounting standard on leasing which requires capitalization of finance leases in the balance sheets of lessee companies as in SSAP21 (ASC, 1984). This accounting policy would tend to increase the financial gearing of lessees as measured by balance sheet data and reduce accounting measures of the rate of return on capital employed, and one might expect these changes to influence the decisions of management, shareholders, suppliers, employees and government.

Management might find leasing a less attractive source of finance because leases are brought on to the balance sheet. They may seek to maintain investment by using alternative sources of finance, such as debt or equity, or they may curtail investment. In addition, management may reduce discretionary expenditures in order to maintain the rate of return on capital employed, or adopt other accounting policies which give more favourable reported results. All these reactions could be the result of information inductance: management making decisions in anticipation of the reactions of shareholders and suppliers of resources.

Suppliers may increase their assessments of the risks of supplying resources to lessees and make the terms of supply (prices, interest rates or credit) more stringent. In the extreme, supplies of resources could be curtailed. These decisions could be made by suppliers of goods and services or by suppliers of finance, such as lessors, banks or debenture holders.

Shareholders may adjust their assessments of the risks and required returns of investing in companies reporting the capitalized values of finance lessees and reassess decisions on shareholdings, with resulting effects on share prices. Employees and their representatives may modify their wage or other claims as a result of changes in reported earnings or rates of return of lessees. Government could modify its taxation and subsidy policies as a result of changes in reported earnings and rates of return, or alter demand or prices paid for goods and services supplied by lessees to the extent that accounting data is used in setting the terms of government contracts.

All these direct decisions and effects are set out in table 6.2. The table also identifies a series of indirect effects which may follow from the direct decisions. Indirect effects may be numerous and difficult to trace but certain potential indirect effects are suggested. For example if management decides to curtail investment because leasing is less attractive and other finance sources are not available or are unattractive, production technology may be changed (to more labour intensive methods) or production may be reduced. In each case such indirect effects may lead on to others. For instance, if more labour intensive production methods are adopted, the demand for labour may increase and employment may rise. Alternatively, an indirect result of a fall in production may be a reduction in the demand for labour and with it employment and perhaps wages. Furthermore, changes in demands for labour, in wages and in the supply of final products, may lead to indirect effects elsewhere. Customers may be faced with reduced supplies of goods and services and prices may rise as a result.

Similar types of potential economic consequences following from other accounting regulation may be set out in the manner of tables 6.1 and 6.2. The large number of decisions and effects listed in tables 6.1 and 6.2 interact with each other in many different ways. This implies that identification of the full extent of economic consequences following from an accounting regulation will be extremely difficult both conceptually and in practice. One approach to this problem is to construct a simple model of the main economic relationship involved, and to use the model to derive predictions of likely economic effects. For our present purposes such a model would also serve to illustrate, from a different perspective, the source and extent of economic consequences.

A Model of Economic Consequences

If management finds leasing less attractive after lease capitalization, the amount of leasing may be reduced, with corresponding effects on other forms of financing and investment. Other effects, on production, the demand for labour inputs and in the final product market, may follow. An illustrative model of the nature of such effects and their inter-relationships is given in figure 6.1.

Figure 6.1 is composed of seven quadrants, each of them interrelated. Quadrant (1) shows the investment demand schedule of a typical lessee company. As a result of lease capitalization, suppliers of finance may increase risk premiums to reflect higher levels of balance sheet gearing. This is shown by the increase in the company's cost of capital from r_1 to r_2. The result is a fall in investment by the company. The same result may occur if the management of lessee companies curtail investment due to information inductance. The effect on investment is a direct economic consequence of lease capitalization. Quadrant (2) illustrates a possible effect on production. The company is assumed to produce

Table 6.2 The potential economic consequences of lease capitalization

Management	Shareholders	Short-term suppliers of resources	Long-term suppliers of resources	Employees	Consumers	Government
Direct effects						
Leasing is less attractive	Increases in estimates of risk	Increases in estimates of risk	Increases in estimates of risk	Reappraisal of demands for wages and conditions of employment	None	Revision of policies on taxation and subsidy
Reduction in amount of leasing activity	Selling of shares	Increases in risk premiums	Increases in risk premiums			Reappraisal of terms of government contracts
Substitution of alternative finance sources	Increases in risk premium	Tightening terms of credit	Tightening terms of credit			
Decrease in investment	Effects on share prices	Curtailing supplies of credit or other resources	Curtailing supplies of credit			
			Selling of debentures			
			Effects on prices of debentures			

Indirect effects						
Change in production technology	Adjustment of portfolios to reflect changed assessments of risk/return	Volume and profitability of suppliers' business affected	Volume and profitability of suppliers' business affected	Changes in wages and conditions due to the changes in demands for labour	Effects on the supplies of goods and services	Changes in government policies in response to changes in other economic variables
Changes in costs					Effects on prices of goods and services	
Changes in prices and output	Responses to changes in earnings and dividends due to the interaction of all other effects	Changes in suppliers' share price and other economic variables	Changes in suppliers' share price and other economic variables	Changes in levels of employment		Investment incentives
Changes in demand for factors of production					Effects on consumer demand	Employment
Chances in discretionary expenditures						Output
						Price and costs

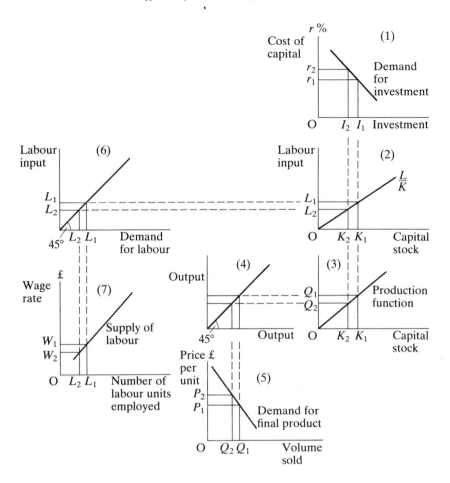

Figure 6.1 A model of the economic consequences of lease capitalization

under conditions of fixed factor proportions, and the line O to L/K shows varying amounts of total factor inputs on this assumption. Reducing the rate of investment from I_1 to I_2 causes the company's capital stock to be reduced, and with it the demand for labour inputs from L_1 to L_2. The demand for labour is transferred, via the construction line of 45° in quadrant (6), to quadrant (7) which illustrates the labour market. Given the supply schedule of labour, the fall in the demand for labour causes wages to fall from W_1 to W_2.

The reduction in the size of the capital stock and the attendant demand for labour causes production to fall. This is shown in quadrant (3) which contains the production function. The production function assumes constant returns to scale and the fall in the capital stock from K_1 to K_2 reduces output proportionately from Q_1 to Q_2. This has the effect of raising price in the market for the company's final product, shown in quadrant (5), from P_1 to P_2.

Figure 6.1 shows a sequence of consequences for a company whose cost of capital increases due to lease capitalization, leading to a fall in investment. Other companies may be affected in different ways. For example companies with no or insignificant leases may find their risk premiums unchanged and may become relatively more attractive to investors. Thus, there may be a migration of capital between companies as a result of the accounting regulation. This analysis does not indicate whether total investment in the economy will change, or whether overall employment or the supply of goods will remain the same. Furthermore, the model and its predictions may be changed by varying the assumptions made on production relationships. For example labour and capital may be substitutable in production, and the companies whose capital stocks are reduced may maintain production by substituting labour for capital. In this case, the demand for labour would rise, and with it wages.

The above analysis has three main purposes. First, it illustrates the extent of potential economic consequences from an accounting regulation and the limitations of considering only direct consequences. Second, the analysis demonstrates that economic theory rather than vague speculation may be used in analysing economic consequences. Third, it shows that such analyses may be useful in deriving predictions of potential consequences, against which empirical evidence of economic consequences may be evaluated by accounting regulators. It is to this topic that we now turn.

ECONOMIC CONSEQUENCES AND ACCOUNTING REGULATIONS

Recognition of the possibility that economic consequences may flow from accounting regulations highlights a number of fundamental questions concerning how accounting standards should be established and what role, if any, considerations of economic consequences should play in the formulation of standards.

One response is to argue that if accounting regulations are ultimately responsible for certain economic effects then that responsibility must be acknowledged and the effects explicitly considered in the process of determining a regulation. This approach requires accounting regulators to adopt a perspective which is broader than purely technical considerations (Rappaport, 1977). For example Buckley (1976) has argued that there is 'little doubt that accounting rules are agents of resource allocation and social policy' and criticized US standards setters for formulating accounting policies in terms of 'abstruse "theoretical" arguments with complete obliviousness of social impact'.

Traditionally, accounting standards setters have sought to make choices between accounting alternatives on purely technical grounds. This is a much cited but largely unspecified approach. Alternatively, standards could be set with the objective of providing information which is suitable for users' decision making. This could be on the basis of what standard setters perceive users to need, or what users demand. Another alternative is to seek to resolve disputes over accounting alternatives by reference to a comprehensive 'conceptual framework' of accounting theory if such a framework could be agreed. Additionally, standard setters might seek to set accounting standards with regard to their economic and social effects. This socio-economic approach embraces the user-decision approach, as we noted at the beginning of this chapter, but goes a good deal further. Finally, standard setters might adopt a strategy which mixes elements of the other approaches or use different approaches for different issues.

As we noted in chapter 4, the ASC recently addressed the issue of how accounting standards should be set (ASC, 1978, 1983). The ASC sought to examine the administrative process by which standards were set in the UK, but did not directly consider the issue of what criteria to apply to choices between accounting alternatives. As regards the economic consequences of accounting standards, the only formal acknowledgement by the ASC of the relevance of this issue was contained in ED29 which specifically requested submissions on the possible economic consequences of proposals on accounting for leases:

> While the ASC has no doubt that capitalisation of assets held under finance leases is the appropriate technical and pracical solution to the accounting problem, it must nevertheless be recognised that there are some who argue that this solution (while technically sound) might have undesirable economic consequences. . . . Commentators who submit reasoned opinions that there would be an unacceptable danger of adverse economic consequences are invited to consider what course should be taken in a standard in place of capitalisation. (ASC, 1981, para. 33)

These views suggest certain conclusions about the ASC's current approach to standard setting in general and economic consequences in particular. It is implied that an analysis of economic consequences is viewed as secondary to the application of technical criteria. Further, economic consequences are considered relevant only as challenges to or disproofs of decisions made on technical criteria.

In the USA, the FASB has taken a much more active interest in the issue of economic consequences. Since 1976 the FASB has sponsored research directed specifically at detection of any effects which accounting standards might be having on securities markets, or management behaviour. Although some of the research has been successful in identifying the existence of certain economic effects, it has done little to clarify the role which analysis of economic consequences might play in standard setting. Rather, investigation of economic consequences tends to emphasize the difficulty of defining that role, as reflected in the following questions.

(1) How much weight should be given to considerations of economic consequences compared with technical or other criteria?
(2) Should the objectives of standard setters be to maximize or minimize socio-economic impact?
(3) What constitutes acceptable or unacceptable consequences following from a standard?
(4) How can choices be made when standards give rise to desirable and undesirable economic effects?
(5) How can a standard setting body specify those economic consequences which it should consider and those which it may ignore?
(6) Are standard setting bodies responsible for acting in the public interest, and what constitutes the public interest?
(7) Should standard setters deliberately mandate what they believe to be an otherwise inferior accounting policy in order to achieve their, or someone else's, public policy objective?

Aside from the methodological issues of applying economic consequences analysis in accounting regulation, the most fundamental question which must be resolved is how far any private sector regulatory body possesses the social legitimacy to make policy choices which favourably or adversely affect different groups. Opinions are divided between those who hold that recognition of economic consequences is necessary to maintain the validity of the rules developed by standard setters and those who fear that such recognition will lead ultimately to the end of private sector regulation of accounting.

In support of explicit recognition of the consequences of accounting choices the following arguments have been put forward:

a politicization of accounting rule making [is] not only inevitable but just. In a society committed to democratic legitimization of authority only politically responsive institutions have the right to command others to obey their rules. (Gerborth, 1972)

If the social welfare impact of accounting policy decisions were ignored, the basis for the existence of a regulating body would disappear. Therefore, the FASB must consider explicitly political (i.e. social welfare), aspects as well as accounting theory and research in its decisions. (May and Sundem, 1976)

Acceptance of this view implies that the decision making processes involved in standard setting are not primarily technical, but are political, involving less the pursuit of correct technical solutions than the achievement of compromise (Hope, 1979) and the successful marketing of accounting rules to affected or interested parties (Horngren, 1973).

Indeed, some have argued that the generation of economic consequences ought to be the purpose of financial reporting, for example improving capital formation, encouraging innovation and risk taking and facilitating domestic enterprises in meeting foreign competition (Mautz and May, 1978).These objectives suggest that accounting standard setters should select accounting alternatives on the basis of the extent to which they give rise to the desired consequences, but there is still the problem of possible conflicts among the different effects of a particular accounting treatment with reference to economic objectives.

As indicated earlier, the notion of accounting standard setting as a political process is not without its critics. Many argue that if it becomes generally accepted that accounting is used to achieve other than purely measurement ends, in as neutral a way as possible, its credibility will be destroyed (Solomons, 1978). Accounting standards could be reduced to satisfying the preferences of specific pressure groups rather than society as a whole. Moreover, effective lobbying on the grounds of alleged economic consequences may become the norm (Sutton, 1984). Alternatively, a search for compromise solutions could cause accounting standards to lack substance and the standard setting process may become stagnant.

SUMMARY

Traditionally accounting regulations have been thought of in terms of their information effects, i.e. the effects which they have on financial reporting following their promulgation. However, interest has grown in the production of financial information to provide an input to decision making. Implicit in the provision of information for decisions is the notion of economic consequences. Of specific interest in recent years has been the question of the extent to which individual accounting regulations can be held responsible for economic and social effects which result from decisions taken on the basis of the information disclosures required by the regulations. Accounting rules can be linked to the effects of decision making to the extent that decisions made in the presence of a rule are different from those which would have been taken in its absence.

Changes in decision making may result from the behaviour of the direct recipients of accounting reports or the decisions of those who gain access to reports. Also relevant is the behaviour of management in anticipating the reactions of others and adjusting corporate affairs accordingly. All these changes can lead to further reactions on other parties, making the identification of a complete range of economic consequences difficult.

A major difficulty in the application of economic consequences analysis in accounting rule making is the choice of appropriate methodologies for undertaking such analysis and for evaluating the significance of economic effects alongside other considerations. Economic analysis may help in this process at least to the extent of making the choices involved in the selection of accounting rules more explicit than at present. In addition, since the economic consequences following from changes in accounting rules may be associated with changes in resource allocation and ultimately with the distribution of income and wealth, well-tried criteria of social welfare may find an application to the economic aspects of accounting rule making.

Ultimately, the most important question is whether private sector bodies can legitimately deal with the choices involved in the assessment of economic questions. Some argue that this is essential to ensure the validity of accounting regulations, others argue that to do so will undermine the basis of a private sector role in regulation. The answer to the question of legitimacy may be different in the case of bodies such as the FASB, which is overseen by a government regulatory agency, the SEC, and from which it derives indirect legal authority, than for bodies like the ASC, which at present lacks the legitimizing support of government, other than in general terms. The importance of the nature of the relationship between legal and professional control of accounting regulation is something which we have discussed elsewhere. However, it must also be said that the political aspect may be so fundamental to accounting standard setting that it is not likely to alter whether the authority for standards stays in the private sector or is transferred to the public sector (Dopuch and Sunder, 1980).

REFERENCES

Accounting Standards Committee 1975: *The Corporate Report.*
Accounting Standards Committee 1978: *Setting Accounting Standards.*
Accounting Standards Committee 1981: *Accounting for Leases and Hire Purchase Contracts,* ED 29.
Accounting Standards Committee 1983: *Review of the Standard Setting Process.*
Accounting Standards Committee 1984: *Accounting for Leases and Hire Purchase Contracts,* SSAP21.
American Accounting Association 1966: *A Statement of Basic Accounting Theory.*
American Accounting Association 1969: 'An evaluation of external reporting practices – a report of the 1966–1968 Committee on External Financial Reporting'. *The Accounting Review,* Supplement to Volume 44.
American Accounting Association 1978: *Report of the Committee on the Social Consequences of Accounting Information,* Committee Reports, Vol. 4.
American Institute of Certified Public Accountants 1973: *Report of the Study Group on the Objectives of Financial Statements* (Trueblood Report).
Arnold, J.A. and Moizer, P. 1984: 'A survey of the methods used by UK investment analysts to appraise investments in ordinary shares'. *Accounting and Business Research,* Vol. 14.
Ball, R.J. and Foster, G. 1982: 'Corporate financial statements: a review of empirical research methodologies'. *Journal of Accounting Research,* Supplement, Vol. 20
Beaver, W.H. 1981: *Financial Reporting – An Accounting Revolution,* Prentice Hall.
Buckley, J.W. 1976: 'The FASB and Impact Analysis'. *Management Accounting,* April.
Cadle, P.J. and Theobald, M. 1985: 'Corporate dividend policies in the UK'. Working Paper, Department of Accounting and Finance, University of Manchester.
Collins, D.W. and Dent, W.T. 1979: 'The proposed elimination of full cost accounting in the extractive petroleum industry: an empirical assessment of the market consequences'. *Journal of Accounting and Economics,* Vol. 1.
Dopuch, N. and Sunder, S. 1980: 'FASB's statement on objectives and elements of financial accounting: a review'. *The Accounting Review,* Vol. 55.
Financial Accounting Standards Board 1978: *Economic Consequences of Financial Accounting Standards,* Stamford, Connecticut.
Gerborth, D.L. 1972: 'Muddling thro' with the APB'. *Journal of Accountancy,* May.
Gordon, M.J. 1964: 'Postulates, principles and research in accounting'. *The Accounting Review,* Vol. 49.
Holthausen, R.W. and Leftwich, R.W. 1983: 'The economic consequences of accounting choice'. *Journal of Accounting and Economics,* Vol. 5.
Hope, A.J.B. 1979: 'Accounting policy: theory or pragmatism or both?'. *Submissions on the Accounting Standards Committee's Document: Setting Accounting Standards,* Vol. II, Accounting Standards Committee.

Hope, A. and Gray, R. 1982: 'Power and policy making: the development of an R and D standard'. *Journal of Business Finance and Accounting*, Vol. 9.

Horngren, C. T. 1973: 'The marketing of accounting standards'. *Journal of Accountancy*, October.

Leftwich, R.W. 1983: 'Accounting information in private markets: evidence from private lending agreements'. *The Accounting Review*, Vol. 58.

Mautz, R.K. and May, W.G. 1978: *Financial Disclosure in a Competitive Economy*, Financial Executive Research Foundation.

May, R.G. and Sundem, G.L. 1976: 'Research for accounting policy: an overview'. *The Accounting Review*, Vol. 51.

Prakash, P. and Rappaport, A. 1977: 'Information inductance and its significance for accounting'. *Accounting Organisations and Society*.

Rappaport, A. 1977: 'Economic impact of accounting standards – implications for the FASB'. *Journal of Accountancy*, May.

Revsine, L. 1973: *Replacement Cost Accounting*, Prentice Hall.

Selto, F.H. 1982: 'Internal adaptions to effects of changes in financial accounting standards'. *Accounting, Organisations and Society*, Vol. 7.

Selto, F.H. and Neumann, B.R. 1981: 'A further guide to research on the economic consequences of accounting information'. *Accounting and Business Research*, Vol. 11.

Sherer, M., Southworth, A. and Turley, W.S. 1981: 'An empirical investigation of disclosure usage and usefulness of corporate accounting information'. *Managerial Finance*.

Solomons, D. 1978: 'The politicization of accounting'. *Journal of Accountancy*, September.

Staubus, G.J. 1977: *Making Accounting Decisions*, Scholars Book Club.

Sutton, T.G. 1984: 'Lobbying of accounting standard-setting bodies in the UK and the USA: a Downsian analysis'. *Accounting, Organisations and Society*, Vol. 9.

Sweringa, R.J. 1977: 'Consequences of financial accounting standards'. *Accounting Forum*.

Taylor, P.J. and Turley, W.S. 1986: 'Applying economic consequences in accounting standards setting: the application of tax incidence analysis'. *Journal of Business Finance and Accounting*, Vol. 13.

Watts, R.L. 1977: 'Corporate financial statements: a product of the market and political processes'. *Australian Journal of Management*.

Watts, R.L. and Zimmerman, J.L. 1978: 'Towards a positive theory of the determination of accounting standards'. *The Accounting Review*, Vol. 53.

Wyatt, A.R. 1977: 'The economic impact of financial accounting standards'. *Journal of Accountancy*, October.

Zeff, S. 1978: 'The rise of economic consequences'. *Journal of Accountancy*, December.

7

Evidence on Economic Consequences

In order to draw conclusions about the existence and nature of the economic consequences following from accounting regulations, evidence must be collected about the effects of actual or proposed regulations. This chapter examines the growing body of empirical research which has sought to provide that evidence. The results of such research can assist accounting regulators in making decisions regarding new accounting regulations, or in assessing the actual consequences of regulations in comparison with their intended or predicted effects.

It is worth emphasizing again, however, that the recognition and observation of economic consequences will not solve the problems of making decisions on possible accounting regulations. The problems of choice may, in fact, be greater if the consequences of alternative courses of action are understood. Most of the studies which have been undertaken have concentrated on testing for the existence of certain consequences associated with individual accounting standards once they are implemented. Although some studies have attempted to forecast likely consequences of proposed standards, relatively little work has addressed the issue of how economic consequences might influence standard setters.

Before reviewing the evidence that has been collected, two further caveats regarding existing research on economic consequences should be noted. First, the great majority of studies have concentrated on the decision making behaviour of specific groups, in an attempt to identify any changes in behaviour following an accounting regulation, rather than either investigating the whole range of effects that might occur, or tracing the results of changes in decisions through to their impact on income distribution or the allocation of resources. Second, almost all of the research has been conducted in the United States. Care must therefore be taken in interpreting the significance of the results of this research in the context of the UK, where the nature and traditions of regulation and the market in which accounting information is used may be different.

Figure 7.1 outlines a classification of the different approaches which have been adopted in economic consequences research according to the different groups of decision makers studied, and the various aspects of the relationship between accounting information and decisions which have been investigated. The different strands of research identified in figure 7.1 provide a framework for the discussion in this chapter.

STOCK MARKET STUDIES

Studies of the stock market effects of accounting reports and corporate disclosure dominate the literature on economic consequences. Lev and Ohlson (1982) have described the market studies literature as representing the 'most concerted and ambitious research effort in accounting history'. The main focus of this research is the relationship between publicly disclosed accounting information and the characteristics of company securities traded in stock markets. Central to the relationship is the use of accounting information by equity investors in their investment decisions. Economic consequences follow as a result of changes in share prices and the allocation of capital to firms. Stock market research has been based on the twin foundations of portfolio theory and its derivative the capital asset pricing model (CAPM), and the concept of efficient capital markets (ECM). More recently, market studies have incorporated developments in the fields of information economics and agency theory.

The CAPM is based on the idea that share prices reflect investors assessments of the risks and expected returns associated with holding shares. Investors will wish to maximize their returns from given levels of risk and will use information to formulate their expectations. The provision of new information may lead to a revision of expectations. Market based studies have investigated the relationship between accounting information and share prices and, in particular, the extent to which capital markets are efficient in reacting to new information. Beaver (1981) has defined an efficient market as follows:

> a securities market is said to be efficient with respect to an information system if and only if the prices act as if everyone observes the signals from that information system. In other words, prices act as if there is universal knowledge of that information. If prices have this property, they 'fully reflect' the information system.

Decision makers and   *Research questions*
principal research issue

A *Investors*
The relationship
between accounting
information and
investors decisions in
stock markets
(stock-market
studies)

1 Do accounting
numbers have an
effect on stock market
variables?

   (a) Earnings data

   (b) Non-earnings
       data

2 Does the choice of
accounting policy by
companies have an
effect on stock market
variables?

3 Do accounting
regulations have an
effect on stock market
variables?

B *Company
management*
The relationship
between information
in accounting reports
and management
decision making
within the company

1 Do accounting
regulations affect
management decision
making behaviour?

   (a) Regulations on
       accounting policy
       (measurement
       and allocation
       issues)

   (b) Regulations
       affecting
       disclosure

2 Are managements'
voluntary choices of
accounting policies
influenced by
economic factors?

3 Do management
attempt to influence
the choice of
accounting
regulations because of
economic factors?

C *Other groups*
The relationship
between accounting
information and the
decision making
behaviour of other
groups

Figure 7.1 Research into accounting information and decision making

Evidence on Economic Consequences

There are three types of capital market efficiency:

(1) Weak-form efficiency: Share prices fully reflect information regarding past share prices.
(2) Semi-strong form efficiency: Share prices fully reflect all publicly available accounting information as well as other non-accounting information.
(3) Strong-form efficiency: Share prices fully reflect all information, accounting or otherwise, whether publicly available or not.

If a capital market is efficient, shares may be thought of as 'correctly priced' in that the prices impound all the relevant information. Thus an investor could not consistently obtain returns in excess of those which are generally expected any more than a firm or consumer in a perfectly competitive market could trade at a price other than the going market one.

Together the CAPM and ECM theories provide a consistent framework for research. CAPM states that the relevance of accounting data to the individual investor is restricted to the prediction of systematic risk, that is the extent to which the returns on an individual security vary with those of the stock market as a whole. Under ECM theory, the information content of accounting data can be inferred from observation of share price movements and changes in the volume of share trading in response to changes in the amount of information available. The majority of empirical tests have been concerned with weak form and semi-strong form efficiency. The chief concerns of these studies have been twofold: to ascertain whether and how quickly the capital market reacts to new information.

Market studies have been classified by Lev and Ohlson (1982) as follows:

(1) studies of the information content of accounting numbers;
(2) studies of voluntary differences in accounting techniques between companies, or of voluntary accounting changes by companies;
(3) studies which test the effects of specific accounting regulations.

Although the first two categories of research do not explicitly consider accounting regulations, some of the research findings are relevant to the subject of regulation and are summarized below.

Information Content Studies

Research of this type has sought to establish whether accounting data provide useful (relevant and timely) information to investors. The studies can be divided into those that have investigated (1) announcements of company earnings, and (2) non-earnings data.

Earnings data. The best-known example of research into the usefulness of earnings data is that by Ball and Brown (1968), who investigated the stock market effects of unexpected changes in annual earnings for a sample of US companies. They identified a significant association between unexpected earnings changes and returns to shares, but found that most of the share price reactions which took place occurred before earnings were announced and hence were in anticipation of the announcement. These anticipatory adjustments suggest that the information contained in earnings data is made public in others ways, for example in interim reports or by press comment. The findings lead to the conclusion that although accounting earnings are relevant to investors (since share prices change in response to them) accounting reports which contain announcements of earnings are not a timely source of information.

Subsequent research which has developed and extended the approach used by Ball and Brown has reached broadly similar conclusions concerning, for example, the effects of quarterly earnings announcements (Brown and Kennelly, 1972), and the relationship between earnings announcements and the variance of share returns (Patell and Wolfson, 1981). Studies outside the United States, for example Australia (Brown, 1970), Britain (Firth, 1976) and Japan (Deakin *et al.*, 1974), have confirmed the relevance of earnings data to share prices. While it may be concluded that accounting earnings and their announcement (both annually and interim) affect share prices, the implications of this conclusion for accounting regulation are not obvious. Information on earnings is clearly used by investors, but what is its social value? To answer that question it would be necessary to investigate the allocations of resources and risks which result from capital market decisions based on earnings data. Also earnings data explain only a part of share price behaviour. Much of what determines share prices, in the statistical sense and by extension in the economic sense, remains unknown, and so the relative importance of regulations affecting earnings measurement and disclosure is not clear.

Non-earnings data. Complementing the research on earnings data, a number of studies have investigated the information content of non-earnings accounting variables. For example the existence of a market reaction to disclosure of management earnings forecasts has been established (Patell, 1976; Ball and Foster, 1982). Unexpected dividend announcements have also been found to give rise to significant market reactions (see Patell, 1976; Griffin, 1976; Aharony and Swary, 1980). Empirical research into the effects of non-earnings items is potentially important for accounting regulation in helping to identify what, beyond earnings, matters to users of financial reports.

Choice of Accounting Techniques by Companies

Another avenue of stock market research concerns investors' reactions to information based on the voluntary choices of accounting policies made by companies' managements. A common theme is present in this research. It concerns the extent to which investors are able to distinguish between changes in accounting policy which are purely cosmetic, i.e. have no effect on cash flows, and changes which reflect events having a real economic substance, i.e. do affect cash flows. If investors are not able to distinguish between these two types of accounting change, management might be able to mislead them through appropriately chosen accounting or disclosure policies. If investors can separate the cosmetic from the real, the possible advantages to management of manipulating accounting policy disappear. Stock market reaction to accounting policies which have only cosmetic (non-cash flow) effects has been studied in two ways. A number of studies have examined cross-sectional differences between accounting policies on, for example, accounting for deferred taxation, depreciation and exploration costs (of oil and gas companies) for samples of companies. These studies have generally concluded that investors are able to distinguish such differences for what they are and to make appropriate adjustments to earnings or key ratios such as price earnings ratios (see Beaver and Dukes, 1973).

Investigation of the stock market effects of accounting-policy switches by companies have generally found no significant reaction. However, since some researchers have detected market reactions to policy switches (Kaplan and Roll, 1972) there remains some doubt concerning investors' ability to identify accounting policy changes with no economic effects. One interpretation of this situation is that observed stock market responses to cosmetic accounting policy changes indicate that the nature of the changes, rather than their effect on the accounting numbers, conveys useful information to investors, for example about management characteristics and motivations. This view calls into question the earlier distinction drawn between those accounting policy changes which are merely cosmetic and those with an economic substance.

One way in which accounting policy changes can have a direct impact on cash flows is if the effects on reported earnings have implications for company taxation. An example of this impact from the US is provided by the adoption of LIFO stock valuation by a number of companies in the 1970s. The possibility of accounting regulations resulting in changes in tax legislation which would subsequently affect companies' tax charges was also raised in the debate concerning both current cost accounting and accounting for leases. The effects of a switch to LIFO stock valuation should be to decrease reported earnings but increase after-tax cash flows under inflationary conditions. Early research reported that investors recognized the cash flow effects and responded as expected, suggesting that the market has the ability to detect real economic effects (Sunder, 1973). However, subsequent research found an association between companies' performance and the adoption of LIFO to help reduce tax charges. Consequently, the stock market may have reacted to the better performance of the companies changing policy and not the change itself.

Effects of Accounting Regulations

Investigation of whether accounting regulations have economic effects could be, as we have already noted, of particular importance in the evaluation of regulations, although such evidence cannot of itself allow the identification of successful or failed regulations. There is increasing recognition, especially by regulatory bodies, that research should be directed towards obtaining evidence of economic effects. It may be that such evidence has most use as 'ammunition' in lobbying exercises, either by regulatory bodies of their constituents, or by interest groups. Two broad categories of accounting regulation have been investigated for stock market effects. The first concerns regulations which reflect choices between alternative accounting policies on issues of measurement or allocation, and the second aspect relates to regulations covering the disclosure of information.

Regulations on accounting policies. A number of accounting standards involve measurement issues and questions about the allocation and recognition of income. In other words, these standards can lead to changes in the amounts shown in accounting statements. The research question is therefore whether these changes are linked to any reaction in the stock market. Tests for stock market responses have been applied to a large number of standards and some examples are quoted below.

Care must be taken in interpreting the results of such tests on individual issues, due to the difficulty of isolating the effect of an accounting standard from all other influences on share prices. For example given results which do not report any evidence of a reaction, a number of possible explanations could be true. It could be that the changed information as a result of the standard is not useful and has been ignored by investors, or that it has already been estimated or obtained by other means and built into share prices, or that there is a reaction but the research method used has failed to identify it. In some cases where initial research has suggested there was a market reaction, later studies have concluded that the apparent response may have been due to other influences.

In the United States, disclosure of information on leasing activity was mandatory under SEC rules before the FASB introduced a standard requiring lease capitalization. The FASB statement thus provides a good example of a change concerning presentation and measurement rather than disclosure. Research has not found any evidence that the requirement for balance sheet reporting of capitalized values for leases gave rise to a significant market reaction (Abdel-Khalik *et al.*, 1981). No equivalent research has yet been carried out in the UK although similar regulations are in force. Studies of certain other US standards, for example accounting for research and development expenditure (Vigeland, 1981) and foreign currency translation (Shank *et al.*, 1980), have also failed to detect stock market reactions to the accounting policies mandated by those regulations.

A subject on which the research findings are more ambiguous is that of accounting for the effects of changing prices (Abdel-Khalik and McKeown, 1978). For example Noreen and Sepe (1981) investigated the period covering the full development of an inflation accounting standard by the FASB, rather than simply looking at the point at which the standard took effect. They concluded that the stock market had reacted at various stages in the development of the standard: the FASB's initial announcement that a mandatory requirement was planned, the subsequent postponement of a decision on its contents and finally the announcement of a new exposure draft on the topic. Conversely, others have concluded that there was no market reaction to the disclosure effects of FAS33 (Beaver and Landsman, 1982).

Research conducted in the UK into the stock market reaction to the current cost accounting information required by SSAP16 has also provided mixed results. Some tests have failed to demonstrate any impact on stock market prices (Appleyard and Strong, 1984; Board and Walker, 1984; Skerratt and Thompson, 1984) but others have suggested that information on current cost earnings did lead to adjustments in investors' expectations about future company performance.

When the stock market research is taken together, the evidence of a stock market reaction to accounting standards is ambiguous. It would appear that, to a large extent, investors may anticipate the effects of alternative accounting policies and that standards which apply more rigid regulation to policy, as distinct from those extending disclosure, do not improve the information set available to investors. If justified, this conclusion may have important implications for the role of accounting standards and other similar regulations.

Regulations on disclosure. Several regulations involving the disclosure of new information have been studied for stock market reaction. The earliest such regulations which have been examined are those contained in the US Securities Act of 1934 (Benston, 1973; Deakin, 1976). In general, the conclusion of studies in this area has been that requirements for new disclosures have information content for investors, for example requirements to disclose segmental data (Collins and Simmonds, 1979; Ajinkya, 1980) and requirements on firms to disclose disagreements with auditors (Fried and Schiff, 1981).

Work by Gonedes (1975) and others casts interesting light on the relative effects of disclosure and accounting policy. Gonedes examined US regulations on the disclosure of extraordinary and special items and found that separate disclosure of such items appeared to have an information content, but their classification by item did not. Interestingly, it is the issue of classification, or measurement, which is likely to prove more troublesome for the regulator than that of whether or not to require disclosure.

Although testing the market effects of accounting disclosures and policies, whether voluntarily decided by management or mandated by regulations, is a valid area for research, some points should be noted regarding the contribution which such tests have made to the discussion of the manner in which regulations should be set (Beaver, 1973; Foster, 1980). In the context of the approach adopted in this book it can be said that the existing research has not provided a theory on which accounting regulators could rely in order to predict those circumstances or issues when a capital market reaction could be expected, or the extent of any anticipated reaction. Investigation of the stock market reaction to the implementation of an accounting regulation may provide results of value in considering its revision, but this does not assist in the initial choice of regulation. More importantly, even where findings on stock market impact have approached unanimity, authors have found it impossible to agree on a generally acceptable evaluation of the desirability or otherwise of that impact. Evidence of changes in stock market variables does not solve the problem of how to interpret the economic welfare implications of the observed impact on the stock market. A further fundamental problem with capital market research as an input to the process of accounting regulation is that it focuses on a single set of decision makers, investors, and on the consequences of their decisions only in terms of impact on the stock market. Economic consequences will not stop at the boundary of the stock market but will extend into other markets, and accounting regulators may need to consider this wider impact rather than narrowly defined stock market effects.

Several groups of decision makers other than investors may alter their behaviour because of changes in the supply of accounting information, and many decisions may be involved. Arguably, the greatest potential for economic effects, following from the decisions of groups other than investors, is associated with management decisions. This is because of their ability to influence economic variables and also because of their role in accounting policy making within the firm. In chapter 6 we discussed some of the ways in which economic consequences might follow from management decisions as a result of accounting changes. Within that general framework, research has been undertaken to identify the effects of accounting policies on management decisions, which can be offered as evidence of the existence of economic consequences. In recent years, a number of studies, based on the agency theory model of managerial behaviour, have also sought to explain management preferences for alternative accounting policies. As we saw in chapter 6, this model of accounting choice is closely associated with economic consequences.

Research into economic consequences following from management decisions may be classified under three broad headings:

(1) management responses to mandatory accounting regulations;
(2) economic consequences associated with managers' voluntary choices of accounting policies;
(3) managers' attempts at influencing accounting regulators through lobbying.

Effects Following Mandatory Accounting Regulations

If, because of the existence of an accounting regulation, managers are forced to adopt policies they would not have chosen voluntarily, they may as a result alter their business decisions in order to minimize the effect of the accounting policy on financial statements. As described in chapter 6, such a response may be explained by the existence of a direct relationship between accounting variables and management objectives or indirectly through information inductance. In this section, we examine the evidence relating to the impact of accounting regulations on management decisions with reference to a number of specific accounting issues. As is the case with the economic consequences literature generally, most of the research relates to the US.

In chapter 5 we described some aspects of the debate which

accompanied the development in the UK of an accounting standard on research and development expenditure and noted in particular the views expressed by management in the aerospace industry about possible economic effects on government contract work. Research in the US has also investigated the R&D issue in terms of whether the FASB standard requiring immediate write-off of all R&D had any effect on the level of R&D expenditures. Although the results of the studies vary, it would appear that there is significant evidence of firms, whose policy before the introduction of the standard included carrying forward some R&D expenditures, reducing their expenditure on R&D following the standard (Horowitz and Kolodny, 1980, 1981; Dukes *et al.*, 1980; Elliot *et al.*, 1984).

Another controversial US accounting standard which has been investigated is FAS8 on foreign currency translation. In this case the main issues were whether the standard's requirement, that all gains and losses arising on translation of overseas investments be recognized in current income, would cause increased fluctuations in the reported earnings of multinational companies and whether managers in such firms would attempt to mitigate these fluctuations by changing their foreign exchange risk management practices. The research studies on this issue have reported that managerial decisions on overseas investment policies, financing and the hedging of foreign exchange risks were affected by the standard (Evans *et al.*, 1978; Shank *et al.*, 1980) and that this behaviour could be linked to information inductance (Wilner, 1982).

Criticism of the standard led to its withdrawal in 1980. It was replaced with new provisions allowing the carrying forward of translation gains and losses, thereby removing the destabilizing effect on corporate income.

The subject of accounting for leases is one that was introduced in the earlier discussion of the effects on stock market prices of an accounting standard requiring capitalization of finance leases. The impact of accounting regulations on this subject on management decisions has also been investigated in both the US and UK. Again the evidence supports the view that management decisions may be altered in response to accounting standards. In the US, research managers were found to have made efforts to restructure finance leases so as to avoid the terms of the standard (Abdel-Khalik *et al.*, 1981). Moreover, the management of substantial proportions of surveyed firms indicated that the standard had caused financing and asset acquisition decisions to be changed. Similar research undertaken in the UK has come to similar conclusions (Taylor and Turley, 1985). Managers in a substantial minority of a sample of companies expected that the introduction of SSAP21 would influence company financing and investment decisions.

Managers' Choices of Accounting Policies

The voluntary adoption of accounting policies by management may be associated with economic consequences. As we saw in chapter 6 a model has been developed which attempts to explain accounting policy choice in terms of factors described as 'contracting costs', 'monitoring costs' and 'political visibility'. The model suggests that firms facing relatively high contracting and monitoring costs are likely to choose accounting policies which tend to report increased accounting income, and firms with relatively high political visibility are more likely to choose income reducing policies. These suggestions have been tested using proxy variables of monitoring and contracting costs and political visibility. Examples of proxy variables are given in table 7.1.

Table 7.1 Proxy variables for contracting and monitoring costs and political visibility

	Proxy variables
Contracting and monitoring costs	Gearing
	Existence of a management compensation scheme tied to accounting earnings
	Interest coverage ratio
	Deviation from dividend constraints
	Owner v management control of the firm
Political visibility	Firm size
	Industry concentration ratio
	Capital intensity
	Systematic risk

A number of examples of accounting policy choices have been investigated on this basis, for example depreciation methods (Holthausen, 1981; Dhaliwal *et al.*, 1982), the treatment of oil and gas exploration costs (Dhaliwal, 1980), the capitalization of interest (Bowen *et al.*, 1981) and overall accounting policy strategy (Zmijewski and Hagerman, 1981).

It is noteworthy that, in general, US empirical findings have proved to be consistent with the predictions of the economic consequences model for two proxy variables: size (a proxy for political visibility) and gearing (a proxy for monitoring and contracting costs). However, the one piece of equivalent (although preliminary) research available for the UK (Ashton, 1985) found no evidence that economic factors determined the choice between methods of accounting for leases in a sample of firms.

Evidence of Management Lobbying

Management preferences for accounting policies will extend to the proposals of accounting regulators for accounting standards. If mandatory accounting regulations give rise to economic consequences, management may seek to influence regulators in their choice of regulations. Several studies have documented the influence brought to bear on regulators by various interest groups including, notably, management. The issue of lobbying and influence was discussed at length in chapter 5 and so this research will not be commented upon further here.

STUDIES OF DECISIONS BY OTHER GROUPS

Although we noted in the previous chapter the potential for the decisions of groups other than investors and managers to be affected by accounting changes, very little research has been undertaken into the existence of such effects. One area of decision making which has received attention in that of risk assessment and credit granting.

A certain amount of evidence has now been collected on the effects of regulations on lease capitalization on credit decisions. Since lease capitalization causes an apparent deterioration in debt-equity ratios, it may have an impact on the assessment of credit risk. At an aggregate level Abdel-Khalik *et al.* (1981) found that the FASB requirement for lease capitalization had no systematic effect on bond risk premiums. In tests of individual decision makers, financial analysts appeared to react to different ways of reporting leases, although loan officers did not appear to respond and did not perceive lease capitalization as affecting levels of gearing (Wilkins and Zimmer, 1983a, 1983b). In the UK, research on the subject of current cost accounting included consideration of users such as government departments, stockbrokers and analysts. These studies provided some evidence of use of current cost information but not of any actual impact on economic decisions and their effects.

There is clearly a need for an increased amount of research into the relationship between information produced as a result of accounting regulations and decisions of a wider variety of groups than is reflected in the traditional emphasis on investors.

SUMMARY

In this chapter we have examined a large amount of empirical research directed at discovering evidence of the economic effects of external financial reports and accounting standards. In the context of accounting regulation this research is potentially very important. If it can be demonstrated that changes in financial reporting practices give rise to economic effects, the case for regulation is strengthened. Also, if evidence can be found that accounting standards affect the behaviour of users of financial reports, the importance of standard setting activities is emphasized. One may extend this argument by suggesting that demonstrating of economic effects should persuade accounting standard setters to take into account economic effects, both actual and potential, in their deliberations and decisions. This does not lessen the difficulties of doing so, but provides a possible motivation for confronting them.

There is undoubtedly ample evidence that information in financial reports is important for stock market decisions. Less clear is the evidence of the stock market effects of variations in firms' accounting policies. Generally, however, the stock market has been found to be able to distinguish cosmetic accounting changes from those accounting changes which give rise to cash flow effects. Equally, studies of the effects of accounting regulations on the stock market have found evidence of such effects, although the available studies are by no means unanimous.

Outside the stock market, aspects of managers decision making in response to accounting changes, including those due to regulations, have been widely investigated. Considerable evidence, almost exclusively from the USA, is available to show the existence of management decisions changing due to accounting changes. Managers may change their decisions because they do not perceive that the stock market behaves as suggested by the efficient markets hypothesis, or because of the relationship between the information in accounting reports and their own rewards.

REFERENCES

Abdel-Khalik, R. and McKeown, J.C. 1978: 'Disclosure of estimates of holding gains and losses to the assessment of systematic risk', in *Studies in Accounting for Changes in General and Specific Prices: Empirical and Public Policy Issues,* Supplement to *Journal of Accounting Research,* Vol. 16.
Abdel-Khalik, R. 1981: *The Economic Effects on Lessees of FASB Statement No. 13, Accounting For Leases,* FASB, Stamford.
Aharony, J. and Swary, I. 1980: 'Quarterly dividend and earnings announcements and stockholders' returns: an empirical analysis'. *Journal of Finance,* Vol. 35.
Ajinkya, B.B. 1980: 'An empirical evaluation of line-of-business reporting'. *Journal of Accounting Research,* Vol. 18.
Appleyard, A.R. and Strong, N.C. 1984: The impact of SSAP16 current cost accounting disclosure on security prices'. In B.V. Carsberg and M.J. Page (eds), *Current Cost Accounting – the Benefits and the Costs,* Prentice Hall International, in association with the Institute of Chartered Accountants in England and Wales, Hemel Hempstead.
Ashton, R.K. 1985: 'Accounting for finance leases: a field test'. *Accounting and Business Research,* Vol. 15.
Ball, R.J. and Brown, P. 1968: 'An empirical evaluation of accounting income numbers'. *Journal of Accounting Research,* Vol. 6.
Ball, R. J. and Foster, G. 1982: 'Corporate financial statements: a review of empirical research methodologies'. *Journal of Accounting Research,* Supplement. Vol. 20.
Beaver, W.H. 1973: 'What should be the FASB's objectives?'. *Journal of Accountancy,* August.
Beaver, W.H. 1981: 'Market Efficiency'. *The Accounting Review,* Vol. 56.
Beaver, W.H. and Dukes, R.E. 1973: 'Delta-depreciation methods: some empirical results'. *The Accounting Review,* Vol. 48.
Beaver, W.H. and Landsman, W. 1982: 'The incremental information content of FAS33 disclosures'. Working paper, Stanford University.
Benston, G.J. 1973: 'Required disclosure and the stock market: an evaluation of the Securities and Exchange Act of 1934'. *American Economic Review,* Vol. 63.
Board, J.G.L. and Walker, M. 1984: 'The information content of SSAP16 earnings changes'. In B. V. Carsberg and M. J. Page (eds), *Current Cost Accounting – the Benefits and the Costs,* Prentice Hall International, in association with the Institute of Chartered Accountants in England and Wales, Hemel Hempstead.
Bowen, R.M., Noreen, E.W. and Lacey, J.M. 1981: 'Determinants of the corporate decision to capitalise interest'. *Journal of Accounting and Economics,* Vol. 3.
Brown, P. 1970: 'The impact of the annual net profit on the stock market'. *The Australian Accountant,* July.

128   *Evidence on Economic Consequences*

Brown, P. and Kennelly, J.W. 1972: 'The information content of quarterly earnings: an extension and some further evidence'. *Journal of Business*, Vol. 45.

Collins, D.W. and Simmonds, R. 1979: 'SEC line-of-business disclosures and market risk adjustments'. *Journal of Accounting Research*, Vol. 17.

Deakin, E.B. 1976: 'Accounting reports, policy interventions, and the behaviour of security returns'. *The Accounting Review*, Vol. 51.

Deakin, E.B., Norwood, G.R. and Smith, C.H. 1974: 'The effect of published earnings information on Tokyo stock exchange trading'. *International Journal of Accounting*, Vol. 10.

Dhaliwal, D. 1980: 'The effect of the firm's capital structure on the choice of accounting methods'. *The Accounting Review*, Vol. 55.

Dhaliwal, D.S., Salmon, G. and Smith, E. 1982: 'The effects of owner versus management control on the choice of accounting methods. *Journal of Accounting and Economics*, Vol. 4.

Dukes, R.E., Dyckman, T.R. and Elliott, J.A. 1980: 'Accounting for research and development costs: the impact on research and development expenditure'. *Journal of Accounting Research*, Vol. 18.

Elliott, J., Richardson, G., Dyckman, T. and Dukes, R. 1984: 'The impact of SFAS52 on firm expenditures on research and development: replications and extensions'. *Journal of Accounting Research*, Vol. 22.

Evans, T.G., Folks, W.R. and Jilling, M. 1978: *The Impact of Financial Accounting Standard No. 8 on the Foreign Exchange Risk Management Practice of American Multinationals: An Economic Impact Study*, Financial Accounting Standards Board.

Firth, M. 1976: 'The impact of earnings announcements on the share price behaviour of similar type firms'. *Economic Journal*, Vol. 86.

Foster, G. 1980: 'Accounting policy decisions and capital market research'. *Journal of Accounting and Economics*, Vol. 2.

Fried, D. and Schiff, A. 1981: 'CPA switches and associated market reactions'. *The Accounting Review*, Vol. 56.

Gonedes, N.J. 1975: 'Risk, information and the effects of special accounting items on capital market equilibrium'. *Journal of Accounting Research*, Vol. 13.

Griffin, P.A. 1976: 'Competitive information in the stock market: an empirical study of earnings, dividends and analysts forecasts'. *Journal of Finance*,Vol. 31.

Holthausen, R.W. 1981: 'Theory and evidence of the effect on bond covenants and management compensation contracts on the choice of accounting techniques: the case of the depreciation switchback'. *Journal of Accounting and Economics*, Vol. 3.

Horowitz, B. and Kolodny, R. 1980: 'The economic effects of involuntary uniformity in the financial reporting of R and D expenditure'. *Journal of Accounting Research*, Vol. 18.

Horowitz, B. and Kolodny, R. 1981: 'The FASB, the SEC and R and D'. *Bell Journal of Economics*, Vol. 12.

Kaplan, R.S. and Roll, R. 1972: 'Investor evaluation of accounting information: some empirical evidence'. *Journal of Business*, Vol. 45.

Lev, B. and Ohlson, J. A. 1982: 'Market-based empirical research in accounting: a review, interpretation, and extension'. *Journal of Accounting Research*, Supplement. Vol. 20.

Noreen, E. and Sepe, J. 1981: 'Market reactions to accounting policy deliberations: the inflation accounting case'. *The Accounting Review*, Vol. 56.

Patell, J.M. 1976: 'Corporate forecasts of earnings per share and stock price behaviour: empirical tests'. *Journal of Accounting Research*, Vol. 14.

Patell, J.M. and Wolfson, M.A. 1981: 'The ex ante and ex post price effects of quarterly earnings announcements reflected in option and stock prices'. *Journal of Accounting Research*, Vol. 19.

Shank, J.K., Dillard, J.F. and Murdock, R.J. 1980: 'FASB No. 8 and the decision makers'. *Financial Executive*, February.

Skerratt, L.C.L. and Thompson, A.P. 1984: 'Market reaction to SSAP16 current cost accounting disclosures'. In B.V. Carsberg and M.J. Page (eds), *Current Cost Accounting – the Benefits and the Costs*, Prentice Hall International, in association with the Institute of Chartered Accountants in England and Wales, Hemel Hempstead.

Sunder, S. 1973: 'Relationship between accounting changes and stock prices: problems of measurement and some empirical evidence'. *Empirical Research in Accounting: Selected Studies, Supplement to Journal of Accounting Research*.

Taylor, P.J. and Turley, W.S. 1985: 'The views of management on accounting for leases'. *Accounting and Business Research*, Vol. 15.

Vigeland, R.L. 1981: 'The market reaction to statement of financial accounting standards no. 2'. *The Accounting Review*, Vol. 56.

Wilkins, T.A. and Zimmer, I.R. 1983a: 'The effects of alternative methods of accounting for leases – an experimental study'. *Abacus*, Vol. 19.

Wilkins, T.A. and Zimmer, I.R. 1983b: 'The effect of leasing and different methods of accounting for leases on credit evaluations'. *The Accounting Review*, Vol. 58.

Wilner, N.A. 1982: 'SFAS8 and information inductance – an experiment'. *Accounting, Organisations and Society*, Vol. 7.

Zmijewski, M.E. and Hagerman, R.L. 1981: 'An income strategy approach to the positive theory of accounting standard setting choice'. *Journal of Accounting and Economics*, Vol. 3.

8

Monitoring Disclosure

Previous chapters have described the structure and nature of regulations produced by different sources of authority in financial reporting and the relationship between the regulatory bodies. A key variable which has been emphasized as important in understanding the need for and success of both professional and legal regulation is that of compliance with the reporting requirements that are imposed. The effectiveness of regulations depends in part on having mechanisms which monitor compliance and take action in the event of non-compliance. Compliance may be encouraged both through positive monitoring of reporting and through the threat of penalties for non-compliance.

The main monitoring mechanism in the case of limited companies is the statutory audit. In this chapter the auditor's responsibilities with respect to both legal disclosure requirements and accounting standards are outlined. The role of investigations by the Department of Trade and Industry is also described. In cases of apparent failure or maladministration in business, the Department has powers to appoint inspectors to investigate a company's affairs. The issues which can give rise to an investigation cover all aspects of business practice, but a number of actual investigations have resulted in criticisms by the inspectors of aspects of accounting disclosure.

Ultimately the main sanction that can be applied to directors for failure to satisfy reporting requirements is legal action, either by those who rely upon the disclosure or by the Department of Trade and Industry which is responsible for the overall regulation of companies. While some cases have involved accounting considerations, it is extremely rare for legal action to be taken as a result of inadequate financial disclosure in its own right. Rather, litigation is normally precipitated by some other aspect of the company's activity, for example financial failure, and accounting disclosures issues may then arise. As a result there is little case law establishing the interpretation of, for example, the concept of a 'true and fair view'. In one instance the Department of Trade and Industry did prosecute the finance director of Argyll Foods Ltd on the basis that the company's 1979 accounts did not comply with the statutory requirement to give a true and fair view (Bird, 1982). Even in this case, however, it has been argued that the Department was forced to prosecute mainly because of the publicity which accompanied the unusual accounting treatment in Argyll's accounts. The Department's reluctance in the matter was evidenced by the fact that the case was heard in Penarth Magistrates Court and so is not a reported case which can be quoted as precedent. When the finance director was found guilty, the Department had established that prosecution should be regarded as a possibility by those preparing accounts, and the summonses against the other Argyll directors were dropped. It is possible that the fact that a successful prosecution had been brought could in itself encourage compliance with disclosure requirements.

THE AUDITOR'S LEGAL RESPONSIBILITIES

The auditor's responsibility in law is to report an opinion on the quality of the accounts, that is the balance sheet, profit and loss account and the notes thereto. 'Quality' in this connection is measured by two criteria: compliance with the requirements of the Companies Act, 1985, and the overriding requirement to show a 'true and fair view'. The detailed rules governing the auditor's responsibilities are contained in section 236 of the 1985 Act. Specifically, the auditor must report an opinion as to whether or not the accounts:

(1) present a true and fair view of the company's results and financial position; and
(2) comply with the requirements of the Companies Act.

In addition the auditor has a duty to report if:

(3) proper books of account have not been kept;
(4) the accounts are not in agreement with the books; or
(5) there are inconsistencies between the accounts and the contents of the directors' report.

Items (1) and (2) will always be reported upon by the auditor, while items (3) to (5) will only be commented upon by exception, i.e. where the auditor thinks something is wrong. The preparation of the accounts and their presentation to shareholders are the responsibility of the directors of the company. The auditor's report is a commentary on the record thus presented.

The above responsibilities indicate that the audit has a primary role in monitoring compliance with the legal disclosure requirements. This role is expressed with respect to the detailed statutory rules but also with concern for the overall picture that is presented by the accounts. The 1985 Act includes the statement that the truth and fairness of the accounts overrides compliance with the detailed rules, so that the latter could be departed from if it is necessary to ensure the former (S.228). The concept of true and fair, and the need for it to be regarded as the overriding criterion, is inherent to the UK system of regulation which does not rely on a detailed codification of how accounts should be constructed, but rather recognizes and relies upon professional judgement in many areas. Judgement of true and fair has been regarded as the domain of the professional accountant, and it is this view which gives rise to the role and status of accounting standards.

In modern times the role of the audit has been interpreted primarily in terms of the annual accounts of a company. The auditor is expected to comment on the content of the accounts, but his report does not state or imply anything about the adequacy of any areas of organizational performance, for example the financial health of the company, its suitability as an investment or the efficiency of management. At present there are certain pressures for an increase in the scope of the investigation and report that auditors should provide. For example recent financial failures have given rise to calls for the auditor to have increased responsibilities with respect to the detection of fraud. Also, there are current proposals that the auditors of banks and building societies should report on the control system operated by the organization, and it is possible that in the longer term these proposals could be extended from the financial services sector to a wider group of organizations. However, these expansions in scope do not alter the fact that the audit is the primary mechanism for monitoring the financial statement produced by companies complying with the relevant legislative requirements relating to those statements.

The formal position in law is that the shareholders of a company appoint and determine the remuneration of the auditor (Ss.384 and 385, Companies Act, 1985). However, while the auditor's position is *de jure* under the control of the shareholders, the real power over appointment, dismissal and remuneration is *de facto* held by the company directors. This situation may undermine the ability of the auditor to form an independent view of the company's accounts in that the auditor may be reluctant to disagree with the directors if it could lead to the loss of the audit. While the power of the directors may weaken the effectiveness of the audit as a means of monitoring compliance, this is more likely with respect to areas of judgement, some of which are covered by accounting standards, than to the factual disclosures required by law.

While the Companies Act states the auditors responsibilities as being to the members of the company, i.e. the shareholders, it should also be noted that the courts have held the auditor to have a duty to other parties as well. A number of cases (recent examples *Jeb Fasteners Ltd* v. *Marks, Bloom & Co.* [1981] 3 All E.R. 289, and *Twomax Ltd* v. *McFarlane and Robinson* [1983] S.L.T. 98) have established that the auditor has a duty of care to third parties, even where at the time of his audit he has no knowledge of their specific existence and interest in the accounts (Kent, 1985). One recent case in Australia which attracted considerable publicity was that of *Cambridge Credit and Another* v. *Hutchinson and Others* (1985) (sometimes referred to as 'Fell and Starkey') where a duty of care to a third party was held and resulted in damages of A$145 million against the partners in an audit firm (still under appeal). The courts seem to regard the audit as a significant control over the public disclosure of accounting information, not just disclosure to shareholders.

Only members of certain approved bodies can be appointed as auditors of limited companies. These are the Institutes of Chartered Accountants in England and Wales, Scotland and Ireland and the Chartered Association of Certified Accountants (S.389, Companies Act, 1985). This restriction on who can audit companies provides another element in the structure of professional and legal regulation. The law relies upon the standards of the profession to enforce the law, or at least to act as agents monitoring compliance with the law. The profession in turn has an incentive to maintain its regulatory standards (including ethical standards) at a high level, in order to ensure that its privileged position will not be altered.

THE AUDITOR AND ACCOUNTING STANDARDS

The auditor's responsibilities with respect to accounting standards arise in two ways:

(1) As noted above, all company auditors are members of four of the professional bodies which issue the accounting standards developed by the ASC. Consequently, there is a direct responsibility on auditors to follow and as far as possible enforce standards, as statements of what is regarded as acceptable practice by the bodies to which they belong.

(2) Accounting standards help define what constitutes a true and fair view by describing accounting methods to be applied to all financial

accounts intended to meet that criterion. Hence, there is an indirect responsibility on auditors to follow accounting standards as part of their legal obligation to report on whether accounts do present a true and fair view. (The relationship between accounting standards and true and fair is discussed in chapter 4.)

The expectations regarding accounting standards which the profession places on its members when acting as auditors are stated in the Explanatory Foreword to SSAPs:

> the onus will be on them not only to ensure disclosure of significant departures but also, to the extent that their concurrence is stated or implied, to justify them. (ASC, 1971, para. 5)

More explicitly, if a company proposes not to comply with an accounting standard the auditor must decide whether he agrees that the non-compliance is justified and approves of the alternative treatment adopted by the company, and also whether the effect on the accounts is material. If he concurs with the company's approach then he should ensure that the non-compliance is disclosed in the accounts, and if adequate disclosure is made then he need not make any reference to the non-compliance in his audit report unless he wishes to draw attention to the item. If he disagrees with the departure from standard practice and its effect is material to the accounts, then the auditor is expected to state his disagreement in his audit report, whether or not the matter is disclosed in the accounts.

Members of the professional bodies who act as directors, and who therefore have responsibility for the preparation of accounts, are also expected to ensure that accounting standards are observed or that departures are disclosed and justified.

The Explanatory Foreword goes on to state that the professional bodies

> may inquire into apparent failure . . . to observe accounting standards or disclose departures therefrom. (ASC, 1971, para. 6)

Thus, the obligation to promote observance of standards is accompanied by the threat of sanction in cases of non-compliance. In practice, however, there is little evidence of this threat being pursued. The profession has not engaged in any positive review of accounts and audit reports for evidence of failures, and investigation will only take place as the result of a complaint being lodged against an auditor. It is probable that cases where the auditor fails to draw attention to non-compliance with a standard are rare. Rather, there may be more grounds for concern that companies do not regard the fact that the auditor will report non-compliance as a significant influence on the decision whether or not to depart from standard accounting practice.

The ASC has traditionally relied upon the professional accounting firms for its power base, as, through the statutory audit requirement, accountants in practice are in a position to promote observance of accounting standards by all companies. Although members of the ASC are drawn from a variety of backgrounds (see table 4.1) a larger number come from professional firms than from any other background, and all the ASC chairmen have been accountants in practice. Auditors have perhaps most to gain from the existence of standards in that, in cases of disagreement with management, they can be referred to as a source of quasi-legal authority. As, to some extent, auditors' livelihood are linked to the strength and status of the profession, they have an interest in ensuring that professional recommendations such as accounting standards are regarded as authoritative and influential in financial reporting, and so have an incentive to promote observance of standards. At the same time, as discussed in chapter 5, the economic relationship between the auditor and management may mean that auditors would prefer to deal with the problem of compliance by pressing for standards which are likely to be acceptable to management.

QUALIFIED AUDIT REPORTS

The principal action an auditor can take if he disagrees with the content of a company's accounts, either because of failure to satisfy the Companies Act requirements or due to non-compliance with an accounting standard, is to 'qualify' the audit report. In cases of extreme disagreement the auditor might resign but, although there might be some temporary adverse publicity, it is likely that the company will be able to find another audit firm.

A qualified report is the auditor's means of drawing the attention of the reader of the accounts to some information which he feels is necessary to an appreciation of the financial position or results of the company, and may be a signal that all is not as it should be regarding the content of the accounts. As a sanction for inadequate financial reporting, however, qualified audit reports suffer from a number of limitations.

Qualifications are sometimes hard to identify in an audit report and may be misinterpreted by non-expert readers. Auditing standards suggest two factors which influence the kind of qualification the auditor should give: the nature of the problem causing qualification and the effect that the problem has on the picture presented in the accounts (Hatherly and Skuse, 1985). These two variables give a matrix of four possible qualified reports, as set out in table 8.1.

Table 8.1   Audit report qualifications

Nature of circumstances	Material but not fundamental	Fundamental
Uncertainty	'Subject to' the problem the accounts give a true and fair view	Disclaimer – the auditor is unable to form an opinion on the accounts
Disagreement	'Except for' the problem the accounts give a true and fair view	Adverse – the accounts are not true and fair

The vast majority of audit qualifications fall into the 'subject to' and 'except for' categories. Non-compliance with a disclosure requirement or an accounting standard would probably lead to an 'except for' report if the auditor disagreed with the company. This 'coded' message in the report may be easily misinterpreted by readers, particularly as the report will go on to say that the accounts show a true and fair view, and so there may be no adverse reaction to the accounts by users. In 1979, the Department of Trade inspectors criticized the auditors of Peachey Properties for reporting in 'hieratic' language, that is 'language which is neither comprehensible as ordinary speech nor adequately defined to a specialist'. While the situation has improved with the introduction of Auditing Standards and Guidelines, audit reports still communicate little information which users of accounts are likely to take note of.

Further evidence that the threat of a qualified audit report does not constitute an effective incentive to comply with professional regulations is provided by the fact that many company managements are prepared to accept qualification for non-compliance with accounting standards. This willingness to endure qualification is probably greater now than when accounting standards were first introduced, as the compliance climate has become more hostile. In particular, SSAP16 on current cost accounting ended up with only some 25 per cent of listed companies complying with its requirements. At one time qualified audit reports were rare and attracted considerable attention and possibly adverse publicity to the company concerned. Their incidence has now increased to the point where a qualified audit report is no longer regarded as significant. It is possible that qualification will only become an effective sanction again if it is accompanied by the likelihood, or even certainty, of some follow-up action, such as review by the Department of Trade or the Stock Exchange.

Many of the circumstances which lead an auditor to consider qualifying his audit report are to do with matters of subjective judgement regarding the accounts, i.e. areas where the law and accounting standards do not lay down definitive rules. It is in these situations that the auditor's professional judgement has the greatest role to play in controlling the quality of financial reporting by companies. Often the outcome will depend on the auditor's ability to resist the pressure to accept the directors' arguments and form an independent opinion. The fact that the directors control the auditors' appointment and remuneration, and the highly competitive market for audit business, will put pressure on the auditor to agree with the directors. However, auditors will be unwilling to set aside their professional judgement and accept the directors' view if there is a possibility that this action could subsequently be uncovered and result in litigation against the audit firm or publicity which would affect its reputation.

DEPARTMENT OF TRADE AND INDUSTRY INVESTIGATIONS

Department of Trade and Industry Investigations supplement the disclosure requirements contained in the Companies Act (Gower *et al.*, 1979). While the statutory framework of disclosure deals with the general provision of information about companies, the Department of Trade and Industry also has the power to appoint inspectors to investigate and report on the affairs of individual companies in certain circumstances. The Department can commence an investigation on its own initiative or following application by the company or its members (see Russell, 1985, pp. 56–60, for a summary of the rules governing appointment of inspectors). The majority of investigations arise in situations where there has been an actual or alleged irregularity in a company's affairs, and, as a result, they are often associated with headline grabbing events and individuals, for example 'Tiny' Rowland, Robert Maxwell and John Stonehouse. Russell (1985) has estimated that an average of 510 cases for possible investigation are considered by the Department each year, but that only about 4 per cent of these go to full investigation. In the years 1971 to 1981 a total of 55 reports of investigations were published. A number of these reports included significant comments relating to financial reporting and disclosure and had implications for accounting regulations.

Normally, the Department of Trade will appoint two inspectors. Sometimes the Department's own staff are used, but more usually one inspector will be a senior partner in a firm of accountants and the other a Queen's

Counsel. The inspectors' task is essentially to establish the facts surrounding an alleged irregularity and to report those facts to the Department. They have the power to require officers of the company to produce documents, and to examine the officers under oath. However, for any legal penalty to follow from the inspectors' findings, legal proceedings must be initiated on the basis of the report, either by the Department or by members of the company.

In the case of public companies the Department's policy is to publish the inspectors' report and in this situation the powers of the inspectors are somewhat more subtle. Because of the publicity which often surrounds the events being investigated, and therefore the inspectors' report, the inspectors have the ability to make influential statements about points of principle or matters of general practice which have been significant in the case of the investigated company.

Thus, while the possibility of inspection may act as a deterrent to malpractice by individuals, the inspection system also has a more general role in the development of regulation of companies, by providing the opportunity for inspectors to give an up-to-date assessment of particular practices or aspects of corporate behaviour. This influence is independent of the question of whether a report includes findings which lead to legal proceedings.

Inspectors' reports have often been critical of accountants and auditors and some of these criticisms have been important influences in the development of professional practice. A number of areas of reporting have been drawn attention to, notably lack of disclosure of information, issues of accounting policy and the judgement and action of auditors. In the case of Pergamon Press (1973) the inspectors criticized the lack of disclosure in Pergamon's accounts regarding interests in and transactions with related companies and concluded that as a result the accounts were misleading. Similarly, in London Capital Group (1977) information concerning advances to directors and associated companies was not disclosed and, in the inspectors' view, the accounts did not show a true and fair view. The inspectors of Court Line (1978) held that the group's 1973 accounts did not show a true and fair view, due to the accounting policies adopted in respect of a number of items in the accounts. Accounting policy was also a major consideration in Rolls Royce (1973) where a change of policy in respect of research and development expenditure had a significant effect on reported results, changing losses into profits. In a number of cases the inspectors have been critical of auditors, for example Pergamon Press (1973), London and Counties Securities (1976) and Court Line (1978). More often than not these criticisms have concerned the auditor's judgement in a situation or his willingness to accept the arguments of management, rather than failure to discover relevant facts.

The inspectors' criticisms have given a continuing stimulus to the importance of accounting standards and it could also be claimed that the succession of critical reports in the mid to late 1970s provided the impetus for the adoption of an Auditing Standards programme and for the setting up of the Joint Disciplinary Scheme by some of the accountancy bodies. However, there is little evidence of inspectors' reports leading to legal action against directors or auditors for failures in respect of financial reporting.

SUMMARY

The effectiveness of regulation depends partly on the degree to which reporting requirements are complied with. To some extent, compliance with regulations will be demanded by those who use information, in order to allow comparison and analysis of the results of different companies. Voluntary compliance, however, cannot be relied upon, and there is a need for mechanisms to monitor the ways in which companies comply with the legal and professional requirements for accounting disclosure.

The main monitoring mechansim for limited liability companies is the statutory audit. Auditors have duties under law to report on company financial accounts in terms of compliance with the requirements of the Companies Act, 1985, and the provision of a true and fair view of the company's affairs and results. As members of professional bodies, auditors have a responsibility to promote observance of accounting standards and comment on non-compliance. Standards are also important to the auditor because of their relationship to the concept of a true and fair view. The auditor has an important role in influencing the quality of disclosure in those areas of reporting not covered by the law or standards.

The principal sanction that an auditor can exercise if he disagrees with the content of the accounts is to qualify his audit report. While companies will, in general, be unwilling to break legal requirements, the threat of a qualified audit report is unlikely to be a major deterrent to directors in those areas covered by accounting standards or unregulated areas of judgement. This is partly because audit qualifications may be misunderstood by readers of accounts and partly because their increasing incidence means they are no longer regarded as unusual events. Qualified reports require some follow-up action to be an effective sanction.

Legal action to follow-up deficiencies in financial reporting is rare. The Department of Trade and Industry has powers to appoint inspectors to investigate companys' affairs, and these investigations have often included consideration of aspects of financial reporting. Although the

140   *Monitoring Disclosure*

inspectors' reports have sometimes been critical of accounting disclosure and auditors' judgement, there is little evidence of a willingness on the part of the Department to pursue legal action as a result. However, statements made by inspectors in the context of the investigation of a specific company often have relevance to more general issues and, because of the publicity these statements attract, can be influential in the development of accounting regulation.

REFERENCES

Accounting Standards Committee 1971: *Explanatory Foreword* to Statements of Standard Accounting Practice, 1971.
Bird, P. 1982: 'After Argyll Foods what is a "true and fair view"? '. *Accountancy*, June, 80–2.
Cambridge Credit and Another v. *Hutchinson and Others* 1985: Commonwealth Law Reports.
Gower, L.C.B., Cronin, J.B., Easson, A.J. and Lord Wedderburn of Charlton 1979: *Gower's Principles of Modern Company Law*, 4th ed, Steven and Sons.
Hatherly, D.J. and Skuse, P.C.B. 1985: 'Audit reports'. In D. Kent, M. Sherer and S. Turley (eds), *Current Issues in Auditing*, Harper Row.
Jeb Fasteners Ltd v. *Marks, Bloom and Co.* 1981: *All England Law Reports*, 289.
Kent, D. 1985:'The auditor's liability to third parties'. In D. Kent, M. Sherer and S. Turley (eds), *Current Issues in Auditing*, Harper Row.
Russell, P.O. 1985: 'Department of Trade investigations'. In D. Kent, M. Sherer and S. Turley (eds), *Current Issues in Auditing*, Harper Row.
Twomax Ltd v. *McFarlane and Robinson* 1983: *Scottish Law Times*, 98.

9

International Aspects
of Regulation

An important source of influence on developments in both legal and professional regulation of financial reporting in recent years has been the existence of international pronouncements concerning financial statements. The extent to which the information contained in UK company accounts has changed as a result of international influences has sometimes been over-emphasized, but it is possible to identify instances where international factors have had a direct impact on both the framework of regulation and also the content of annual accounts.

International considerations can have an influence on national accounting rules in a number of ways:

(1) Even in the absence of any recommendations or pronouncements from international bodies, the comparison of existing domestic accounting practices with those in other countries can lead to a reassessment of current practice and subsequently to changes in practice or the development of new regulations. For example, the US experience with respect to standardization on foreign currency translation may have been influential in the drafting of a standard on the same subject in the UK.

(2) The accounting profession has become increasingly international, and has developed its own international organizations, such as the IASC. These bodies increase both the opportunity and pressure for domestic regulations to be influenced by what is happening elsewhere in the world. The growth of international accounting firms and formal links between firms in different countries has also enhanced the transfer of ideas and practices.

(3) A number of other international bodies, for example the United Nations and the World Bank, have become involved in developing pronouncements on accounting disclosure and promoting them at an international level. These recommendations are often aimed primarily at

multinational companies, but are intended to influence the accounting system in individual countries.

(4) Through membership of the EEC the system of accounting in the UK has become directly linked to the system in other member states, and certain developments and changes have been required as a result of EEC legislation, most notably so far the Companies Act, 1981.

The main purpose of this chapter is to assess the significance of two main international influences on UK accounting practice: the EEC and the IASC. After considering the pressures which have led to the increased proliferation of international recommendations on accounting, the structure and operation of the EEC and IASC regulations are outlined, and the impact of the pronouncements of each of these bodies on actual practices in the UK are assessed.

PRESSURES FOR INTERNATIONAL REGULATION

Given that we are primarily concerned with the regulation of accounting in the UK, it would be inappropriate to attempt to provide a detailed consideration of the role of international standardization of accounting practice, the obstacles to achieving such standardization or the success of individual bodies active in this area (see Samuels and Piper, 1985, chapter 4). However, some appreciation of the pressures which have led to the development of international regulations will be helpful in assessing their impact on domestic accounting rules in the UK. Many of the pressures for and objectives of regulation are basically the same at the international level as they are at the level of national legislation and standards, but international factors add an additional dimension to the control of accounting practice.

Increasing the Comparability of Financial Statements

As with national regulation, international accounting rules can be justified, first of all, by the need to compare the financial statements of different companies, and the fact that this comparison should not be prejudiced simply because the accounts are prepared in different countries. The business environment is increasingly international, and the use of accounting information across national boundaries creates a pressure for that information to be understandable to the user wherever he may be. For example, a British financial institution may consider investing funds on the New York Stock Exchange. In order to determine the advisability of such an investment, or to evaluate performance once an investment is made, the information relating to the investment should ideally be consistent and comparable with that available in respect of competing alternatives in the UK or in other countries. It is obviously desirable from the user's point of view if consistency is ensured in the production of the accounting information rather than having to make subsequent adjustments or assumptions himself. Additionally, for a UK company trying to raise funds in an overseas market, it is beneficial if the same set of accounts satisfies national requirements in both the UK and the other country concerned.

So international usage of accounting information, which is an increasing part of the modern business environment, provides a role for international regulations to try to promote comparability and consistency between accounts produced in different countries.

Multinational Companies

The trend towards international business has meant that in most countries a large proportion of economic activity is carried out by companies which have operations in other countries as well. These links may be the result of a company establishing an overseas branch or subsidiary, or taking-over an existing business in another country. They may be for the duration of a particular project or contract, or permanent in nature. They may involve activities which are closely related to each other or businesses which are extremely diversified. Many of the largest multinational companies can properly be described as 'international' in the sense that the nature and scale of their activities makes it difficult to identify the company with a single home-base country.

The existence of multinational companies presents another source of justification for international regulation of accounting. In fact, multinationals give rise to two somewhat different pressures for standardization of accounting practice.

First, it can be argued that, if similar standards of reporting and accounting conventions were required in different national environments, there would be considerable advantages to multinational companies in terms of the preparation and consolidation of financial statements, the introduction of management information systems, international performance evaluation and investment appraisal.

Second, a converse argument is that differences in reporting practices between countries give multinationals an opportunity to make transfers and adjustments in order to exploit the relative advantages of different accounting conventions when reporting the company's performance, for example to minimize the amount of taxation paid in particular countries. International standardization is therefore felt necessary in order to limit the power of multinationals to take advantage of inconsistencies in reporting requirements between countries.

Professional Accounting Firms

Professional accounting firms also stand to gain certain benefits from standardization of accounting across national boundaries. Many accounting firms are themselves multinational and have grown in this way in response to the increasing demands of international business. The provision of professional services, including the audit of multinational companies, would be made easier with international standardization, as would the training and transferability of professional staff.

Efforts to create international standards often involve considerable professional involvement, for example the IASC and the Groupe d'Etudes, which are mentioned in later sections, are bodies representing professional institutions from different countries.

Common Market Objectives

As an extension of some of the pressures discussed above, there are certain factors which are specific to the context of regulation in the EEC. Regulation of accounting is seen as one means of promoting the wider objectives of the community, namely the removal of competitive advantage, the free movement of capital and labour and the promotion of trade between EEC member states. These objectives which may be called the 'common market' objectives of the EEC, have been referred to in the development of European accounting legislation:

> This situation (of diverse accounting practice) may be prejudicial to the fusion of national markets into a common market operating as an internal market.

> Otherwise competition . . . will continue to be distorted artificially.

> . . . these differences may also be prejudicial to the rational orientation of capital investment. (Commission of the European Communities, 1971)

Thus the objectives of increasing comparability of companies and promoting the consistency of accounting regulations in different countries have received particular emphasis in the context of the EEC.

Progress in International Regulation

Despite the considerable pressures for international standardization of accounting, it is not easy to achieve, largely because of the great diversity in accounting systems used in different countries, both in reporting practices and in the conceptual foundations underlying those practices. There is a danger that international regulations can become simply codifications of differences, or indecisive compromises. As the majority of the bodies who have issued international guidelines on accounting have no power to enforce their recommendations, they are dependent mainly on voluntary compliance. Rigid definitive standards are even more difficult to implement at an international level than within an individual country.

In the last ten to fifteen years, there has been a noticeable increase in both the number and variety of bodies drafting codes or recommendations for accounting and promoting them at an international level. The following sections outline the procedures and objectives followed by two international organizations which are important from a UK perspective, the EEC and IASC, and evaluate their influence on UK practice. Mention is also made of some of the other international bodies which have issued proposals concerning accounting and external reporting.

THE EUROPEAN COMMUNITY

EEC regulations on accounting form one part of a broader programme for the harmonization of company law in member states. This programme of harmonization is intended to ensure that certain basic rights and requirements apply to all companies in the Community, and to protect the interests of shareholders, employees, creditors and other third parties. As indicated above, the underlying philosophy of the EEC is directed towards the creation of a unified business environment, and to facilitate this, attempts have been made to make all European companies subject to the same laws, requirements for disclosure of information and taxation.

In accounting, the term 'harmonization' has come to refer to the work of the EEC in trying to regulate accounting practice. Because the EEC has approached accounting in a very detailed way, and because the directives of the EEC carry legal power, the potential for effective standardization across national boundaries is greater than that associated with the pronouncements of any other international body (Nobes and Parker, 1981, chapter 12).

Harmonization is achieved through the development of EEC legislation, which is binding on the member states. Normally legislation is implemented through a directive, which, when adopted by the EEC Council of Ministers, individual countries are under obligation to introduce into national legislation.

Development of EEC Directives

The production of a directive, from initial proposal to adoption, can be a very lengthy process. The Fourth Directive was adopted in July 1978, but this was 13 years after the first study group on harmonization of accounting was appointed, and several more years elapsed before the directive was enacted in the national legislation of some countries. The Fifth Directive is still in proposal form, a revised draft having been issued in 1983, 11 years after the first draft. The length of the legislative process can be attributed to a number of factors.

First, although implementation of EEC legislation is mandatory on all members states, this does not mean that regulations can be imposed on countries easily. Rather the acceptability of the contents of a directive must be ensured before its adoption by the Council of Ministers. If a proposal is unacceptable in a particular country, it will not be adopted and the need to ensure acceptance of a directive can delay its development.

Another factor is that the implementation of EEC legislation inevitably threatens national sovereignty to some degree. Member states have an emotional as well as a practical interest in lobbying to maintain their existing procedures and regulations rather than being forced to accept those of another state.

The development of EEC legislation involves reconciling and finding a consensus between a very wide variety of interests, professional, commercial, political and governmental. In addition, a directive, once introduced, is intended to be relatively permanent, and cannot be changed easily. Consequently considerable attention is devoted to finding a solution which will be long lasting.

A further factor is the nature of the subject matter of the directives. In the area of accounting, the EEC directives have been concerned with the complete structure of financial statements, in contrast to an approach based on individual reporting issues. The attempt to introduce one directive, which would provide comprehensive regulations dealing with the format and content of accounts, valuation methods and publication of accounts, meant that the full diversity of accounting principles and practices in member states had to be reconciled before the legislation could be introduced.

The main elements in the process through which directives are produced and implemented are summarized in figure 9.1. Because the directives ultimately affect national legislation, the process of development involves legal and political considerations as well as technical accounting matters, and a wide variety of professional, commercial and governmental interests will seek to influence the content of a directive.

The first step in the process is the preparation of a proposed directive

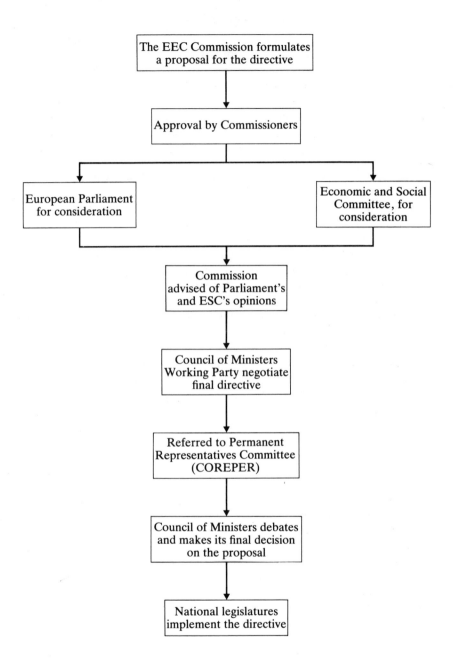

Figure 9.1 The development and implementation of an EEC directive

for adoption by the commission. The proposals will take account of existing practice in member states and, in the case of accounting matters, the work of developing an outline draft directive may be delegated to the Groupe d'Etudes, which has represented the professional accounting bodies in the EEC. Once adopted, the draft becomes public, and is submitted to the European Parliament and the Economic and Social Committee for comment. Both bodies will discuss the draft and report views to the Commission, which then reconsiders the proposals and produces a revised draft.

At this stage, representatives of the individual governments of the member states become involved. A Council of Ministers Working Party takes the revised draft and negotiates a final directive. These negotiations are held in private and the negotiating positions of the individual governments are not made public. Once the negotiations have been successfully completed, another body of government representatives takes over, the Committee of Permanent Representatives (COREPER), with the objective of resolving any remaining political and legal issues regarding implementation.

The final stage in the development of a directive is adoption by the Council of Ministers, which comprises the relevant ministers from all EEC countries. On adoption, the directive stands as an order to member states to ammend their laws to incorporate its requirements. In fact the EEC has been described as the

> only . . . international organisation presently promulgating accounting standards (which) has the ability to enforce its recommendations. (Daley and Mueller, 1982)

The stages outlined above involve two distinct phases. First there is the work of the EEC permanent civil service in creating exposing and revising a draft directive. Second the process is then transferred to the EEC representatives of the individual governments. The first phase is the development of a 'European' position, the second is the acceptance of that position by the individual countries. The national accounting bodies in the separate states have the opportunity to attempt to influence the drafting of the directive through membership of the Groupe d'Etudes, but also to present views to their own national government in order to influence the latter stages of development.

European Professional Accounting Bodies

For many years, the two main international bodies representing the accounting profession in Europe have been the Union Européen des Experts Comptables, Economiques et Financiers (UEC), which covers all

European countries, and the Groupe d'Etudes, which has been restricted to EEC countries.

The UEC is the longer-established organization, having been founded in 1951. Its activities have covered professional issues in accounting, auditing, ethics and taxation, and it has issued standards and recommendations. In recent years, however, it has been restricted mainly to auditing and ethics, i.e. the main areas of professional behaviour. This is due to the fact that the wider issues of accounting and taxation have been under consideration by the EEC and development of a European professional position has been left to the Groupe d'Etudes.

The Groupe d'Etudes was established in 1961 to assist the development of harmonization proposals, and to represent the profession, in the EEC. Much of the work of the Groupe, which is mainly carried out by working parties, has been undertaken at the request of the EEC Commission. This work, which has included development of draft proposals for directives, is not published, but the Groupe may also initiate and publish its own work and submissions on published proposals. The activites of the Groupe have had most direct relationship with the work of the Commission, but the position it has adopted will also be likely to carry weight with the government negotiators (Rutteman, 1983). It has also had a role in the implementation and interpretation of adopted directives.

Proposals now exist for uniting the UEC and the Groupe into a single body. Separate organizations were appropriate when the EEC was first created, with only six members, but as the size of the community has grown the case for a single body to represent the European accounting profession has strengthened. Also the overlap between the UEC and the Groupe has increased as the EEC has begun to develop directives on issues such as liberalization of the profession. A new organization is to be formed called the Federation Européenne des Experts Comptables (FEE) and it is planned that it will be in operation by the beginning of 1987. It will have an executive and two main committees: an EEC Committee, which will carry on the work of the Groupe, and a Coordinating Committee, which will deal with congresses, seminars, education and publications. Thus, the creation of the FEE will affect the structure of the international profession in Europe, but the role of the profession will remain largely the same.

EEC Directives and the UK

A total of ten company law directives have been developed, although not all have yet been adopted. Table 9.1 outlines brief details of the areas covered by the directives. Two have particular relevance to financial reporting and disclosure: the Fourth on company accounts, and the

Table 9.1   EEC directives on company law

Directive	History of Development*	Subject Matter
First	Draft: 1964 Adopted: 1968 (OJ 1968 L65)	Powers of a company and its directors (ultra vires rules)
Second	Drafts: 1970, 1972 Adopted: 1977 (OJ 1978 L25)	Formation, maintenance increase and reduction of capital and payment of dividends
Third	Drafts: 1970, 1973, 1975 Adopted: 1978 (OJ 1978 L295)	Mergers between public companies within one member state
Fourth	Drafts: 1971, 1974 Adopted: 1978 (OJ 1978 L222)	Detailed rules for the format, content valuation methods and publication of annual accounts
Fifth	Drafts: 1972, 1983 (OJ 1983 C240)	Structure, management and audit of public companies
Sixth	Drafts: 1972, 1975 Adopted: 1982 (OJ 1982 L378)	Supplements the Third Directive and deals with scissions
Seventh	Drafts: 1976, 1978 Adopted: 1983 (OJ 1983 L193)	Consolidated accounts for groups of companies
Eighth	Drafts: 1978, 1979 Adopted: 1984 (OJ 1984 L 126)	Minimum qualifications for auditors
Ninth	Draft: 1984 (OJ 1984 L311) Not yet adopted	Control of groups and protection of minorities, creditors and employees
Tenth	Proposal: 1985 (OJ 1985 C23) Not yet adopted	Regulation of cross border mergers Supplements the Third Directive

*References are to the Official Journal of the European Communities.
  In addition, a number of other directives have been adopted or proposed on matters such as the annual accounts of banks, the annual accounts of insurance companies, and conditions for admission of securities of stock exchange listing.

Seventh on group accounts. Some of the remaining directives are relevant to other professional aspects of accounting, notably the Fifth and Eighth which cover certain aspects of auditing.

The development of both the Fourth and Seventh Directives shared similar histories. Initial drafts of the directives threatened to impose major change in UK practice, but after negotiation the final adopted directives accommodated most of the existing UK approach and so the initial threats were not realized. The same could be said from the perspective of other countries as they too have successfully negotiated provisions which protect national practices. While directives have narrowed some of the differences between countries, they have not resulted in absolute standardization (Turley, 1982). The most significant impact in the UK has been that implementation of the directives means that some aspects of reporting, previously covered by professional regulation, are now included in the law. As a result the potential scope of future legal regulation of accounting has increased.

The Fourth Directive was enacted in UK legislation in the Companies Act, 1981. For the first time uniform formats for accounts were established and certain accounting principles were given legal status. In addition, disclosure requirements were expanded and a three-tier classification of companies was introduced as a means of allowing exemptions from disclosure according to the size of the company. Although the government took advantage of many of the options permitted to member states, in order to minimize the disturbance to existing practice, some of these changes still represent important developments in the regulatory framework.

The requirement for conformity with uniform statutory formats for accounting statements is an area where the UK has had to adapt to the European influence of countries such as France where a rigid structure for accounts has been in force for many years. However, although the UK now has a 'Euro-structure' for accounts, the UK version remains more flexible than that in many countries, for example in the amount of information which can be disclosed in the notes rather than on the face of the financial statements.

The inclusion of accounting principles in statute is also an area in which the UK framework has become more European. But the content of the specific principles outlined in the directive indicates that this is an area in which the UK has had a greater influence on the rest of the EEC. The first draft of the directive, proposed in 1971, included requirements that annual accounts should reflect the company's position 'as accurately as possible' and 'conform to the principles of regular and proper accounting'. The equivalent provisions in the final directive are that the accounts should show 'a true and fair view' and be prepared on the basis of a number of 'general principles'. The true and fair view is stated as an overriding requirement which can justify departure from other reporting obligations. In addition, the stated general principles are those of going concern, consistency, accruals and prudence, which were already established as 'fundamental concepts' by SSAP2. Thus the UK negotiators conceded increased statutory control but preserved the main content of the UK approach to principles. Acceptance of the concept of a true and fair view was extremely important to maintenance of the UK philosophy of disclosure, but has caused problems of interpretation in some other EEC countries more accustomed to rigid legal prescription of the content of the accounts.

The classification of companies may be an important area of development in UK reporting requirements. The exemptions provided to small and medium companies by the 1981 Act were not of major significance, but more concessions may be introduced in the future. For example, the possibility of reducing the disclosure requirements for small companies is currently being debated (Department of Trade, 1985a), as is the applicability of accounting standards to small companies (Carsberg *et al.*, 1985).

In the development of the Seventh Directive on group accounts, the principal issue was the criteria for consolidation of a group's financial statements. In particular, there was a clear conflict between the UK approach, based principally on legal control as measured by equity share ownership, and that found in Germany, where emphasis is placed on management influence and economic control rather than legal rights. The adopted directive provides a compromise between these positions. It requires the legal criterion of a minimum percentage of ownership but allows member states the option of applying the criterion of economic control as well. A wide range of optional conditions and exemptions are contained in the directive, to accommodate differences in approach in different member states. There is even an exemption which appears to be designed specifically to cope with the unusual structure of one major company, Royal Dutch Shell. The main change to the UK approach is that group accounts will be required where a minority shareholding is accompanied by an agreement with other shareholders which gives voting control, although it is likely that this will apply only to legally enforceable agreements.

With respect to the preparation, audit and publication of group accounts, the majority of the requirements in the directive are consistent with existing practice in the UK. The provisions governing the format and content of accounts, accounting principles and the true and fair view parallel those contained in the Fourth Directive on company accounts, and were applied to groups as well as individual companies by the 1981

Companies Act. Some individual areas of accounting practice currently governed by accounting standards may be affected by the Seventh Directive, notably goodwill, associated companies and merger accounting.

In the case of accounting for goodwill, the accounting standard (ASC, 1984) was developed in the knowledge that European legislation would require some restriction in existing practice, and the standard achieved this in advance of the directive. The main restriction is that goodwill arising on consolidation can no longer be carried forward as an asset indefinitely, it must be written off, either on acquisition of the subsidiary company, or over its useful economic life. In anticipating the directive, the accounting standard has ensured that no further change in practice is required, but implementation of the directive will mean that another area of accounting practice will be covered by legal regulations.

The same is true of accounting for associated companies, which has been the subject of a standard since 1971. The provisions of the directive are consistent with the requirements of the standard, which were revised in 1982 (ASC, 1982). The directive will not involve any changes in UK practice, but legal backing will be given to the standard.

The option for member states to permit the use of the technique of merger accounting in certain circumstances was included in the directive mainly for the benefit of the UK, and is unlikely to be utilized in other countries. Again the subject is covered by an accounting standard (ASC, 1985a). Some of the conditions of the standard are less restrictive than the directive, concerning the circumstances in which merger accounting can be used, when one company acquires another, notably with respect to the amount of the consideration that can be in a form other than equity share capital. Implementation of the directive will require some revision of the standard, a point accepted by the ASC when the standard was issued (ASC, 1985b, para. 16).

The timetable for implementation is that member states are required to change their laws to give effect to the directive by 1st January 1988, but the rules need only apply to accounts for financial years beginning on or after 1st January, 1990. The UK government has indicated that it intends to utilize the full period before applying the requirements of the directive, despite the fact that, as indicated above, implementation will not involve fundamental changes in approach or practice (Department of Trade and Industry, 1985b).

It is clear that while EEC directives have provided a significant influence on the regulation of accounting practice in the UK, that influence has been accommodated by developments within the existing pattern and approach, rather than by radical changes of direction. While EEC legislation has resulted in some changes in the structure and content of financial accounts, the main impact has been that statutory regulation now extends into many areas which were previously subject only to professional control. The approach to implementation of both the Fourth and Seventh Directives has been to leave the existing framework as far as possible unchanged.

The broad approach to implementation which has been adopted is to make the minimum changes possible and so far as is consistent with that to allow maximum flexibility.

(Department of Trade and Industry, 1985b, p.2)

THE INTERNATIONAL ACCOUNTING STANDARDS COMMITTEE

The IASC was formed in 1973 by professional bodies representing nine countries: Australia, Canada, France, Germany, Japan, Mexico, the Netherlands, the United Kingdom and Ireland (treated as one professional unit) and the United States. Since then the IASC has grown considerably, and it now has a membership of over 90 accounting bodies from about 70 different countries. Although the size has expanded, much of the power within the IASC has remained with the original members as they provide a majority of the board which establishes International Accounting Standards (IASs), but from 1987 the influence of the founder members will be reduced.

The IASC operates from a secretariat based in London and is funded partly (90 per cent) by the board member bodies and partly (10 per cent) by the International Federation of Accountants (IFAC), which collects subscriptions from all the member bodies. Membership of IFAC and IASC are the same, but they have tended to cover different functional areas of accounting. The IASC has been responsible for developing accounting standards while IFAC has confined its working to auditing, ethics and management accounting.

The nature of the IASC, as a body representing the accounting profession in different countries, has a number of implications for its operations. The IASC has, of course, no power in itself to enforce its standards. Rather, application of international standards depends on the willingness of the national professional bodies to promote them, and also on the power of those bodies in their national environments. In some countries accounting disclosure is subject to tight legislative control, almost to the exclusion of professional recommendations, and the power of the national profession will be slight. Even in the United States the IASC does not have a direct link with the main national standard setting body, as it is the American Institute of Certified Public Acountants (AICPA) and not FASB which is a member of IASC, although FASB is likely to take account of IASC developments indirectly. Paradoxically, in those countries where the profession is strong and has traditionally had a major role in regulating practice, there is a danger that the national body will not want to surrender its authority to the IASC and so will not promote the international standards as fully as possible. Alternatively, it is possible that IASs will have little impact in countries where the profession is strong, because it is these professional bodies which will have the strongest influence on the development of the standards, so that the content of a standard may be little different from existing national practice.

As a professional body, the IASC may also suffer in terms of international representativeness. Certainly when it was first formed it could not claim global representativeness, since only one member could be described as a developing country, although this problem has been alleviated as the IASC has grown.

The above points indicate some of the difficulties facing the IASC, but they should not be taken to imply that international standards do not have an important role. A considerable amount has been achieved since 1973 both in the production of standards and in the promotion of their acceptance. A total of 24 international standards have been produced, and these are listed in table 9.2. International standards are now officially recognized in Italy, and in Canada many companies listed on the Toronto stock exchange now disclose compliance with the IASC standards. The IASC has also had an influence on the development of consistent national standards on some issues, for example the UK and US standards on foreign currency translation. Overall, however, the power of the IASC remains less than that of the EEC for enforcing standardization internationally (Nobes, 1985).

The Procedures of the IASC

The IASC sets standards through a main board, which at the present time includes representatives from 13 countries, the nine founder members plus four others, as listed in table 9.3.

The manner in which a standard is set, once a topic for possible standardization has been selected, involves a number of stages which are similar to those followed by the ASC in the UK. These procedures are set out in table 9.4. Broadly, the IASC structure involves the IASC Board, steering committees on individual topics, and liaison with national standard setting bodies. There is also a consultative group which meets regularly with the IASC Board to discuss matters of principle and policy. This group includes representatives of international organizations covering trade unions, stock exchanges, and financial analysts, as well as the World Bank, the United Nations (UN) and the Organization for Economic Co-operation and Development (OECD).

Table 9.2   International Accounting Standards issued to 31 December 1985

	Issued
1 Disclosure of accounting policies	Jan. 1975
2 Valuation and presentation of inventories in the context of the historical cost system	Oct. 1975
3 Consolidated financial statements	June 1976
4 Depreciation accounting	Oct. 1976
5 Information to be disclosed in financial statements	Oct. 1976
6 Accounting responses to changing prices	June 1977
7 Statement of changes in financial position	Oct. 1977
8 Unusual and prior period items and changes in accounting policies	Feb. 1978
9 Accounting for research and development	July 1978
10 Contingencies and events occurring after balance sheet date	Oct. 1978
11 Accounting for construction contracts	Mar. 1979
12 Accounting for taxes on income	July 1979
13 Presentation of current assets and current liabilities	Nov. 1979
14 Reporting financial information by segment	Aug. 1981
15 Information reflecting the effects of changing prices	Nov. 1981
16 Accounting for property plant and equipment	Mar. 1982
17 Accounting for leases	Sep. 1982
18 Revenue recognition	Dec. 1982
19 Accounting for retirement benefits in the financial statements of employers	Jan. 1983
20 Accounting for government grants and disclosure of government assistance	Apr. 1983
21 Accounting for the effects of changes in foreign exchange rates	July 1983
22 Accounting for business combinations	Nov. 1983
23 Capitalization of borrowing costs	Mar. 1984
24 Related party disclosures	July 1984

Table 9.3   Countries represented on the
IASC board

Australia
Canada
France
Germany (Federal Republic)
Italy
Japan
Mexico
The Netherlands
Nigeria
South Africa
Taiwan
United Kingdom and Ireland
United States

Table 9.4   Stages in the development of an International
Accounting Standard

---

1 A steering committee (SC) of three or four IASC
members, is formed to consider the accounting issue
2 The SC prepares an outline for consideration by the
board, including a recommendation as to whether to
proceed to a standard
3 On the basis of the Board's comments, a first draft of the
exposure draft is prepared; this is reviewed by the
Board and released to IASC members for comment
4 The first draft is amended following comments received;
if approved by two-thirds of the Board the exposure
draft is published by IASC members
5 Comments received on the ED are considered and a
revised draft standard prepared by the SC; approval
by three quarters of the Board is required for adoption
as an international standard

Objectives of International Accounting Standards

The stated objectives of the IASC, as contained in its constitution are:

(a) to formulate and publish in the public interest accounting
standards to be observed in the presentation of financial
statements and to promote their acceptance and observance;

(b)   to work generally for the improvement and harmonization of regulations, accounting standards and procedures relating to the presentation of financial statements. (IASC, 1983a, para. 8)

From these objectives may be seen both a concern for the dual aspects of the quality of information in financial statements and the degree of comparability between statements produced in different countries, and also a suggestion that international standards are seen as a vehicle for promoting the more general objective of international harmonization of accounting.

This latter point is important in assessing the success of the IASC. Some commentators have been somewhat pessimistic regarding the contribution of the IASC, pointing to its lack of enforcement power and to the degree of divergence in the ways in which member bodies in different countries attempt to promote international standards. To do so, however, is to see the standards as important in themselves, rather than as part of a more general process of promoting international harmonization. IASC standards will be used in different ways in different countries: adopted as national standards; as a basis for developing national standards; as a basis of comparison with existing national standards; or as an input to the legislative process of regulation. Some of these uses may promote harmonization in the sense of narrowing areas of difference, without involving rigid adherence to the IASC's standards. It therefore makes sense to look at the IASC in terms of its overall contribution to harmonization rather than compliance with individual standards:

> The essence of IASC's work is the worldwide harmonization and improvement of accounting principles used in the preparation of financial statements for the benefit of the public. The achievement of this is not adversely affected by the more detailed requirements of some countries nor the need for adaptation to national circumstances. (IASC, 1983a, para. 13)

When the IASC was established the intention was to produce basic standards which would be capable of rapid acceptance and implementation internationally. The IASC has stated that it 'concentrates on essentials' and that its standards should not be 'so complex that they cannot be applied effectively on a worldwide basis' (IASC, 1983b, para. 10). In fact, some of the standards have been in areas which would not be regarded as basic or essential, for example 'Accounting for Construction Contracts' (Nobes, 1985). Also, in other more fundamental areas the need for compromise may result in a somewhat bland statement on what are complex issues, for example inflation accounting.

Acceptance of international standards depends not only on the accounting profession, but also on the attitude of multinationals and in some cases government regulatory agencies. There is also considerable variation in the degree of acceptance of different standards, as illustrated by the examples in table 9.5.

The figures in table 9.5 indicate that acceptance of international standards in some controversial areas, such as changing prices and segment reporting, is less than in others such as disclosure of accounting policies and depreciation. Also, it would appear that acceptance is largely dependent on conformity with existing national regulations. On average some 21 countries accept an international standard because it conforms with existing regulations compared with only 12 who actively adopt the standard.

International Accounting Standards and the UK

Formally, the position of the UK accountancy bodies is that they regard international harmonization as important and support the work of the IASC (IASC, 1983a, para. 13). The responsibilities of members of the IASC, as set out in the *Preface to Statements of International Standards*, include that they will use their best endeavours to ensure compliance with international standards, to persuade national authorities that international standards should be followed in all material respects, and to ensure that auditors satisfy themselves that financial statements comply with international standards (IASC, 1983b, para. 4).

In practice in the UK, as in many countries, these obligations tend to be followed to the extent that it is convenient. All international standards, when published in the UK, carry a preface indicating the relationship between the standard and UK regulations. Now SSAPs also include a section referring to any relevant international standards where appropriate. For example, SSAP23 on Accounting for Acquisitions and Mergers includes the following paragraph:

> The requirements of International Accounting Standard No. 22 'Accounting for business combinations' which relate to accounting for acquisitions and mergers accord very closely with the content of the United Kingdom and Irish Accounting Standard No. 23 'Accounting for acquisition and mergers' and accordingly compliance with SSAP 23 will ensure compliance with the requirements of IAS 22 which relate to accounting for acquistions and mergers in all material respects. (ASC, 1985a para. 40)

Table 9.5 Examples of the extent of acceptance of international accounting standards

	Adopted in substance	Conforms in substance with national standards and local requirements	Presently under consideration	No action taken or planned	No response
1 Disclosure of accounting policies	16	31	3	5	5
4 Depreciation accounting	15	31	6	2	6
14 Reporting financial information by segment	9	17	15	12	7
15 Information reflecting the effects of changing prices	6	18	12	16	8
17 Accounting for leases	12	15	19	7	7
Average IAS nos 1–23	12	21	12	7	7

Source: IFAC Newsletter, Vol. 9, No 3, September 1985.
The above figures record the responses of 60 member bodies to an IFAC survey, out of the total membership of 91.

The effect of international standards on UK practice, or on the behaviour of the ASC, is difficult to measure. Some cases can be quoted where an international standard has had an important influence on the development of a UK standard. For example, IAS3 on Consolidated Financial Statements was a major influence on the development of SSAP14, Group Accounts, and on the revision of SSAP1. There are also cases where differences exist between an IAS and the related SSAP, as in the case of IAS9 which requires disclosure of the amount of research and development expenditure, something which is absent from the equivalent UK standard SSAP13. Also some subjects have been covered by international standards but no UK standard has been introduced, nor has the international standard been adopted, for example reporting on segments of a business.

Understandably, the UK bodies are not willing to subordinate their authority for setting standards to the IASC and differences between IASs and SSAPs are likely to remain. Where differences do exist, the UK bodies are clear that 'the United Kingdom and Ireland accounting standard would prevail' (ASC, 1986, para. 14), and there is no suggestion that non-compliance with international standards should be regarded as a significant consideration by auditors when preparing their report, unlike SSAPs, where non-compliance could lead to an audit qualification. International standards do provide a significant input into the deliberations of the ASC, both in raising possible topics for inclusion in the ASC agenda, and also in providing one source of authority which may be referred to as standards are developed, but compliance with international standards will be determined on the basis of domestic considerations.

OTHER BODIES

A wide range of international organizations and committees are involved in attempting to promote regulations for accounting and disclosure (Brennan, 1981). We have described the two which have had most relevance to practice in the UK, but there are many more. Some are global organizations while others are concerned with a particular region; some are professional bodies while others are public organizations (Samuels and Piper, 1985, pp. 109–19). Two which may be mentioned here because of their status as global public bodies are the UN and the OECD.

The UN's involvement in financial reporting is carried on through its Commission on Transnational Corporations. In 1976 it established a group to look at reporting, and the following year published proposals on *International Standards of Accounting and Reporting for Transnational Corporations* (UN, 1977). In addition, the UN Commission envisaged that these proposals would be used as a basis for the development of a set of international standards. A working group of experts was established in 1979, with representatives from 34 countries, including 22 from Asia, Africa and Latin America, a balance which contrasts sharply with the representation on the IASC Board. It is intended that standards should be developed covering information to be disclosed in financial statements, accounting policies, information on companies within a group, segmental reporting and non-financial information, with the objective of improving 'the availability and comparability of information disclosed by transnational corporations' (UN, 1982, para. 38). Thus, the main emphasis of the UN activity is on increasing disclosure as a means of ensuring the accountability of large multinationals. As the main intergovernmental organization in the world, the UN proposals could provide the ultimate form of international standardization. However, the existing progress suggests that the prospects for achieving a set of standards which will be acceptable by governments and corporations worldwide would seem remote.

The OECD has also produced a code of conduct for multinational companies (OECD, 1976). These guidelines, published in 1976 and revised in 1979, cover many aspects of the activities of companies, including industrial relations, competition and taxation and include a section dealing with disclosure of information. In contrast with the UN publication, however, the code does not include a detailed listing of the items of information which should be disclosed. Rather it addresses the general issue of ensuring the sufficient disclosure of information to allow understanding of the structure, activities and policies of the organization, and suggests the various aspects of organizational activity about which disclosure should be made. While the OECD shares the UN emphasis on disclosure, it does not regard itself as a standard setting body but rather as a forum for promoting other international efforts towards harmonization. As such, its chances of success, with both governments and multinational companies may be higher than the UN (Zund, 1983).

The UN and OECD do not have direct power to enforce adherence to their recommendations. While they do have considerable influence, compliance with their codes is voluntary. Both organizations are also more notable as political than as accounting institutions and this will be reflected in the development of and reaction to their recommendations. For example there is the possible conflict between developed countries and developing nations regarding the activities of multinationals and the use of the accounting standards to control them. The problems of achieving a consensus on a global scale are enormous, and will often result in compromise regarding the content of standards. However, despite the difficulties of development and compliance it is likely that these bodies will continue to show an interest in accounting regulation in the future.

SUMMARY

The business environment is becoming increasingly international and this trend is reflected in the growth of interest in the harmonization of international standards of reporting for business enterprises. Pressure for harmonization comes from global considerations, such as the worldwide activities of multinational companies, international movement of capital, growth in the international accounting firms, and regional considerations, as in the desire to harmonize accounting within the EEC. A wide variety of bodies have become involved in issuing recommendations or rules concerning accounting. Some, for example the UN and OECD are concerned primarily with reporting by multinationals. Others, such as those of the EEC and the IASC are attempting to improve the consistency of accounting reporting more generally.

The two main sources of international influence on UK developments in financial reporting have been the European Economic Community and the International Accounting Standards Committee. The directives of the EEC ultimately carry the force of law. They have considerably reduced the diversity in reporting practices between EEC member states, but have not resulted in complete standardization. The UK has been able to maintain the fundamentals of its approach to financial reporting within the constraints of the directives, both in terms of the general approach to reporting, as expressed in the true and fair view, and also in more detailed areas of accounting practice. The main significance of the EEC directives has been that the boundaries between statutory and professional regulation of accounting have been redrawn, with new areas, such as accounting principles, coming under legislative control.

The standards of the IASC also provide an important influence on the work of the ASC. International standards do not have the same status as EEC directives, in that the IASC had no powers of enforcement. There is a large degree of overlap between the contents of international standards and UK accounting standards but, where there is conflict, it is clear that national considerations will prevail. None the less the international standards can influence the development of SSAPs, in placing items on the ASC's agenda and in providing an additional source of authority to which the ASC might refer.

REFERENCES

Accounting Standards Committee 1982: 'Accounting for associated companies', SSAP1, April. Reproduced in *Accounting Standards 1985/86*, Institute of Chartered Accountants in England and Wales, London, 1985.

Accounting Standards Committee 1984: 'Accounting for goodwill', SSAP22, December. Reproduced in *Accounting Standards 1985/86,* Institute of Chartered Accountants in England and Wales, London, 1985.

Accounting Standards Committee 1985a: 'Accounting for acquisitions and mergers', SSAP23, April. Reproduced in *Accounting Standards 1985/86,* Institute of Chartered Accountants in England and Wales, London, 1985.

Accounting Standards Committee 1985b: 'Statement by the Accounting Standards Committee on the publication of SSAP23. Accounting for acquisitions and mergers', TR 567, April. Reproduced in *Accounting Standards 1985/86,* Institute of Chartered Accountants in England and Wales, London, 1985.

Accounting Standards Committee 1986: 'Explanatory foreword to accounting standards', revised, London.

Brennan, W.J. 1981: 'Survey of national, regional and international institutions'. In F.D.S. Choi (Ed.), *Multinational Accounting: A Research Framework for the 80's,* UMI Research Press, Ann Arbour, Michigan.

Carsberg, B.V., Page, M.J., Sindall, A.J. and Waring, I.D. 1985: *Small Company Financial Reporting,* Prentice Hall International, in association with the Institute of Chartered Accountants in England and Wales, London.

Commission of the European Communities 1971: 'Proposal for a Fourth Directive on the annual accounts of limited liability companies'. *Bulletin of the European Communities,* Supplement No. 12.

Daley, L.A. and Mueller, G.G. 1982: 'Accounting in the area of world politics'. *Journal of Accountancy,* April.

Department of Trade and Industry 1985a: *Accounting and Audit Requirements for Small Firms – A Consultative Document,* London, July.

Department of Trade and Industry 1985b: *The EC Seventh Company Law Directive on Consolidated Accounts – A Consultative Document on Implementation,* London, August.

International Accounting Standards Committee 1983a: *International Accounting Standards Committee Objectives and Procedures,* London, January.

International Accounting Standards Committee 1983b: *Preface to Statements of International Accounting Standards,* London, January.

Nobes, C.W. 1985: 'Is the IASC successful?' *The Accountant,* 21 August.

Nobes, C.W. and Parker, R.H. 1983: *Comparative International Accounting,* Philip Allan, Deddington.

Organization for Economic Co-operation and Development 1976: *International Investment and Multinational Enterprises. Guidelines for Multinational Enterprises.* Paris, revised 1979.

Rutteman, P. 1983: 'What role the Groupe d'Etudes?' *Accountancy,* July, 16–17.

Samuels, J.M. and Piper, A.F. 1985: *International Accounting: A Survey,* Croom Helm, London.

Turley, W.S. 1982: 'International harmonization of accounting: the contribution of the EEC Fourth Directive on company law.' *International Journal of Accounting Education and Research,* Vol. 18/2, Fall, 13–27.

United Nations 1977: *International Standards of Accounting and Reporting for Transnational Corporations,* New York.

United Nations 1982: *International Standards of Accounting and Reporting. Report of the Ad Hoc Intergovernmental Working Group of Experts on International Standards of Accounting and Reporting,* New York.

Zund, A. 1983: 'Endeavours towards the harmonization of standards of accounting and reporting in the OECD and UNO – a critical appraisal'. In M. Bromwich and A.G. Hopwood (eds), *Accounting Standards Setting*, Pitman, London.

10

Regulation of Accounting in other Countries

International regulations are concerned primarily with the removal of differences in accounting practice between countries, and we have described the effect of such regulations in the UK. In addition to the diversity of practices employed in the preparation and presentation of accounts, there are also major differences in the underlying systems of regulation found in individual countries. Indeed, there are often strong links between differences in the regulatory systems and differences in the detailed practices. The principle subject of this book is the regulation of accounting in the context of the UK, but it is also appropriate to compare the UK approach with the manner in which accounting is controlled and regulated in other countries. It is interesting to consider not only how the system of regulation varies internationally but also why such differences exist.

The systems in six other countries are outlined in this chapter, illustrating a diversity of different approaches to accounting regulation. Three of these countries, the United States of America, Australia and Canada, share an Anglo-American background with the UK while the others, France, Germany and the Netherlands, represent major countries and traditions in continental Europe.

DIFFERENCES IN REGULATION BETWEEN COUNTRIES

Differences in the systems by which financial reporting is regulated in different countries result from several factors, for example the nature of the legal and fiscal systems, the forms of organization which businesses typically adopt and the associated pattern of corporate financing, and the importance of the accountancy profession.

In the UK and USA, for example, the legal system places considerable reliance upon case law and precedent at the expense of statute law, whereas most countries of continental Europe have a heavy preponderance of detailed statute law. These differences find echoes in company laws. In the USA there are no statutory requirements for accounting which bear comparison with the UK Companies Acts. Instead, the SEC, the Federal regulatory agency with responsibility for the securities industry, has the function of ensuring that investors are supplied with information necessary for investment decisions (Carsberg and Eastergard, 1983). To this end, the SEC is empowered to impose disclosure requirements but in practice it has devolved most of the responsibility for prescription on accounting matters to private sector regulatory bodies. In sharp contrast, countries such as France and Germany have company laws which prescribe in detail and with precision on matters of accounting disclosure and measurement. The relationship between financial reporting and tax law also varies between countries and helps to explain differences in the systems of regulation. In many Continental European countries the law requires an equivalence between the items recorded in published financial accounts and those recorded for tax purposes. Correspondingly, there is a tradition of much greater statutory regulation of the contents of financial reports than in the UK.

The dominant form of business organization in the UK and the USA is the public limited company with widespread shareholdings, whilst, for example, in West Germany and Japan banks provide a much larger proportion of corporate finance, either directly by loans or through shareholdings. The numerical supremacy of small, individual shareholders in the USA and UK is partly responsibile for the importance of mandatory public disclosures of audited financial information which meets the criteria of truth and fairness (and their US equivalents). A statutory requirement for external verification by audit is less critical where financial institutions are the providers of finance or where internal sources of finance dominate, as in France where family-based businesses are important (Nobes and Parker, 1983a).

The existence of a large and well-established accountancy profession is a notable influence on accounting regulation. Proportionately, and absolutely, the accountancy professions in the UK and USA are large relative to those in other developed industrial countries and on the whole considerably longer established. Also, they are much more numerous and influential in the management of companies in the UK than in other comparable countries (Armstrong, 1984). These factors open the way for the accountancy professions in the UK and USA to have important direct and indirect roles in accounting regulation which may be denied to the professions in other countries (Johnson, 1980).

In the USA, like the UK, there is a mixture of public and private sector regulation of financial reporting. However, in the USA, legal regulation of financial reporting derives not from companies' legislation specifically, but from legislation designed to regulate the securities industry. US companies' legislation normally does not embrace the content and form of periodic financial statements nor are audits required by legislation enacted in individual States. Neither has the US Congress interested itself in regulation of accounting disclosure except on infrequent occasions. The key legislation is contained in the Securities Act, 1933 and the Securities Exchange Act, 1934 which were enacted in response to the financial crisis of 1929 and after. The Securities and Exchange Commission (SEC) was set up to administer the 1933 Act, and the 1934 Act gave the SEC authority to prepare and administer regulations governing the financial disclosures mandated by both Acts (Benston, 1976). It has five members who are appointed by the President. Since its founding, the SEC has issued a great many documents on regulatory and accounting matters as 'Accounting Series Releases' and latterly 'Staff Accounting Bulletins'. These generally relate to security regulation rather than general accounting matters. Companies with equity or debt securities quoted in the USA must file annual reports with the SEC on Form 10–K and quarterly reports on Form 10–Q. Quarterly financial reports containing less information than annual reports are also required by the stock exchanges. These quarterly financial reports are unaudited but the SEC requires them to be included in the annual audited financial statements and considers it to be part of the information on which the company is monitored. Thus, the auditor is considered to be associated with quarterly reports. Although regulation S–X contains rules for the preparation of financial reports by regulated companies, the SEC has, since its inception, limited its role in regulation to that of supervisor and has allowed private-sector regulatory bodies to play a major role in the formulation of rules and guidelines for accounting and auditing. Three phases are recognizable in the activities of these private accounting regulators.

The AICPA's Committee on Accounting Procedure

The Committee on Accounting Procedure was established in 1936, but it was in 1939 that a reconstituted committee adopted a more vigorous regulatory role. Prior to 1939, the US professional accountancy bodies had been quite active in considering accounting principles but had failed to achieve any important degree of standardization (Zeff, 1972). Public criticism of the profession's failure in this respect mounted during the 1930s and was given added sharpness in April 1938 when the SEC issued 'Accounting Series Release No.4' (reproduced as reading (4) in Previts, 1980), which established the criterion of 'substantial authoritative support' to be applied to accounting principles in judging whether financial statements would be accepted for filing. Unless a source of authority acceptable to the SEC was created, it was clear that the responsibility for establishing such principles would devolve to the SEC (Zeff, 1972). From January 1939, the Committee on Accounting Procedure issued a series of Accounting Research Bulletins (ARBs) which sought to provide substantial authoritative support for practice. The committee addressed itself to specific accounting issues on an *ad hoc* basis and succeeded in eliminating many questionable practices. However, the ARBs tended to recommend the acceptability of alternative practices which were not dependent upon differences of fact or circumstances. The Committee's failure to deal firmly with the problem of variety in accounting and the lack of any formal version of generally accepted accounting principles led to its demise.

The Accounting Principles Board

In 1959, the AICPA replaced the Committee on Accounting Procedure with the Accounting Principles Board (APB). The creation of the APB brought with it a separate Accounting Research Division whose function was to support the APB and develop and document generally accepted accounting principles. The composition of the APB involved an important and controversial development. The AICPA specified that only the managing partners of the largest eight firms of public accountants could represent their firms on the APB. This was designed to ensure the support of the dominant firms of accountants for the APB's pronouncements. Implicit in this was that each of the eight or nine largest firms was entitled to nominate one member of the 18-man APB. Although an active research programme was begun, it petered out and the APB lapsed into a pattern of activity similar to that of the Committee on Accounting Procedure, and was criticized for the extent to which it was dominated by the accountancy profession to the exclusion of the opinions of other interested parties.

Financial Accounting Standards Board

The FASB was set up in 1973 in an attempt to make good the perceived deficiencies of the APB. It is composed of seven members who serve full-time for five years and are required to sever prior business or professional appointments. Originally four members were drawn from the profession and three from other backgrounds, but this structure has now been dropped, so that the seven members are appointed irrespective of the nature of their background. Appointment to the FASB is made by the Financial Accounting Foundation (FAF) which is board of trustees elected by various accounting and business bodies, for example the AICPA, the Financial Executives Institute and the Securities Industry Association. In addition the FAF appoints an advisory body, the Financial Accounting Standards Advisory Council (FASAC) to act as a consultative body providing contact between the FASB and the wider business community. The FASB produces and issues Statements of Financial Accounting Standards (SFAS), Statements of Concepts (general concepts used in the development of standards) and Interpretations (to extend, explain or provide clarification of SFASs). The process of developing statements has many similarities with the procedures of the ASC, including the publication of exposure drafts for public comment. The activities of the FASB are financed by voluntary contributions from public accounting firms and other organizations and individuals.

The SEC, which has the authority to regulate financial disclosure, requires financial statements to be prepared in accordance with accounting principles which have 'substantial authoritative support'. The pronouncements of the FASB have been acknowledged by the SEC in ASR No. 150 to satisfy this criterion. Thus, FASB statements have influence and force partly because the SEC, the government agency, approves of them, and it is possible that if the SEC does not agree with a standard developed by the FASB, it will require amendment. The staff of the SEC regularly monitor the activities of the FASB and on occasion have intervened in the development of accounting standards on controversial topics (e.g. the disclosure of replacement cost information and oil and gas accounting) (Carsberg and Eastergard, 1981). The overall structure of regulation in the USA, which we have briefly described above, is summarized in figure 10.1.

The system of regulation in the USA, and the procedures of the FASB, provide a number of interesting points of comparison with the UK.

(1) The role of the SEC: Although company legislation in the USA includes less detailed regulation of accounts than in the UK, the government exercises much greater control over disclosure in practice, through the agency of the SEC. This point of comparison is important when the issue of compliance with standards is considered, in that the position of the SEC gives much greater authority to SFASs than accompanies accounting standards in the UK.

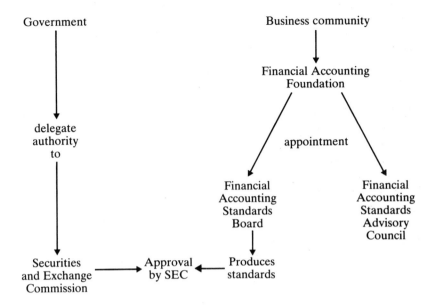

Figure 10.1   The structure of regulation of accounting in the USA

(2) Independence of the FASB: The ASC is clearly identified as a body of the UK accounting profession. In contrast the FASB has been structured to make standard setting institutionally independent from the profession. Again this point relates to compliance and enforcement, in that standards may be more acceptable or authoritative if produced by an independent body.

(3) Justification of standard practice: Accounting standards in the USA include justification of the recommended practice, with reference to the economic consequences of the policy, and any dissenting opinions on the FASB. This attempt to provide a rational justification for policy choice is a more formal part of the process than with the ASC, although there has been some development in this direction in recent SSAPs, such as foreign currency translation and leasing.

(4) Public hearings and public meetings: The ASC has experimented with public hearings on certain issues, e.g. inflation accounting, but with little public response. In the USA in contrast, public hearings have been a long-established practice, and are treated more seriously, with presentations often being made by senior executives from major industrial companies. In addition, the meetings of the FASB itself are open to the public, while the ASC meets and votes behind closed doors.

Points (3) and (4) illustrate a more developed approach to the marketing of accounting standards in the USA, and in particular the desire to show that the standards emerge from a 'due process' of open government, a factor which has become increasingly important in the UK.

(5) The resources of the FASB: The staff of the FASB vastly outnumber their ASC equivalent. While ASC members are part-time volunteers, the FASB members are full-time and paid, and are supported by a large secretariat. The total annual budget of the FASB approaches $10 million in comparison to some hundreds of thousands of pounds for the ASC. Further, all of this money is raised by voluntary contribution.

(6) Accounting standards programme: A final point of comparison is the issues that have been covered by standards produced by the FASB and ASC. Many issues have resulted in similar standards, sometimes as a result of collaboration to some extent, as in the case of foreign currency translation, but one statistic which stands out is that in 13 years the FASB has issued some 86 standards, at an increasing rate, while the ASC has produced 23 in 16 years.

Overall the US system reflects a greater commitment to standards, and a concern with making the process of standard setting acceptable, as well as the product, perhaps due to the greater potential threat of increased public-sector regulation if the private-sector FASB fails.

REGULATION IN CANADA

Financial reporting in Canada has been influenced by the close historical links with the UK, the federal political structure of the country and the extensive economic links with the US, through trading and investment (Zeff, 1972). The system of regulation and the nature of the accounting profession illustrate the influence of the UK traditions, while accounting practice reflects the US influence. The accounting profession has direct responsibility for the preparation of authoratitive statements on account-ing practice. In 1945, the Canadian Institute of Chartered Accountants (CICA) established the Accounting and Auditing Research Committee to formulate accounting standards. This committee was divided into two in 1973, to separate accounting and auditing, and since then it is the Accounting Research Committee (ARC) which has the authority to establish accounting standards in its own right.

The status of the CICA recommendations under Canadian law is of interest. The main statute concerning companies regulation is the Canada Business Corporation Act, 1975. This Act includes requirements con-cerning the maintenance of accounting records, and the preparation, audit and presentation of financial statements. Company financial statements must be prepared in accordance with the standards established by the CICA and contained in its handbook. Thus, accounting standards approved by the ARC assume the virtual status of law. Public companies are also subject to Securities Acts, but again the policy is that CICA recommendations are authoritative in the interpretation of the law. The legal status of accounting standards in Canada can be defined as follows:

> Where the term 'generally accepted accounting principles' is used, either in Securities Legislation, Regulations, or Company Law and Regulations, the Securities Administrators will regard pronouncements by the Accounting (and Auditing) Research Committee of the Canadian Institute of Chartered Accountants to the extent set out in the research recommendations in the 'CICA Handbook' as 'generally accepted accounting principles'.
> (National Securities Administrators National Policy 27, 1972)

The ARC has a membership of 22. Although this number includes representatives of the professional bodies of financial analysts, financial executives, certified accountants and management accountants, and two academics, the CICA has a large majority of the membership. At least two-thirds of the members must be CICA members, and one-half must be in public practice. It is interesting that legal recognition of accounting standards has been obtained despite the dominance of the ARC by the accounting profession. Indeed it is the technical expertise of the profession which has been used to justify the status of ARC recommendations. Proposals for accounting standards are prepared and evaluated by a process similar to those of the FASB and ASC (see Price Waterhouse, 1982, for a summary of ARC's procedures). The ARC meets in secret, does not hold public hearings and gives little information on the reasons for choice in individual standards. These aspects of the process have more in common with the procedures of the ASC than those of the FASB. Since 1974 there has also been an Advisory Board, comprising representatives of the broad spectrum of business interests, to provide a wider forum for discussion of accounting issues. A two-thirds majority of the ARC is required for adoption of a standard, which is then published in the CICA handbook and, as indicated above, is thus accorded considerable legal authority. The accounting standards that have been adopted show many similarities with accounting principles applied in the US, which is perhaps not surprising given the similarities and overlap between the business environment in the US and Canada. However, current ARC pronouncements cover a smaller range of subjects than has been regulated by the FASB.

Overall, the most notable aspect of regulation in Canada is the quasi-legal authority which has been delegated to a private body to establish accounting standards, and which has been formally recognized in statute to a much greater degree than in the UK.

In common with the United States and Canada, Australia has a federal system of government and this has influenced the structure and administration of companies legislation in that, for many years, the individual states operated separate companies acts. It was not until 1961 that a uniform set of companies acts was introduced in the separate states (Holzer, 1984). In addition, the historical influence of the relationship with the UK has been reflected in the approach to and content of regulations (Standish, 1983). Traditionally, Australia has followed the UK pattern of a balance between professional and legal regulation. This structure has now been changed to a significant degree with the creation in 1984 of the Accounting Standards Review Board (ASRB) which has authority for recommending statutory backing for standards. The main statutory control of company reporting is through the federal Companies Act, 1981 and the associated Companies Code, which have applied in all the states since 1982. The legal requirements continue to reflect the UK influence, for example the Act includes a paramount provision that financial statements should show a true and fair view of a company's affairs. The rules concerning the form and content of accounts are not contained in the Act, but in the Companies Code. In addition, stock exchange listing requirements include some additional disclosures. Administration of the Code is governed by the National Companies and Securities Commission (NCSC), in conjunction with the Corporate Affairs Commission in each state. The NCSC has power to regulate company affairs and securities markets and, in substance, follows a role similar to that of the SEC in the United States.

Professional statements have been promulgated by the Australian Accountancy Research Foundation (AARF), which was established in 1966 jointly by the Institute of Chartered Accountants of Australia (ICAA) and the much larger Australian Society of Accountants (ASA). The AARF develops accounting standards and, to the end of 1985, 18 have been produced. To begin with the standards tended to be adaptations of statements by the ICAEW but more recently the AARF has pursued a more independent line, although still with considerable UK and US influence.

Until recently, accounting standards have not had any direct force of law, although it should be noted that the Code contains a requirement for both the directors and the auditors to report whether the accounts comply with accounting standards and the reasons and effect of any non-compliance. In this situation, compliance with accounting standards could have been taken as, prima facie, necessary for a true and fair view. However, the possibility of standards having a more direct legal sanction has now arisen with the creation of the ASRB.

Accounting Standards Review Board

The ASRB was established in 1984 by the Ministerial Council. It has seven members: a chairman, one representative of each of the ASA and ICAA and four other members. The ASRB's role is to evaluate accounting standards with a view to recommendation for statutory backing. It has the power to consider existing and proposed standards from professional bodies or others, determine priorities among possible standards, sponsor development of standards and conduct public hearings or other consultations in evaluating a standard. Interestingly the ASRB has stated a number of criteria for the assessment of standards. In order to be considered acceptable a standard should be:

(1) relevant to informed decision making and consistent with community requirements and expectations regarding directors' accountability;
(2) well formulated and logically derived;
(3) consistent with approved accounting standards;
(4) practicable, having regard to the possible commercial and economic consequences of implementation.

The creation of the ASRB has broken new ground regarding the government's role in accounting regulation in Australia, but in doing so it has also raised a number of additional issues (Standish, 1985). It is not clear exactly what areas of accounting are to be covered by standards accorded statutory backing. For example, should they include all generally accepted principles, or be restricted to controversial or topical areas of practice, and what is the relationship between standards and the statutory disclosure requirements? The prospect of statutory backing can also be expected to have an impact on the work of the AARF in developing standards. It is intended that the ASRB should consult closely with the AARF and regard it as the primary source of accounting standards. For its part, the AARF will be likely to be influenced by the need to produce standards which are acceptable to the ASRB and to employ a greater degree of legalism in the way in which standards are drafted.

The model of the ASRB provides an interesting comparison with the position both in the United States, where legal backing for standards comes from the SEC rather than from statutory backing on the recommendation of a body concerned solely with accounting standards, and in Canada, where legal backing is achieved through a general requirement rather than specific approval of individual standards. It is also interesting as a development in a system which for many years has followed a similar pattern in the UK.

REGULATION IN FRANCE

The structure of financial reporting in France has been influenced by a variety of sources: company and tax law, labour law, accounting standards from the accounting profession, the Stock Exchange, the EEC, and the National Accounting Plan (Collins and Pham, 1982). Overall, the structure of regulation involves greater reliance on legal control than in the countries discussed so far.

Companies legislation in France contains relatively few accounting requirements. Companies are required to keep minimum books of account and the law provides a definition of distributable profit and requires accounts to be audited. There is no list of generally accepted accounting principles but rather a list of certain restricted practices. The main purpose of the accounting provisions of company law is to provide a basis for sharing out profit rather than to ensure the disclosure of information for users.

Accounting is seen as the basis for taxation and tax law is highly prescriptive. It provides for the form and nature of financial statements and defines detailed methods to be employed in calculating profit. Many of these methods coincide with the details of the National Accounting Plan (Plan Comptable) ('the Plan'). The Plan was formulated in 1947 by the French Government as an attempt to standardize accounting, in order to provide information which could be aggregated for macro-economic planning. It was revised in 1957 and 1979, the latter revision incorporating the EEC Fourth Directive, and contains a detailed numbered listing of accounts items, official accounting terminology, detailed instructions on the contents of accounts and valuation methods for assets and liabilities. The main principles reflected in the plan are conservatism and adherence to legal form rather than economic substance. In fact, seventy separate variants of the plan exist for different economic sectors and these rather than the main plan are mandatory on companies.

While the Plan does provide a somewhat rigid and legalistic approach to accounting, this approach is derived from a clearly stated set of objectives, which reflect the importance of the government as opposed to private shareholders in the French financial system, and the government's use of information. These objectives differ from those traditionally assumed in the UK both in their content and in the fact that they are stated explicitly. The stated objectives include:

(1) to promote national economic and fiscal policies;
(2) to assist in eliminating fiscal inequalities;
(3) to provide data for the study of market trends;
(4) to aid development of fairer taxation;
(5) to aid governmental authorities;
(6) to provide shareholders, creditors and suppliers with a basis for exercising judgement.

The plan is administered by the National Accounting Board (Conseil Nationale de la Comptaibilité) which is an official agency of the Ministry of Finance and Economy. The Ministry appoints the Board's chairman and meets its expenses. Other members include accountants, industrialists and civil servants. It is the Board, and not professional accountancy bodies, which has authority to establish accounting standards. The two professional accountancy bodies in France came into being relatively recently and have rather distinct functions. The Ordre des Experts Comptable et Comptable Agréés (1945) is the professional body of accountants, as distinct from auditors, who are covered by the Compagnie Nationale des Commissaires aux Comptes (1967) and have rather distinct functions. Each has important disciplinary and administrative roles to play in regard to their own members, but neither is as powerful or influential on accounting regulations as the professional bodies in the UK. Although an Accounting Standards Committee was created in 1964 by the Ordre and has issued a number of recommendations, these are unlike UK standards. The main roles of the profession are to ensure compliance with accounting regulations formulated by other bodies and to make recommendations where other regulations are lacking.

Despite vigorous attempts to broaden the base of share ownership, the Stock Exchange is relatively small compared with the London or New York Exchanges and many companies remain dominated by family shareholdings. Moreover, French companies have relied upon bank financing to a much greater degree than their UK or US counterparts. Thus, it is not surprising that there has been little market influence on financial reporting. As an effect of the Companies Act, 1966, a Commission for Stock Market Operations (Commission des Operations de Bourse (COB)) was set up, modelled on the SEC. The chairman of COB is appointed by the President of the Republic, and its wide responsibilities include regulating the information supplied by companies to holders of securities and the public, and ensuring minimal disclosure standards for new issues and take-overs. COB believes it has a role in the improvement of accounting standards, and has exerted considerable influence on financial reporting by encouraging the publication of consolidated accounts.

As we have already noted, the EEC has affected regulation in France through the influence of the Fourth Directive on the Plan. Perhaps the most notable feature of this has been the introduction of the concept of 'true and fair' (or 'image fidèle') which is widely viewed as a significant change of philosophy from the traditional French approach, and one that may have future ramifications for financial reporting.

REGULATION IN THE FEDERAL REPUBLIC OF GERMANY

The main element in the system of regulation in West Germany is the high degree of legal prescription which governs company financial reporting (Beeny, 1975). Detailed provision of accounting requirements by law has a long history (Macharzina, 1983), both for companies generally and for special categories of company, and relies on the application of a uniform chart of accounts. The dominant characteristic of accounting regulation in Germany is the legal principle that values of profit, assets and liabilities reported in financial accounts may not be higher and lower respectively than their counterparts allowed for tax purposes. Thus, financial reporting is very heavily constrained by tax law, and the role of the accounting profession is restricted to the interpretation of the law.

The legality of interpretations are judged by the courts on whether they represent generally accepted accounting principles. Formally, there is no official institution which has the authority or responsibility for establishing these principles, although the German Institute of Accountants, through its professional committee, has published pronouncements, comments and releases on accounting matters and the law since the 1930s.

The integration of the EEC Fourth Directive has extended considerably the generally accounting principles in German law but the directive has been implemented with less flexibility over acceptable practice than in the UK. The German tradition has been retained, in which accounting regulation is governed by the law with the accounting profession having a supplementary and subsidiary role.

REGULATION IN THE NETHERLANDS

The approach to the regulation of accounting in the Netherlands has been characterized by a high degree of flexibility with high professional standards (Nobes and Parker, 1981). This approach differs from that followed in most other continental European countries and has more similarities with the system in the UK, although there are also some interesting differences between the two countries. The extremely legalistic structure of regulation, exemplified by France and Germany above, and in particular the role of tax law, has not been an important factor in the regulatory frameworks in either the Netherlands or the UK. Rather, control of accounting practice has come from company law and from the accounting profession.

Prior to 1970, there were very few legal requirements imposed on the form and content of company accounts. Subsequently, the legal requirements included provisions that the accounts should be drawn up fairly and systematically, and that they should provide information which would permit a sound judgement on the financial position, profit and loss, solvency and liquidity of a company. These provisions have some similarity with the UK approach of requiring a 'true and fair' view and adoption of this concept as a result of the EEC Fourth Directive has thus been easier than in some countries. Before implementation of the directive, the bases used to value assets and liabilities were specified in only general terms in law as those regarded as acceptable in economic and social life, reflecting the flexibility of the Dutch approach.

The accounting profession is involved in regulation through the membership of the Dutch Institute of Registered Accountants in a Tripartite Committee, with the Dutch Employers Association and the Central Trade Union Council, which was set up at the request of the government to examine reporting standards and consider guides on principles of reporting. The Committee publishes 'Observations on the Law on the Annual Accounts of companies'. These observations are for guidance and are not mandatory on companies and auditors need not ensure that they are followed. So the intention is not to promote acceptance of a rigid model for external reporting, but to assist judgement in the context of freedom and flexibility.

Dutch law also provides for an Enterprise Chamber in the courts, for adjudication on, amongst other things, the legality of financial statements. The chamber hears specific cases brought by, for example, shareholders or trade unions and although judgement applies only to the defendent company, the court may also make statements regarding general principles.

The framework of regulation in the Netherlands thus involves a combination of legislation, the pronouncements of the Tripartite Committee and the rulings of the Enterprise Chamber. The Chamber provides a form of control which we have not observed in the other countries reviewed above, but may have a particular role in the Dutch system because of the general permissive character of the legal and professional regulations governing accounting (Klassen, 1980).

SUMMARY

As one of the purposes of looking at other countries is to draw attention to the diversity that exists in systems of regulation, it would be inappropriate to draw generalizations from the survey in this chapter. Perhaps the most interesting element in the comparative analysis of different national frameworks for accounting is the variety which exists with respect to the relationship between the law and the accounting profession.

In France and Germany, the role of the profession as an independent source of regulation is very much subsidiary to the law, although the profession can have influence on the development of law. In contrast, in those countries which share an Anglo-American background with the UK, the formal role of the law has been much less, and greater reliance has been placed on the profession as the appropriate body to regulate and oversee the development of practice. However, the relationship between the law and the professional regulations is much more complicated than is implied by simply looking at the traditional sources of authority on accounting matters in different countries.

In the United States, Canada and Australia we have seen that although professional regulations have a major role, they are increasingly depen- dent on some form of legal backing for their authority. In Canada this is achieved through general legal backing for all standards, in the United States the SEC gives effective legal backing and in Australia, although there is an SEC equivalent body, there is now a separate government board with the responsibility for recommending standards for statutory backing.

The effect of the EEC Fourth Directive has been to narrow many of the areas of difference between the formal requirements in the different European countries but the underlying approaches still reflect very dif- ferent traditions. The reliance on legal prescription and uniformity in France and Germany contrasts with the flexibility of the approach found in the Netherlands and the UK, and reflects different underlying objec- tives for financial reporting.

International precedents may also provide some possible innovations in the UK in future. In particular, the experience of other English-speaking countries with a variety of forms of legal backing for professional stan- dards, and the Dutch approach of controlling flexibility by having a type of accounting court, may be relevant to possible development in the UK in future.

REFERENCES

Armstrong, P. 1984: 'The rise of accounting controls in British capitalism'. Working paper, Department of Management, The Polytechnic, Huddersfield.

Beeny, J. 1975: *European Financial Reporting I: Germany*, ICAEW.

Benston, G.J. 1976: *Corporate Financial Disclosure in the UK and the USA*, Saxon House for the ICAEW.

Carsberg, B.V. and Eastergard, A. 1983: 'Financial Reporting in North America'. In C.W. Nobes and R.H. Parker (eds), *Comparative International Accounting*, Philip Allan.

Collins, L. and Pham, D. 1983: 'Research into the processes of accounting standard setting in France.' In M. Bromwich and A. G. Hopwood (eds), *Accounting Standard Setting*, Pitman.

Holzer, P. 1984: *International Accounting*, Harper and Row, New York.

Johnson, T. 1980: 'Work and power'. In G. Esland and G. Salaman (eds), *The Politics of Work and Occupations*, Oxford University Press.

Klassen, P. 1980: 'An accounting court: the impact of the enterprise chamber on financial reporting in the Netherlands'. *The Accounting Review*, Vol. 55.

Macharzina, K. 1983: 'Financial reporting in West Germany'. In C. Nobes and R.H. Parker (eds), *Comparative International Accounting*, Philip Allan.

National Securities Administrators, 1972: National Policy 27, Ottawa.

Nobes C.W. and Parker R.H. 1983a: 'Financial reporting in France'. In C.W. Nobes and R.H. Parker (eds), *Comparative International Accounting*, Philip Allan.

Nobes C.W. and Parker, R.H. 1983b: 'Financial reporting in the Netherlands'. In C. W. Nobes and R. H. Parker (eds), *Comparative International Accounting*, Philip Allan.

Previts, G.J. 1980: *The Development of SEC Accounting*, Addison-Wesley.

Price Waterhouse, 1982: *International Survey of Accounting Principles and Reporting Practices*, Butterworth.

Standish, P. 1983: 'Financial reporting in Britain and Australia'. In C.W. Nobes and R.H. Parker (eds), *Comparative International Accounting*, Philip Allan.

Standish, P. 1985: 'In Australia the law sets standards'. *Accountancy*, November 114–15.

Zeff, S. 1972: *Forging Accounting Principles in Five Countries*, Stripes.

11

Future Developments

The framework of financial reporting is constantly changing. With each new Companies Act the boundaries between statutory regulation and professional regulation are redrawn. With each new accounting standard, rules are applied to areas which had previously been governed by convention and professional judgement. Changes in the law and the development of standards bring with them questions of principle concerning the concepts which should be applied and of consistency between the law and accounting standards and between different standards.

The financial environment of business is also changing more rapidly today then ever before, with the creation of new financial instruments and relationships which existing accounting practice has no established conventions for recording. Developments in information technology could move financial reporting into a new era in which the data base or on-line access replace the traditional set of periodic accounting statements. Such developments raise questions about concepts of reporting, the role of standardization and the use of financial information in decision making.

Accountants cannot ignore change in their environment, they are forced to react as they are confronted with the impact of change on accounting statements. The last two decades provide ample evidence of the need for continual development in accounting practice. The question is not whether accounting practice will change in coming years, but rather how it will change and develop. Will accounting practice provide leadership in financial reporting, developing concepts or proposing innovations which anticipate the demands which will be placed on practice, or will it react passively and be seen increasingly to provide irrelevant information? Will developments in accounting standards be dependent on a 'bush-fire' approach where issues are dealt with as they become controversial or will developments be planned in a more coherent and structured way? How will the changes which have occurred in statutory regulations in recent years affect the process of evolution in reporting practices – will they strengthen professional developments or constrain them?

The answers to these questions are not easy to predict, and it would be inappropriate to attempt to do so here. The principal areas which have provided the subjects addressed in this book have been the structure of the framework for financial reporting, the authority of reporting requirements, compliance with those requirements, the manner in which new requirements are developed and their effects. In this chapter a number of issues which are relevant to the way in which these areas will appear in the future are outlined, but predictions of the outcomes of these issues are not attempted. For convenience the discussion is split into sections considering changes in the framework for regulating financial reporting, developments in the work of the ASC and changes in the nature of financial reporting, but these categories should not be thought of as totally independent.

THE FRAMEWORK FOR REGULATION OF ACCOUNTING PRACTICE

The principal issue regarding future developments in the regulatory framework concerns the relative roles of legal and professional regulations. In the discussion in chapter 3 of recent changes in the statutory regulations relating to accounting, the point was made that although there has been a redistribution from professional to statutory control as a result of implementing EEC directives, the underlying philosophy remains one of reliance on professonal regulation within a statutory framework. The main alternatives to continuation with this approach are that increased reliance will be placed on statutory regulation, that legal backing will be used to support professional regulations or that new agencies will be created to have a role in the development, approval or enforcement of regulations.

An Increasing Reliance on Statutory Regulations

The failure of the ASC to introduce and enforce a standard on accounting for the effects of changing prices has resulted in some loss of credibility for the ASC regarding its ability to provide an effective form of regulation in controversial areas of accounting practice. If this failure was to be repeated, then loss of confidence in professional regulation could lead to greater reliance on statutory control. This would result in a more inflexible system than at present, in terms of both the freedom of companies to depart from regulations and also the ability of the system to react quickly to changes in the reporting environment. Professional regulations would become means of interpreting the practical implications of statutory provisions but would not have a role in going beyond statute and providing a lead in the development of financial reporting.

Legal Backing for Accounting Standards

The authority of accounting standards could be strengthened through some form of legal backing. Bromwich (1985) suggests that more formal legal recognition of standards would give the ASC a 'political mandate' from society. The problems of compliance and enforcement could be approached by using the law to enhance the status of accounting standards, in one of a number of ways.

First, the Canadian model could be followed and a general statutory requirement introduced for accounts to be prepared in accordance with relevant accounting standards as developed by the ASC and approved by the CCAB bodies. This approach would confer on the ASC and the professional bodies direct legal authority for regulation, and would imply confidence in their procedures and expertise for producing solutions on accounting issues. It would give the standard setters greater power to carry out the role that they attempt to serve at present and remove some of the constraints which currently affect the development of standards. A general statutory requirement to follow standards would preserve the existing structure of regulation regarding the development of rules governing accounting practice but would change the relative status of standards and the Companies Act requirements.

A second, somewhat different alternative would be for legal recognition to be given to individual standards, for example by statutory instrument, either as they are developed or when they have been proved to work in practice (Bromwich, 1985). Under this approach authority would not be given to the ASC directly. Rather, the statements it produces would be subject to government review before legal recognition was granted and so the balance of authority would remain firmly with government. If recognition was only granted after a standard had been proved in practice then the problem of compliance would not be dealt with, as non-compliance would be likely to lead to legal recognition being withheld. Thus the status of the standard setting process itself would not be enhanced, and the process could become one of preparing possible inputs to the statutory mechanisms rather than providing an independent source of regulation.

A number of standards have passed into statute through changes in the law in recent years, for example the fundamental concepts referred to in SSAP2, but there is a difference between the contents of individual standards being incorporated into law over time and explicit legal recognition of an accounting standard in its own right. The ASC has also seen the law as a possible way out of its inability to implement an inflation accounting standard. The ASC suggested to the CCAB bodies that they request government to introduce a general requirement for accounts to reflect the effect of changing prices, to provide the basis for the ASC to regulate practice in this area (ASC, 1985). However, the CCAB reaction was unenthusiastic and the request was not pursued.

A final way in which legal backing for accounting standards may arise is through the courts. Reliance by the courts on accounting standards as a basis for evaluating accounting practice will enhance the status of standards both individually and in general. There is a lack of established case law in which accounting standards have been used as evidence but this may change as the continuing increase in litigation involving accountants may lead to more cases reaching the courts. In the judgement in one recent case (*Lloyd Cheyham & Co. Ltd.* v. *Littlejohn & Co.*, 1985), Justice Woolf held accounting standards to be important evidence in assessing accounting practice.

> While they [accounting standards] are not conclusive, so that a departure from their terms necessarily involves a breach of the duty of care, and they are not as the explanatory foreword makes clear, rigid rules, they are very strong evidence as to what is the proper standard which should be adopted and, unless there is some justification, a departure from this will be regarded as constituting a breach of duty. (Woolf, 1985)

Increased clarification of the legal status of accounting standards would be welcome although it should be noted that, while judgements such as Justice Woolf's in some ways strengthen the ASC's authority, they also emphasize its reponsibilities in developing standards which are acceptable to society.

Creation of Additional Agencies

The current framework for regulating accounting practice could also be changed through the introduction of new agencies or elements in the overall structure. This could involve the development of new bodies, or reorganization of the existing agencies. Some alternatives that have been proposed are described below.

A securities and exchange commission. Perhaps the idea that is discussed most frequently is the possibility of introducing an additional tier in the regulatory framework, between statutory and professional regulation, by creating a government-backed agency with responsibility for oversight of business behaviour, including reporting standards. This idea attracts consideration both because of the fact that, as noted in chapter 10, many other countries already have such bodies, for example the United States and Australia, and also because of the proposals for a Securities and Investment Board (SIB) in the UK, with supervisory powers relating to the securities industry. Drawing on international precedent is not easy, however, because there are notable differences between the overseas bodies, and any change in the UK system should take account of the existing structures that operate in this environment. It is also not clear that SIB provides an appropriate national precedent. The SIB is intended to be a self-regulatory body but with legal authority delegated to it. Part of the reason for its introduction was to provide protection for investors and regulation of securities business in an environment where diversity of financial instruments and financial advisors was increasing. The accounting community in the UK is already quite cohesive and a case could be made that if the intention is to preserve self-regulation, it would be more appropriate for the government to deal directly with the accounting profession through the ASC, perhaps reorganized in some ways, than to impose an additional element in the hierarchy of regulatory agencies. The creation of a new agency could detract from, rather than enhance, professional self-regulation and any new agency would be faced with the same choice discussed above as to whether to recognize accounting standards in general or approve standards individually.

An accounting court. Another possible innovation in the existing structure would be to establish an accounting court, with responsibility for adjudicating in cases of disputes over the applicability of accounting standards. Bromwich (1985, p. 119) sees this possibility in terms of an informal professional body, but there is also international precedent for a more official structure in the Dutch Enterprise Chamber, which is described in chapter 10. The facility to judge issues of accounting principle and practice in their own right could be an advantage in comparison with the current position, where accounting issues tend to find their way into the courts only in connection with problems of business failure or financial loss. Review of more instances involving the application of standards to particular circumstances could lead to improvements in existing standards and in the consistency between different standards.

A review body. A further suggestion that has been proposed is that the structure of the ASC should be reorganized to separate the production of accounting standards from their approval. Hope and Briggs (1982) suggest a watchdog 'policy review board', which would consist of individuals from a wide spectrum of backgrounds and interests and would have responsibility for setting broad policy and approving standards, and an 'accounting standards board' which would develop the proposed standards. The rationale behind this approach is that the development of standards relies on the technical expertise of acountants, but the approval of standards for application to company accounts should involve representation of wider interests of society. Reflecting a concern that standards should be seen to emerge from 'due process', the ASC has reorganized its structure and representativeness in recent years, but it still relies heavily on individuals from an accounting background, either in professional practice or in industry and so remains more representative of those concerned with the production of accounting statements rather than their use. Further changes may be unlikely until more experience has been obtained of the current structure. Bromwich (1985, p. 118) also discusses the possibility of a 'review panel' in the context of approval of individual standards for legal backing.

THE WORK OF THE ACCOUNTING STANDARDS COMMITTEE

The work of the ASC would of course be affected by any changes in the structure of the regulatory framework and in the status of accounting standards as a result. Even if the structure remains as it is at present, it is possible to identify a number of issues which could be significant in the way in which the ASC carries out its function.

The use of SORPs. The ASC now has the vehicle of statements of recommended practice to supplement accounting standards, but it remains to be seen exactly how this form of regulation will be utilized. When introduced, the justification for SORPs was that some issues were not fundamental to a true and fair view and so standardized practice was not necessary but recommended practice could be stated. In practice it may be difficult for the ASC to limit the use of SORPs to this separate class of issues. There will be a temptation to use the non-mandatory SORP as a way of getting around the difficulty of non-compliance on controversial issues, or as a means of experimenting in the hope of leading ultimately to an accounting standard. Care will be needed if the opportunity that SORPs provide for promoting innovations in financial reporting is to be exploited (Bromwich, 1985, p. 114).

Development of concepts. The ASC may devote more effort to developing the conceptual foundations on which accounting standards should be based (McMonnies, 1985). A review of SSAP2, which is concerned with accounting principles and policies, is currently underway. The prospects for achieving a conceptual framework which could be utilized by the ASC were discussed in chapter 5. Although an overall agreed framework might be unlikely, there could be scope for further development of concepts beyond the position currently outlined in SSAP2. For example, in the *Review of the Standard Setting Process* (ASC, 1983), the link between accounting standards and the true and fair view was re-established. This implies a concept of universality, i.e. that all standards should apply to all accounts required to give a true and fair view, but the ASC might find this approach difficult to follow in practice. The concept of substance over form has been applied in SSAP21 on accounting for leasing transactions, and the concept of materiality is also under review by the ASC.

Further development of concepts should be welcomed if it can help to ensure consistency between standards, and identify more explicitly the nature of the choices being made by the standard setters, but no agreed conceptual framework will be found which enables the 'correct' choices to be made.

The work programme of the ASC. The agenda of topics being addressed by the ASC must be kept under review, in order to ensure that the work of the ASC is seen as relevant to emerging issues in the business environment. Bromwich (1985, pp. 109–11) makes a number of recommendations concerning the way in which the ASC should develop its methods of operating. He suggests that the ASC should give attention to developing a longer term and more structured work programme, rather than adopting a 'fire fighting' approach as issues arise. He also recommends that a greater role should be given to research on accounting problems, with the appropriate time that is needed, and that the role of working parties should be to brief the ASC on all aspects of an issue, not simply to develop preferred solutions.

The choice of topics that the ASC deals with in the immediate future, the way it develops proposals on them and the nature of those proposals, has been made more important as a result of the failure in the area of accounting for the effects of changing prices. The ASC lost some credibility in the successive stages of the attempt to implement an inflation accounting standard and eventually had to concede its inability to enforce a standard. As a result it has ground to make up in the development of standards on other issues, although it is to be hoped that the experience of inflation accounting does not lead the ASC to be reluctant to address potentially controversial issues.

Legalism. Another factor that may confront the ASC increasingly in the future is a legalistic attitude to the way standards are interpreted and applied. This attitude is already apparent in the US where advice is given on how to construct business affairs in order to avoid the requirements of standards. One example in the UK is that of accounting for leases, where it appears that implementation of SSAP21 is being affected by the rigid definition of finance leases contained in the standard (Lennard, 1985). Increased use of 'avoidance' procedures, similar to tax avoidance in taxation legislation, could be of concern to ASC. It would call for great care in the wording of standards and the possibility of 'antiavoidance' provisions, and to some extent could undermine the 'professional' element on which self-regulation by the profession currently relies.

Increasing internationalization. The work of the ASC in future is likely to be affected by the increasing internationalization of business. This factor was evidenced in the case of foreign currency translation, where the development of SSAP20 was to large extent coordinated with the efforts of the IASC and the FASB on the same subject. European considerations have also had an impact on the ASC's work, not least in the fact that implementation of European legislation has resulted in the need to review a number of existing accounting standards.

DEVELOPMENTS IN FINANCIAL REPORTS

In looking to the future it is appropriate to consider not only possible developments in the structure of accounting regulations and the process by which those regulations are produced, but also possible ways in which the content of the information disclosed might change.

Disclosure of Information

Throughout this century there has been a trend of increasing the amount of information companies are required to disclose. This trend has been evident in the periodic changes in the legal requirements governing accounts and, more recently, in certain accounting standards.

One interesting aspect of the work of the ASC has been the explicit inclusion in standards of requirements for disclosure of the accounting policy associated with particular aspects of reporting. Information of this nature is likely to be of assistance to users of accounts in 'seeing through' differences in the results of different companies which are attributable purely to the adoption of different accounting policies. It is possible that there will be increasing emphasis in future on supporting the figures in the accounts with explanation of the basis of the disclosures and measurements, particularly with respect to those areas of judgement which have a significant impact on the accounts.

Disclosure of information in addition to the figures in the accounts is also likely to be of importance in dealing with the problem of legalism referred to above, and the related issue of 'window dressing'. It is possible for companies to arrange their affairs in a manner which means that, by applying a strict interpretation of the law, the accounts may not include some information which would be necessary to reflect the underlying economic substance of the arrangements. Financial advisors have been inventive in creating new ways of avoiding disclosure, particularly by structuring relationships between companies in ways which avoid the legal definition of a subsidiary. Increased disclosure of information in the notes to the accounts could help alleviate this type of problem without jeopardizing the legality of the financial statements by incorporating information into the balance sheet or profit and loss account directly.

New Forms of Reporting

A number of suggestions have been advanced for innovations in the type of reports that should be produced by companies. Some idea of the potential for innovation can be given by referring to a number of discussion papers published in the late 1970s which referred to possible extensions in the type of information companies should disclose. (For a full discussion of a number of alternative forms of reporting, see Lee, 1981.)

In 1975 the ASC published a discussion document, *The Corporate Report* (ASC, 1975) which attempted to consider the role and structure of corporate disclosure and the types of groups who might be interested in and have a valid claim to receive information about company activity. After discussing the objectives and uses of financial reports the document outlined a number of possible new areas for development in reporting:

Statement of value added
Employment report
Statement of exchanges with government
Statement of foreign currency transactions
Statement of corporate objectives
Statement of future prospects
Social reporting
Disclosure and disaggregation

The government published its own consultative document *The Future of Company Reports* two years later (Secretary of State for Trade, 1977).

This green paper referred to many of the areas listed above and also included consideration of a number of other specific areas of accounting measurement and reporting, for example accounting for leasing transactions, pension commitments and research and development expenditure, and the possibility of legal backing for SSAP 10 on statements of source and application of funds.

Both *The Corporate Report* and *The Future of Company Reports* reflected a general philosophy of increasing disclosure as part of the public accountability of companies. They indicate the potential scope for extending disclosure as many of the areas referred to above have not been followed up with actual requirements in law or accounting standards. The general thrust of *The Corporate Report* was not taken up by the ASC, although some accounting standards have regulated specific areas of accounting practice such as foreign currency translation and leasing transactions (Tweedie, 1981). There has been no attempt to standardize practice with respect to, for example, value added statements, which remain a matter for voluntary disclosure by companies and in whatever form the company chooses.

As regards action by government, legislation has introduced some requirements regarding the inclusion in the directors report of a statement on certain aspects of employment policy and a statement of future prospects, but these tend to be restricted to minimal disclosures. Other possible legislative changes in reporting requirements suggested in *The Future of Company Reports* were not followed up partly due to a change of government in 1978. The new government had a different approach to the role of legislation in promoting innovations in financial reporting, as reflected in a further consultative document *Company Accounting and Disclosure* (Secretary of State for Trade, 1979).

This paper was mainly concerned with the implementation of the EEC Fourth Directive, but did refer to some of the items raised in the 1977 green paper. For example, with respect to employee reporting, the document concluded:

> This process of experimentation and evaluation could be undermined by the introduction of rigid statutory requirements relating to disclosure to employees, and the Government propose to treat this matter as one for companies and employees to deal with themselves.
>
> (Secretary of State for Trade, 1979, p. 8)

The extent to which companies can be relied upon to experiment and innovate in expanding disclosure, and the extent to which legislation or other regulations will be necessary to overcome the natural reluctance of management to disclose, are issues which are likely to be important in the future development of financial reporting.

Smaller Companies

In contrast to the above, it is also possible that the future will see some restrictions on disclosure. It is likely that greater differentiation in accounting requirements will be applied to companies of different sizes. Since 1981 a three-tier classification of companies has been recognized on the basis of size, as defined by a number of criteria, and the nature of ownership. The Companies Act, 1981 allowed small private companies to limit the amount of information they disclosed, by filing 'modified' accounts. An extension of this allowance would be to reduce the amount of information that such companies have to report in the accounts distributed to shareholders. The government is currently looking at the possibility of reducing the disclosure requirements which apply to small companies (Department of Trade and Industry, 1985).

In the area of accounting standards it is possible that some standards might be made to apply only when a company reaches a certain size. While the ASC has stated that standards should apply to all accounts required to give a true and fair view, this approach must be coupled with consideration of cost and benefit, and it may be argued that the obligation to comply with standards could impose unwarranted costs on small companies (Stacy, 1985). On this basis it would seem that exemptions would be most appropriate with respect to those standards which require the disclosure of information, as these may entail costs associated with the recording of information, and this approach would be consistent with the idea of limiting the legal disclosure requirements.

SUMMARY

The main issues which are likely to be of importance in the development of the framework of regulation of financial reporting in the foreseeable future are those which have been most prominent throughout the review of the development of the existing framework contained in this book. They are the mixture of statutory and professional regulations, the problem of compliance with non-statutory requirements and the influence this has on their development, and the boundaries between areas of reporting subject to legally or professionally mandated rules and those left to voluntary disclosure.

In particular, a major consideration is whether there will be any shift in the balance between the roles of the law and accounting standards, or whether attempts will be made to maintain the existing roles but with new measures to make them effective, for example legal backing for standards. The issue of regulation or de-regulation will also be relevant to possible changes in the structure of reporting, for example the introduction of new types of statements or the removal of some disclosure requirements. The ASC must re-establish its authority following the failure to proceed with a standard on inflation accounting, confront the possibility of an increasingly legalistic attitude to the interpretation of standards and develop conventions regarding the role of the Statement of Recommended Practice.

REFERENCES

Accounting Standards Committee 1975: *The Corporate Report – A Discussion Document*, London.

Accounting Standards Committee 1983: *Review of The Standards Setting Process*, London.

Accounting Standards Committee 1985: Policy Statement by the Accounting Standards Committee on Accounting for the Effects of Changing Prices, TR 604, ICAEW, London.

Bromwich, M. 1985: *The Economics of Accounting Standard Setting*, Prentice Hall International in association with The institute of Chartered Accountants in England and Wales, Hemel Hempstead.

Department of Trade and Industry 1985: *Accounting and Audit Requirements for Small Firms – A Consultative Document*, London, July.

Hope, A. and Briggs, J. 1982: 'Accounting policy making – some lessons fromt he deferred taxation debate'. *Accounting and Business Research*, Vol. 12, 83–96.

Lee T.A. 1981: *Developments in Financial Reporting*, Phillip Allan, Deddington.

Lennard, A. 1985: 'Classifying leases: more guidance needed'. *The Accountants Magazine*, November, 486–8.

McMonnies, P. 1985: *The Authority of Accounting Standards*, Gee & Co., Wokingham.

Secretary of State for Trade 1977: *The Future of Company Reports*, Cmnd 6888, HMSO, London.

Secretary of State for Trade 1979: *Company Accounting and Disclosure*, Cmnd 7654, HMSO, London.

Stacy, G. 1985: 'Universality can hinder progress'. *The Accountant*, 2 May, 12–13.

Tweedie, D.P. 1981: 'Standards, objectives and The Corporate Report'. In R. Leach and E. Stamp (eds), *British Accounting Standards – The First Ten Years*, Woodhead Faulkner, Cambridge.

Woolf, The Hon. Mr Justice, 1985: Judgement in the High Court of Justice, Queens Bench Division. In *Lloyd Cheyham & Co. Ltd* v. *Littlejohn & Co.*, at the Royal Courts of Justice, London, 30 September (Case ref. 1984 NJ 4032).

Appendix 1

The main accounting requirements of the Companies Act 1985 are contained in sections 221–62, which provide rules and obligations regarding the preparation, publication and audit of accounting statements, and in Schedule 4, which establishes the formal regulations on structure and content of the statements. Sections 263–81 lay down rules covering the distribution of profits and assets and schedule 7 covers matters to be dealt with in the directors' report. The principal provisions are summarized below.

PREPARATION AND PUBLICATION OF ACCOUNTS

The directors of every company are required to maintain adequate records to enable accounting statements to be prepared. Accounts must be prepared for each accounting period and presented to shareholders in a general meeting for approval. Approved accounts are signed by two directors and made public by filing with the Registrar of Companies. The filed statements comprise the profit and loss account and balance sheet and notes thereto, the directors' report and the audit report.

Companies with subsidiaries (holding companies) must produce group accounts combining the results and position of the company and its subsidiaries. This requirement does not apply if the holding company is itself a subsidiary of another company. 'Subsidiary' status is defined in the legislation.

The Act requires the accounting statements to give a 'true and fair view' of the company's performance and position. This requirement overrides the other provisions of the Act and its schedules regarding the information to be included in the accounting statements.

A number of general principles to govern the preparation of accounts are included in the legislation: accruals, prudence, going concern and consistency. There are also rules dealing with stock valuation and depreciation. Accounting policies adopted by the company shall be disclosed in the notes to the accounts.

Accounting statements are to be presented in accordance with the prescribed formats included in the Act. There are two possible balance sheet formats (vertical or horizontal layout) and four profit and loss formats (combinations of vertical or horizontal and operations or expenditure headings). There are a large number of options regarding whether individual items of information are disclosed on the face of the accounting statements or in the notes.

The following information is required to be disclosed in the profit and loss account or related notes.

Income

Turnover (and analysis between substantially different geographical markets and different classes of business); other operating income; income from investments (distinguishing investments in group companies, related companies and others) and interest receivable.

Expenses and Charges

(*Note*: depending on the formats chosen, certain expenses may be classified under cost of sales, distribution expenses and administrative expenses or as changes in stock levels, staff costs and other operating charges). Depreciation; auditors remuneration including expenses; details of directors' emoluments, number of directors in bands of £5000, emoluments of UK chairman and highest paid UK director (some exemptions if total directors' emoluments do not exceed £60,000); average number of employees, expenditure on wages and salaries, social security costs and other pension costs, and number of employees in bands of £5000 over £30,000; interest payable (distinguishing that payable to group companies, banks, and other); hire of plant and machinery; taxation on ordinary activities (separating UK corporation tax, UK income tax and overseas tax).

Appropriations

Transfers to and from reserves; dividends paid and proposed.

Other Matters

Extraordinary income and charges and related taxation; effect of any prior year items; exceptional transactions; amounts written off investments; basis of foreign currency translation; comparative figures; any additional information for a true and fair view; departures from the Act's requirements, with reasons.

DISCLOSURE IN THE BALANCE SHEET

The following information is required to be disclosed in the balance sheet or related notes.

Fixed Assets

Intangible assets (separating development costs, concessions and patents etc. and goodwill); tangible assets (separate amounts for land and buildings, plant and machinery, fixtures and fittings, assets under construction); investments (distinguishing shares and loans in group companies, related companies and others); details of subsidiaries and related companies.

(For each of the relevent items above, the accounts must show opening and closing balances, revaluations, acquisitions and disposals, transfers, depreciation and other adjustments).

Current Assets

Stocks (separate amounts for raw materials, work in progress, finished goods and payments on account); debtors (separate amounts for trade debtors, group companies, related companies, others, prepayments and accrued income); investments; cash at bank and in hand.

Liabilities

Creditors, falling due within one year and after more than one year (under each, show separately debentures, bank loans and overdrafts, trade creditors, bills of exchange payable, amounts due to group and related companies, taxation and social security, accruals, and deferred income, others); provisions for liabilities and charges (pensions and similar obligations, taxation and deferred taxation).

Capital and Reserves

Details of authorized and allotted share capital; share premium account; revaluation reserve and details of movements; other reserves and movements; profit and loss account.

Other Matters

Charges on the company's assets; contingent liabilities; capital expenditure commitments and plans; other financial commitments; details of transactions involving directors; comparative figures; accounting policies; basis of foreign currency translation; departures from the Act's requirements, with reasons; any additional information for a true and fair view.

THE DIRECTORS' REPORT

Information Regarding the Company or Group

Principal activities and any change; a fair review of the business during the year and at the year end; proposals regarding dividends and transfers to reserves; significant events since the year end; likely future developments; details regarding changes in fixed assets and, in certain circumstances, market value.

Information Concerning the Directors' Interests

The names of directors during the year; interests (including directors' families) in shares and debentures at the beginning and end of the year; interests in contracts.

Other Matters

Political and charitable donations; policy on employment of disabled persons; action regarding consulting, informing and involving employees.

THE AUDITOR'S REPORT

The auditor must report an opinion on whether the accounting statements give a true and fair view and whether they are prepared in accordance with the requirements of the Act.

In addition he must make reference in his report if proper books of accounts have not been kept; the accounts are not in agreement with the books; all the necessary information and explanations have not been obtained; or information contained in the directors' report is not consistent with the accounts.

The auditor must provide details of certain items if omitted from the accounts. For modified accounts (see below) the audit report must include a statement that the company qualifies for exemption and the accounts have been properly prepared.

EXEMPTIONS

Certain exemptions from disclosure are permitted in the accounting statements for filing purposes of small- and medium-sized companies (defined in the Act). The rules for these 'modified accounts' are contained in Schedule 8 to the Act. Full accounts must be provided to shareholders even though modified accounts are filed with the Registrar.

Special rules also exist for application in the case of the accounts of certain special categories of companies, including banking, insurance and shipping companies. Special category accounts are dealt with in Schedules 9, 10 and 11.

Appendix 2

SSAP1: Accounting for associated companies. (Issued Jan. 1971, amended Aug. 1974, revised Apr. 1982.) Requires the use of the equity method of accounting for associated companies. The revised standard uses the concept of 'significant influence' to define associated company status, as opposed to the holding of between 20 per cent and 50 per cent of the equity voting rights used in the original standard.

SSAP2: Disclosure of accounting policies. (Issued Nov. 1971.) Specifies four 'fundamental accounting concepts' which should underlie the preparation of financial statements, namely going concern, accruals, consistency and prudence. Requires disclosure of adoption of different concepts and also of accounting policies relating to items which have material effect on the financial statements.

SSAP3: Earnings per share. (Issued Feb. 1972, revised Aug. 1974) Requires disclosure of earnings per share on the net bases (profit after tax, minority interests and preference dividends, but before extraordinary items). Fully diluted earnings per share should also be shown where a company has contracted to issue further shares. Applies only to companies listed on a recognized stock exchange.

SSAP4: The accounting treatment of government grants. (Issued Apr. 1974.) Allows grants relating to fixed assets to be credited to revenue either by reducing the cost of acquisition of the asset by the amount of the grant, or by treating the grant as a deferred credit and transferring it to revenue over the useful life of the asset.

SSAP5: Accounting for value added tax. (Issued Apr. 1974.) States that turnover in the profit and loss account should exclude VAT on taxable outputs, and that irrecoverable VAT on inputs should be included in the cost of the related item.

SSAP6: Extraordinary items and prior year adjustments. (Issued Apr. 1974.) Defines extraordinary items as those 'which derive from events or transactions outside the ordinary activities of the business and which are both material and expected not to recur frequently or regularly; and prior year adjustments as those arising from 'changes in accounting policies and from the correction of fundamental errors'. Requires that the profit and loss account should show separately: profit before extraordinary items; extraordinary items (less attributable taxation); and profit after extraordinary items. Prior year adjustments should be shown in a statement immediately following the profit and loss account.

SSAP8: The treatment of taxation under the imputation system in the accounts of companies. (Issued Aug. 1974.) Requires separate disclosure in the profit and loss account of (1) United Kingdom corporation tax, split between tax on the income of the year, tax on franked investment income, irrecoverable Advance Corporation Tax (ACT) and relief for overseas taxation, and (2) overseas taxation. Also regulates the effect of ACT on balance-sheet items.

SSAP9: Stocks and work in progress. (Issued May 1975.) Applies the lower of cost or net realizable value to valuation of stocks and work in progress. Long-term contract work in progress to be valued at cost plus attributable profit less foreseeable losses and progress payments. Accounting policies and analysis of stocks and work in progress by main categories to be disclosed.

SSAP10: Statements of source and application of funds. (Issued July 1975.) Applies only to companies with a turnover of at least £25,000 per annum. Requires inclusion of a source and application of funds statement in the financial statements, showing the effect of profit, dividends, share issues and loans raised, acquisitions and disposals of fixed assets, changes in working movements in net liquid funds.

SSAP12: Accounting for depreciation. (Issued Dec. 1977, revised Nov. 1981.) Requires depreciation of assets with a finite useful life by allocation of the net cost as fairly as possible over that useful life, and disclosure of details of accounting policy and the amount of depreciation. Revised with the publication of SSAP19 on investment properties.

SSAP13: Accounting for research and development. (Issued Dec. 1977.) Research expenditure to be written off in the year of expenditure. Development expenditure should also be written off as incurred but may be deferred if certain conditions specified in the standard are met. Companies should also disclose the amount of the movement in deferred development expenditure.

SSAP14: Group accounts. (Issued Sep. 1978.) Group accounts should be prepared in the form of a single set of consolidated financial statements. The standard also requires uniform group accounting policies and specifies rules regarding accounting dates and situations where subsidiaries may be excluded from consolidation.

SSAP15: Accounting for deferred taxation. (Issued Oct. 1978, revised May 1985.) Deferred taxation should be computed using the liability method. Provision should only be made for deferred taxation arising from timing differences between accounting profits and taxable profits and only to the extent that it is possible that a liability or asset will crystallize, based on reasonable assumptions and all relevant information.

SSAP16: Current cost accounting. (Issued Mar. 1980, mandatory status suspended June 1985.) Applies to listed companies and large unlisted companies (as defined by the Companies Act, 1981). Requires presentation of current cost accounts either as supplementary to the historic cost accounts or as the main accounts with supplementary historic cost information. Uses the concepts of maintenance of operating capability and value to the business as the basis for adjustments in the profit and loss account and revaluations in the balance sheet. Profit and loss adjustments are for depreciation, cost of sales, monetary working capital and gearing. The first three lead to calculation of current cost operating profit and the fourth to current cost operating profit attributable to shareholders.

SSAP17: Accounting for post balance sheet events. (Issued Aug. 1980.) Sets out conditions under which material post balance sheet events should lead to adjustments to the financial statements, and conditions where the nature and an estimate of the financial effect of the event should simply be disclosed.

SSAP18: Accounting for contingencies. (Issued Aug. 1980.) Material contingent losses should be accrued in the accounts where it is probable that the loss will occur and the amount of loss can be estimated with reasonable accuracy. Material contingent gains should be disclosed if probable to occur, but not accrued, and material contingent losses not accrued should also be disclosed. The manner of disclosure is also covered by the standard.

SSAP19: Accounting for investment properties. (Issued Nov. 1981.) Provides that investment properties should not be depreciated, except where held on lease, and should be included in the balance sheet at their open market value.

SSAP20: Foreign currency translation. (Issued Apr. 1983.) Distinguishes translation for the purposes of individual companies from consolidated financial statements. Individual companies should translate using the temporal method (using the exchange rates ruling at the date to which a transaction or valuation relates) and exchange gains and losses, except where investment is hedged, should be reported as part of the profit or loss from ordinary activities. Consolidated financial statements should be prepared using the closing rate method and exchange differences recorded as a movement on reserves. The method used and details of exchange gains and losses should be disclosed.

SSAP21: Accounting for leases and hire purchase contract. (Issued Aug. 1984.) Distinguishes operating leases and finance leases and governs accounting by both lessors and lessees. The main provision is that finance leases should be capitalized and appear in the lessee's balance sheet as both an asset and an obligation to pay future rentals. These values are then reduced by depreciation and future payments respectively. Detailed requirements for disclosure of accounting policy and details of lease transactions are also included in the standard.

SSAP22: Accounting for goodwill. (Issued Dec. 1984.) Purchased goodwill should not be carried in the balance sheet as a permanent item. It should normally be eliminated from the accounts on acquisition (immediate write-off), but may be ammortized through the profit and loss account over its useful economic life. No amount should be attributed to non-purchased goodwill in balance sheets.

SSAP23: Accounting for acquisitions and mergers. (Issued Apr. 1985.) Defines the circumstances in which the use of merger accounting to account for business combinations is permitted but not required. The circumstances involve considerations of the nature of the offer, the proportion made up of equity share capital and the levels of holding before and after the offer. In other circumstances acquisition accounting should be used.

STATEMENTS OF STANDARD ACCOUNTING PRACTICE ISSUED AND
SUBSEQUENTLY WITHDRAWN

PSSAP7: Accounting for changes in the purchasing power of money.
(Issued May 1974, withdrawn 1977.)

SSAP11: Accounting for deferred taxation. (Issued Aug. 1975, withdrawn
1977.)

Appendix 3

SUMMARY OF STOCK EXCHANGE DISCLOSURE REQUIREMENTS

The Stock Exchange's 'Listing Agreement – Companies' contains a number of requirements for disclosure of information in the annual report and accounts of listed companies, some of which are also required by law or by SSAPs. The main points are summarized below.

GENERAL

The annual report and accounts must be issued within six months following the end of the financial period to which they relate.

COMPANY AND GROUP STRUCTURE, MANAGEMENT AND CONTROL

(1) Details of the directors' interest at the end of the year in the capital of any member of the group.
(2) Details of any substantial interests in the share capital (5 per cent or more of full voting shares) other than directors.
(3) Information on significant contracts in which any director has a material interest.
(4) Information on significant contracts involving a corporate substantial shareholder (30 per cent or more of voting rights).
(5) Disclosure of any waiver of dividends and/or emoluments by directors or shareholders.
(6) The principal country of operation for each important subsidiary.
(7) Details concerning each company (other than subsidiaries) in which the group interest in the equity capital is 20 per cent or more.

(8) A statement indicating the company's position regarding close company status for taxation purposes.
(9) Particulars of any authority for the purchase by the company of its own shares.

ACCOUNTING

(1) A statement by the directors of the reasons for any significant departures from standard accounting practices (i.e. SSAPs).
(2) A geographical analysis of turnover and trading results for operations outside the UK.
(3) A statement of interest capitalized during the year and the treatment of any related tax relief.
(4) Details of bank loans and overdrafts and other borrowings and the timetable over which they are repayable.
(5) An explanation of any material differences between actual results and any published forecast.

INTERIM REPORTS

To prepare a half-yearly or interim report to be sent to share holders or published in newspapers within the six months following the date of the notice of the annual general meeting.

Glossary

AAA	American Accounting Association
AARF	Australian Accountancy Research Foundation
ACT	Advance Corporation Tax
AICPA	American Institute of Certified Public Accountants
APB	Accounting Principles Board
ARB	Accounting Research Bulletin
ARC	Accounting Research Committee
ASA	Australian Society of Accountants
ASC	Accounting Standards Committee
ASRB	Accounting Standards Review Board
ASSC	Accounting Standards Steering Committee
CACA	Chartered Association of Certified Accountants
CAPM	Capital asset pricing model
CCA	Current cost accounting
CCAB	Consultative Committee of Accountancy Bodies
CICA	Canadian Institute of Chartered Accountants
CIPFA	Chartered Institute of Public Finance and Accountancy
COB	Commission des Operations de Bourse
COREPER	Committee of Permanent Representatives
CPP	Current purchasing power
DTI	Department of Trade and Industry
ECM	Efficient capital markets
ED	Exposure Draft
EEC	European Economic Community
FAF	Financial Accounting Foundation
FASAC	Financial Accounting Standards Advisory Council
FASB	Financial Accounting Standards Board
FEE	Federation Européenne des Experts Comptables
IAS	International Accounting Standards

IASC	International Accounting Standards Committee
ICAA	Institute of Chartered Accountants of Australia
ICAEW	Institute of Chartered Accountants in England and Wales
ICAI	Institute of Chartered Accountants of Ireland
ICAS	Institute of Chartered Accountants of Scotland
ICMA	Institute of Cost and Management Accountants
IFAC	International Federation of Accountants
MIB	Marketing of Investments Board
NCSC	National Companies and Securities Commission
OECD	Organization for Economic Co-operation and Development
R&D	Research and development
SEC	Securities and Exchange Commission
SFAS	Statement of Financial Accounting Standards
SIB	Securities and Investments Board
SOI	Statement of Intent
SORP	Statement of Recommended Practice
SRO	Self-regulatory organization
SSAP	Statement of Standard Accounting Practice
TFRC	Taxation and Financial Relations Committee
UEC	Union Européenne des Experts Comptables, Economiques et Financiers
UN	United Nations
USM	Unlisted Securities Market

Index